GREYHOUND NATION

Edmund Russell's much-anticipated new book examines the coevolution of people and domestic animals. Using greyhounds and their owners in England from 1200 to 1900 as a case study, Russell shows that history and evolution are two names for the same process: evolution in domestic animals was a historical process, and human history was an evolutionary process. Challenging the popular notion that animal breeds remain uniform over time and space, Russell shows that greyhounds varied and changed just as much as their owners. Some changes were physical and others cultural. People and dogs alike evolved in response to the forces of modernization, such as capitalism, democracy, and industry. They also evolved in response to each other. Human history and animal evolution were not separate processes, each proceeding at its own rate according to its own rules. They intertwined in subtle and fascinating ways.

Edmund Russell is Professor of History at Boston University, where he focuses his research on environmental history, the history of technology, US history, and biology. He is the author of *Evolutionary History: Uniting History and Biology to Understand Life on Earth* (Cambridge University Press, 2011) and coeditor of the Cambridge Studies in Environment and History series.

Studies in Environment and History

Editors

J. R. McNeill, *Georgetown University*
Edmund P. Russell, *Boston University*

Editors Emeritus

Alfred W. Crosby, *University of Texas at Austin*
Donald Worster, *University of Kansas*

Other books in the series:

(continued after Index)

GREYHOUND NATION

A Coevolutionary History of England, 1200–1900

Edmund Russell

Boston University

CAMBRIDGE
UNIVERSITY PRESS

CAMBRIDGE
UNIVERSITY PRESS

University Printing House, Cambridge CB2 8BS, United Kingdom

One Liberty Plaza, 20th Floor, New York, NY 10006, USA

477 Williamstown Road, Port Melbourne, VIC 3207, Australia

314–321, 3rd Floor, Plot 3, Splendor Forum, Jasola District Centre,
New Delhi – 110025, India

79 Anson Road, #06–04/06, Singapore 079906

Cambridge University Press is part of the University of Cambridge.

It furthers the University's mission by disseminating knowledge in the pursuit of
education, learning, and research at the highest international levels of excellence.

www.cambridge.org
Information on this title: www.cambridge.org/9780521745055
DOI: 10.1017/9781139049269

First published 2018

Printed in the United States of America by Sheridan Books, Inc.

A catalogue record for this publication is available from the British Library.

ISBN 978-0-521-76209-0 Hardback
ISBN 978-0-521-74505-5 Paperback

For my siblings,

*MARY, CATHERINE, PATRICK, ELIZABETH, SUSAN,
VIRGINIA, AND MICHAEL*

Whoever would write the history of dogs must write the history of man.
Hugh Dalziel, 1888

CONTENTS

FIGURES

ACKNOWLEDGEMENTS

This book was a puppy that matured into a bigger dog than I expected. I was originally writing a book about working-class dogs in England. Authors in the nineteenth century described whippets as "the poor man's greyhound." To understand that description, a chapter on greyhounds seemed necessary. When I dug into greyhound history, I realized that the most fundamental assumptions of breed histories are mistaken. Historians often portray breeds of animals, and varieties of plants, as uniform, isolated, and static. My research convinced me that isolated, uniform breeds were a recent development. Before the nineteenth century, breeds lived in porous, diverse populations. Projecting today's ideas about breeds onto the past obscured some of the most important features of animal history. An effort to tell a more accurate story, and to demonstrate how evolution and history are two facets of the same coin, led to the book in your hands.

Audiences at the University of British Columbia, Juniata College, Virginia Tech, University of Kansas, University of Oklahoma, Massachusetts Institute of Technology, Cambridge University, University of Virginia, Royal Institute of Technology (Stockholm), University of Michigan, Virginia Commonwealth University, and the annual meeting of the American Society for Environmental History heard presentations of portions of this paper. My gratitude goes to audience members for helpful comments.

This material is based on work supported by a sabbatical leave from the University of Virginia and the National Science Foundation under grant number SES-0220764. Any opinions, findings, and conclusions or recommendations expressed in this material are those of the author and do not necessarily reflect the views of the National Science Foundation. The University of Kansas provided financial support from my Joyce and Elizabeth Hall Professorship funds. I thank those institutions for their support.

I conducted research on this book during a year (2002–2003) at Cambridge University. There I had the good fortune to become a visiting fellow at Clare Hall, a visiting scholar in the Department of History and Philosophy of Science, and a visiting research fellow at the Centre for History and Economics, King's College. Thanks go to all three of those organizations for welcoming me into stimulating environments in which to work and learn. At the Kennel Club (London), the librarians made a wealth of material available to me. Ms. Sybil Churchill gave me a tour of the club, answered questions, and allowed me visit her home in Gloucestershire to use her private collection on the Ladies' Kennel Association. Jeff Sampson helped me understand dog genetics.

Some material in this book previously appeared in Edmund Russell, "Coevolutionary History," *American Historical Review* 119 (Dec. 2014): 1514–28.

This book builds on the work of many scholars but owes a special debt to Harriet Ritvo. By grounding animal history in social history, she helped inspire my approach and led me to sources. Other scholars also had a significant impact on the framework developed in this book. P. B. Munsche and Emma Griffin influenced my thinking about hunting. Charles Darwin and Stephen Palumbi helped me understand evolution under domestication. William Durham shaped my ideas about cultural evolution and coevolution. Charles Elton, G. Evelyn Hutchinson, Maurits Ertsen, and F. J. Odling-Smee helped me develop ideas about niche construction.

Jenny Kane, Alex Dinn, Anna Russell, Margaret Russell, and Elizabeth Hammeteman helped with research, and I am most grateful to them. I discussed ideas in the book with Brian Balogh, who always had sage advice. Pamela Gordon helped me analyze translations of text in ancient Greek. Katherine Clark, Jonathan Clark, Victor Bailey, Deborah Gershenowitz, John McNeill, Lucy Sankey Russell, and an anonymous reviewer read part or all of the manuscript and offered suggestions that improved it.

Credit for the idea of studying canines goes to our dog, Riley. I was thinking about evolutionary history one day when, as I stood with him in our driveway, I realized that his ilk provided a splendid case study. Riley was, literally, my companion throughout the project. He lived eighteen energetic years and died one month before I completed the manuscript. We miss him.

As always, the advice and support of my wife, Lucy, made this work possible.

Thank you.

1

INTRODUCTION

The goal of this book is to understand how people and other species have shaped each other. It uses the history of wolves and people as a case study. Wolves (*Canis lupus*) make a good case study because it is easy to see the impact of people on their traits. People modified the traits of wolves to create dogs (that is, domestic wolves).[1] People further changed the traits of domestic wolves to fashion breeds.[2] Any breed would make a good case study. This book uses greyhounds in England because they have a long, documented history. The story in this book begins around 1200 CE, when greyhounds appeared in a written document. It ends around 1900, when kennel clubs initiated a new era in human–greyhound coevolution by banning cross breeding.

Overview

The thesis of the book is that people and greyhounds evolved and coevolved from 1200 to 1900. Neither people nor greyhounds were fixed. They evolved (that is, their traits changed). Some evolution came in response to broad social and ecological forces, such as economics, politics, infrastructure, and habitats. As social and ecological forces changed the world, people and greyhounds adapted. Human and greyhound populations also evolved in response to each other. People shaped greyhounds with certain traits, those traits circled back to shape human traits, which sparked further change in greyhounds, and so on.

The term for this kind of evolution, in which *traits of two or more populations change in response to each other*, is **coevolution**.[3] Charles Darwin referred to this process as **coadaptation**.[4] A classic example, identified by Darwin as well as the biologists who introduced *coevolution* as a synonym in 1964, is the interaction between plants and pollinators. The body parts of insect pollinators often match the anatomy of flowers almost perfectly. It seems unlikely that one stayed constant while the other adapted to it, so

1

insects and plants likely adapted to each other. As Darwin put it, "I can understand how a flower and a bee might slowly become, either simultaneously or one after the other, modified and adapted to each other in the most perfect manner, by the continued preservation of all the individuals which presented slight deviations of structure mutually favourable to each other."[5]

Darwin's *On the Origin of Species* was an extended analysis of evolution and coevolution under domestication. As he explained,

> It is, therefore, of the highest importance to gain a clear insight into the means of modification and *coadaptation*. At the commencement of my observations it seemed to me probable that a careful study of domesticated animals and of cultivated plants would offer the best chance of making out this obscure problem. Nor have I been disappointed; in this and in all other perplexing cases I have invariably found that our knowledge, imperfect though it be, of variation under domestication, afforded the best and safest clue. I may venture to express my conviction of the high value of such studies, although they have been very commonly neglected by naturalists.[6]

Greyhound Nation follows Darwin's lead in focusing on evolution and coevolution of people and domestic organisms. It differs from *On the Origin of Species* in examining the historical forces that led people to value different traits at different times in non-human populations.

English law inadvertently divided human–greyhound coevolution into two major periods. The first lasted from 1200 to 1831. I call it the **patrician era** because the only people who could legally own greyhounds were royals, aristocrats, and large landowners. The second period stretched from 1831 to the present. I call it the **modern era**. In this period, all classes of people legally owned greyhounds. The overall trend for human and greyhound evolution was from more to less variation. Greyhounds, and the people who interacted with them, varied more in 1200 than they did in 1900.

One reason for this narrowing was a loss of human and greyhound **niches**. The idea of niches comes from biologists, who have used *niche* in multiple ways.[7] Some ecologists have described niches as *occupations*. Badgers have jobs to perform in the economy of nature. Other ecologists have described niches as something like *habitats*, or the conditions in which organisms live (e.g., a marsh). Other ecologists use *niche* in other ways.

This book combines the occupational and habitat concepts of niches. It uses *niche* to mean a *job–habitat combination*. I refer to the job aspects of a niche as the *job dimension*. I refer to the habitat aspects of a niche as the *habitat dimension*. Each niche in this book, then, has two dimensions – a job and a habitat.[8] If we know the job and habitat of an organism, we know its niche. Every population in this book had a niche. This holds true for people as well as for greyhounds. People in the book, such as men who hunted with greyhounds, held jobs. (Here, *job* includes unpaid work.) They performed their job in a specific habitat, such as a forest.

Niches have evolutionary consequences. Every niche rewards a different combination of traits. Some traits are **physical**, such as the size of a greyhound. Other traits are **behavioral**, such as the speed of a greyhound. Physical and behavioral traits optimal for one job were suboptimal for another. Large greyhounds were optimal for hauling down deer but suboptimal for catching rabbits (momentum carried them past quick-turning rabbits). Greyhound owners adapted greyhounds to specific niches. The more niches, the greater the variation in greyhounds. The same held true for human populations. Human behavioral traits suited to chasing deer, such as standing still and waiting for greyhounds to bring prey to hunters, worked poorly when chasing hares that ran far away. **Niches shaped evolution when human and canine populations adapted to them.** More jobs for people and greyhounds meant more variation in human and greyhound populations.

Niches disappeared because of long-term historical trends. Economics, politics, culture, technology, and ecology all shaped niches for people and greyhounds. They spawned a wide variety of niches (job–habitat combinations) in the medieval period. People and greyhounds used a variety of methods to pursue a variety of prey in a variety of habitats (e.g., they chased deer in forests and hares in open countryside). Each method of pursuing each species in each habitat created a different niche. Each niche called for a different package of traits in people and greyhounds. Varied niches rewarded varied traits in people and greyhounds. Historical forces narrowed the range of prey pursued over time, which narrowed the range of jobs, which narrowed variation in niches, which narrowed variation in human and canine populations. For example, deer hunting disappeared by the eighteenth century. Without deer hunting niches for people and greyhounds, traits needed for deer hunting faded. Populations evolved.

The most radical narrowing came from modernization. This book uses *modern* because greyhound owners applied the term to themselves and their greyhounds in the nineteenth century. Modernity changed the evolution of people and greyhounds. Key modern forces included capitalism, democracy, mass communication, industrial infrastructure, bureaucracy, and standardization. Mild versions of these processes appeared in the last half-century of the patrician era (1776–1831), which leads me to term this half-century the **transitional period**. The forces of modernity roared after 1831. Modernization did more than remake human society. It remade evolution.

In addition to eliminating jobs, modernity narrowed job descriptions within occupations. In the early modern period, coursers used many sets of rules to govern coursing (pursuing animals with greyhounds while spectators bet on performance). By the late nineteenth century, they standardized rules for coursing hares. Narrowing of job descriptions (the rules to follow while coursing) narrowed the range of behavioral traits in human and canine populations. Modernity also narrowed variation in habitats. In the early modern period, greyhound owners adapted their dogs to their own estates. This practice created great national variation. In the late nineteenth century, greyhound owners across England adapted their dogs to a single estate that hosted the premier coursing championship, the Waterloo Cup. Narrowing of job descriptions, plus standardization of habitats, rewarded narrowing of traits in some human and canine populations.

A radical change in job description came in the 1880s. Before that decade, greyhound job descriptions were silent on ancestry. Greyhounds of mixed ancestry were common and prized. In the 1880s, two organizations closed the breeding pools of some greyhounds. The Kennel Club closed the breeding pool of show greyhounds. The National Coursing Club closed the breeding pool of coursing greyhounds. Now, descending from two parents registered as greyhounds was essential in job descriptions for greyhounds working in shows and coursing. Half a millennium of cross breeding came to a halt for these important greyhound populations, reducing the variation available to breeders of registered dogs up to the present. This break with tradition makes 1900 a logical ending point for this book's narrative.

Significance

The findings in this book are significant in several ways. First, they show that historical change is evolution. Differences in terminology, and the cultural divide between humanities and science, have obscured this fact. The logic for the equivalence is simple. Historical change involves change in human ideas and behaviors. Some ideas and behaviors become more common, and others become less common. Ideas and behaviors are human traits. **Evolution** means *change in the frequency of traits in populations.* Ergo, historical change (change in the frequency of ideas and behaviors in human populations) is evolution.

Second, historical forces are evolutionary forces. Politics, economics, culture, and technology do more than shape human experience. They also shape evolution. They change the frequency of thoughts and behaviors in human populations. They shape evolution in non-human populations, too. They affected the frequency of traits in greyhounds. As for greyhounds, so for all dogs. As for dogs, so for all domestic plants and animals. Historical forces have created niches (job–habitat combinations) for all breeds of all domestic organisms since their domestication. Each niche rewarded a different package of traits, creating variation among populations.

This study shows that many historical fields can extend their analyses to include evolution in non-human populations. For legal historians, it shows that a change in the law affected greyhound evolution by enabling all classes of people to shape greyhounds to meet their goals. For political historians, it shows that democracy shaped greyhound evolution by spawning a backlash among patricians. (Anti-democratic elites isolated the breeding pool of greyhounds to reassert patrician control over animal sports and breeding.) For economic historians, it shows that capitalism shaped greyhounds. (Profit-seeking entrepreneurs created dog shows, which rewarded different greyhound traits from hunting and coursing.) For historians of technology, it shows that greyhounds were biotechnologies. They were tools shaped to do particular jobs in particular ways. The book also shows that technological change shaped evolution in indirect ways. The spread of railroads enabled greyhounds from distant regions to mate, homogenizing greyhound traits on a national scale. For environmental historians, it shows that ecological change affected greyhound evolution. Loss of habitat for deer and other species reduced the jobs available to greyhounds, which reduced the range of traits needed in greyhounds.

Third, evolution falls into historical periods. Evolutionary biologists are accustomed to dividing evolution into long periods of time, such as the Pleistocene. Recently, biologists and other scientists have recognized that we have entered a new epoch called the Anthropocene. Scientists and historians debate the beginning of this period. Industrialization? After World War II? The beginning of agriculture? I am less interested in debates over timing than in the reality of human impact. People now shape the evolution of organisms around the globe. We do so directly and indirectly, intentionally and accidentally. This fact forces us to recognize that the same forces that shape human history also shape evolution. Not surprisingly, this pattern divides evolution of many non-human populations into the same historical periods as human history. The reason is simple. Domestic plants and animals work in the human economy. Economic change alters job markets for domestic organisms as well as people. Change in jobs rewards change in traits of employees, both human and non-human.

Fourth, evolutionary biologists should build human social forces into their models. Now that people have created an "evolution explosion," as biologist Stephen Palumbi dubbed it, we need to take the causes of that explosion seriously. Treating humanity as one large, undifferentiated population will not do. People did not have the same impact on evolution 30,000 years ago that we do now. Change in the scale of impact is not due to change in our genetic makeup. It is due to change in social forces. Ancient agricultural economies had different impacts on the evolution of domestic populations from capitalistic economies. Some evolutionary studies, then, should focus on the differences in evolutionary impacts created by differences in economic systems. The same goes for differences in political, cultural, and technological systems.

Fifth, we should understand breeds as evolving populations rather than fixed types. Many authors embrace what I call the **statue history of breeds**. In this recounting, breeds have three defining traits. First, breeds were *uniform*. The traits of breed members varied little. Second, breeds were *isolated*. Breed members mated with other breed members to create new breed members. If they mated with a member of another breed, the offspring did not belong to the breed. Third, breeds were *static*. Breeders changed the traits of organisms when developing a breed, after which breed traits stayed the same.

Historians have argued that the greyhound breed, in particular, exemplified these features throughout time. They describe greyhounds as originating 8,000 years ago in the Mediterranean. Ancient greyhounds were purebred, meaning members had uniform traits and were isolated from other breeds. Today's greyhounds descended from ancient purebreds with no change. As one greyhound historian put it, "my dog . . . is of the same type, and does the same things, as those Greyhounds of Egypt and Greece so many thousands of years ago."[9] Once created, greyhounds resembled the Venus de Milo (albeit without losing their forelegs). The world around them went through wrenching changes, but greyhounds did not. They were living statues that remained the same for thousands of years. At least, that is the received wisdom.

Greyhounds – and surely other breeds – were not uniform, isolated, or static. They were varied, porous, and changing. These population features were not mistakes. People did not aim to make greyhounds a "true" breed and fall short. Variation, porosity, and malleability were virtues. They helped people achieve their goals. Conversely, the people who interacted with greyhounds were not uniform, isolated, or static. They, too, were varied, porous, and changing. These features helped greyhounds meet their "goals" (survival and reproduction).

Sixth, we should stop projecting today's breed concept onto the past. We distort our understanding of history when we assume that greyhounds – or other breeds of animals or varieties of plants – were uniform, isolated, and static. They were not. Changing a linguistic habit will help. Historians commonly refer to animals and plants using the singular, as in *the* greyhound. This habit encourages us to see organisms as fixed types throughout time and space. *Seeing members of a group as uniform and static* is **essentialism**. A synonym is **typological thinking**.[10] One can trace it to Plato's concept of ideal **types**, in which one perfect form of each thing in the world exists (often out of sight). Variation is seen as incidental rather than important. When applied to people, we call typological thinking **stereotyping**. Stereotyping is no more accurate for non-human populations than for people. *The* greyhound never existed, except in people's heads.

Biologists refer to the opposite of typological thinking as **population thinking**. Population thinkers see variation and change in populations, rather than uniformity and stasis. This book embraces population thinking. Greyhounds had similarities, but they were not identical. This book replaces the singular (*the* greyhound) with the plural (greyhounds) to highlight that greyhounds were varied individuals rather than a fixed type.[11] It is a history of greyhounds, not of *the* greyhound.

Literatures

This book contributes to several fields. One is the young field or research program known as evolutionary history. This field situates evolution in human history. It analyzes how historical forces have shaped the traits of human and non-human populations. A subset of evolutionary history is coevolutionary history, or the analysis of how human and non-human populations have shaped each other. This book advances coevolutionary history by, among other things, incorporating cultural evolution.[12]

This book adds to environmental history, the field that studies the interaction between people and the rest of nature. Traditionally, environmental historians focused on the impact of human actions on (a) the ecology (distribution and abundance) of non-human species, and (b) the impact of pollution on human health. Evolutionary and coevolutionary history, including the ideas in this book, expand environmental history by assessing history as an evolutionary process.[13]

The book contributes to the history of technology. The most direct way is by highlighting the importance of organisms as technology. We have developed a habit of equating technology with machinery, but this concept is too narrow. Domestic animals and plants are technologies. People shape them to work for humans. Before tractors, draft animals pulled plows and wagons. Draft animals were biotechnologies in the root meaning of the word (live technologies). Recovering their history is important because, among other things, it tells us how social forces might shape the traits of biotechnologies created through genetic engineering. The traits of genetically modified organisms are not just the result of technical decisions. As historians of technology have stressed, the design of technology incorporates social values. The same holds true for domestic plants and animals. Another way this book intersects with the history of technology is in demonstrating the unintended impact of technology (railroads) on evolution (change in animal traits).[14]

This book extends ideas about periodization and transformation in British history. I am an environmental historian, a historian of technology, and an American historian. I took up the study of English dogs to broaden my horizons. I do not pretend to be an expert on the sceptered isle. I am sure British historians could offer a deeper, more nuanced interpretation of social change than this book offers. My contribution, I believe, is to show that (a) well-studied historical processes had little-studied impacts on evolution, and (b) evolution played an important role in British history.[15]

This book contributes to the young field of animal studies. Scholars in the field employ a variety of approaches, but it seems fair to say that cultural constructivism plays a key role. Such studies, including those that show how people projected ideas about themselves onto animals, informed my approach. I found, however, that it was impossible to analyze culture outside its material context. Breeders adapted animals to economics, technology, and ecology as well as to their wishes. These realities, as much as desires for social status, shaped animal traits. In addition, breeders ran into biological limits. If they could, they surely would have bred out the need for animals to drink, eat, and defecate. They did not. The material world set limits on the ability of people to realize their dreams. The idea of prices, which animals exacted in return for enabling people to achieve their goals, offers a way to balance cultural construction with material realities.[16] Within animal studies, some key works have appeared on the history of dogs. This book adds to that body of work.[17]

The book joins a thriving literature in sports history. Scholars in this field have stressed the extent to which sports reflected, and helped to promote, social change. They have identified the nineteenth century as a revolutionary period. Team sports, formal rules, national governing organizations, and enthusiastic gambling were common features. The world of coursing and dog shows saw similar developments, which shaped evolution of greyhounds as well as human experience. Sports had evolutionary consequences.[18]

For biologists, this book proposes a model for incorporating human social forces into evolutionary models. The idea that people shape evolution is not mine. Natural historians before Charles Darwin, such as the Comte de Buffon, suggested this idea. Although often forgotten, Darwin built his argument for evolution by natural selection atop evidence of evolution by human selection. Recently, biologists have argued that human beings have become the world's most powerful evolutionary force. When biologists study anthropogenic evolution, however, the human side of the story may lack the sensitivity to variation seen in studies of non-human populations. Biologists might identify "people" or "culture" as the actors in anthropogenic evolution. These claims are correct, but they work at the same level of analysis as attributing natural selection to "nature." They are so general they offer little predictive value (a requirement for scientific hypotheses).[19]

This book contributes to the literature on cultural evolution and coevolution.[20] It follows the lead of others in pointing to memes as heritable instructions for behaviors. It emphasizes that coevolving populations can shape each other through more than affecting survival or reproduction (key elements of evolution through natural and sexual selection). The greyhounds in this book did not affect human survival or reproduction. Through what mechanism, then, did greyhounds affect their coevolving populations of people? This book focuses on two mechanisms: *creating opportunities* for people to have behavioral traits, and *exacting prices* for desired behaviors.

This book adds to the literature on niche construction, including human niche construction. Biologists traditionally saw environments as fixed. They assumed populations adapted to environments. Recently, they have shown more appreciation for the degree to which organisms adapt environments to themselves. Beavers build dams to adapt environments to themselves. This process is known as niche construction. When people do it, it is called human niche construction. This book argues that human niches can fruitfully be divided into two dimensions: jobs and habitats. It suggests that coevolving populations co-construct niches for each other.[21] Co-construction of niches helped to shape human and greyhound evolution.

Clearing the Fog

Common misunderstanding about evolution might make arguments in this book puzzling. Here are examples of misconceptions. Evolution is biological (or genetic) determinism. Evolution involves only genetic or physical traits. Evolution happens only through natural selection. The unit of evolution is species. Evolution is speciation. Evolution takes millions of years. Evolution must be accidental. People cannot affect evolution. This section clears up these points of confusion. Readers with deeper knowledge of evolution may wish to skip to the next section.

As noted earlier, **evolution** means *change in the frequency of traits in populations. Change in frequency* means a trait becomes more or less common in a population. **Traits** are *features of organisms.* Some traits are **physical**. Rough fur is an example. Other traits are **behavioral**. Running, eating, sleeping, and killing prey are behavioral traits. Any change in frequency in any trait – large or small, permanent or temporary – is evolution. In this book, greyhound populations evolved with respect to physical and behavioral traits. Human populations evolved with respect to behavioral traits, but not physical traits (so far as we know).

This book does not make most of the arguments mistakenly thought essential to evolution. It does not argue that people or greyhounds became new species. It discusses change within populations of two species, *Homo sapiens* and *Canis lupus*. It does not argue that genes determined human behavior. So far as I know, none of the human behaviors in the book were under genetic control. Genes probably influenced greyhound behavior, but we do not know this. No one was measuring gene frequencies. Even if genes did affect behavior, they were not solely responsible. Training shaped greyhound behavior. Neither people nor greyhounds in this book evolved through natural selection (in the usual sense of non-human selection). Greyhounds evolved through two other kinds of selection named by Darwin: *methodical selection* (selective mating) and *unconscious selection* (keeping high-performing individuals and killing the rest). Drift (random change in traits) and sampling effects (population bottlenecks) probably affected greyhound evolution, too. People evolved through choice (they decided to behave in certain ways). People and greyhounds evolved over months, years, and centuries.

People and greyhounds in this book **inherited traits** through at least two mechanisms. One was **memes**, meaning *instructions for behavior*. Examples are the rules that governed wagering on the outcome of coursing contests. Memes shaped human behaviors, and some greyhound behaviors, in this book. Unlike genes, memes pass promiscuously. Inherited through learning, rather than from mating, memes pass among non-relatives and across space and time. The other inheritance mechanism was probably **genes**. It seems likely that variation in alleles (gene versions) was responsible for some variation in greyhound traits (e.g., coat length and behaviors). But because no one was measuring gene frequencies, this book has little to say about genetic inheritance.

People shaped the traits of greyhounds through three mechanisms. One was **breeding**. The meaning of *breeding* changed over the period covered in this book, but people consistently used breeding to develop greyhounds with desired traits. The second mechanism was **training**. People inculcated memes in greyhounds through training. These memes affected the frequency of behavioral traits in greyhounds. A third mechanism was **creating opportunities to behave in certain ways**. This mechanism was implicit in creating jobs. People created the chance for greyhounds to hunt deer, and some took advantage of the opportunity.

Greyhounds shaped human behavior through two mechanisms. One was **creating opportunities to behave in certain ways**. Greyhounds created the chance for people to hunt deer, and some people took advantage of the opportunity. A second mechanism was **exacting prices for desired behaviors**. Greyhounds demanded food, water, and shelter in exchange for hunting deer. Put slightly differently, greyhounds trained people by rewarding certain human behaviors, such as supplying good food, with good performance.

Chapters

Chapter 2, "Patrician Coevolution (1200–1776)," examines a half-millennium in which greyhounds coevolved with a tiny sliver (1 percent) of the English population. Patricians used their seats on the throne and in Parliament to grant themselves a legal, class-based monopoly on greyhound ownership and breeding, which created a class-based monopoly on greyhound evolution and human–greyhound coevolution. Greyhounds evolved to suit the goals of patricians, and patricians evolved to suit the needs of greyhounds (survival and reproduction). Patricians and greyhounds co-constructed a variety of niches. Jobs included hunting a variety of prey species and coursing. Patricians tailored human and greyhound traits to specific jobs in specific habitats on specific estates. Fine-tuning traits to these niches created wide variation in human and greyhound traits on a national scale. A decline in the number of hunted species reduced the range of jobs available to greyhounds and people over the patrician era, which narrowed the range of niches, which narrowed variation.

Chapter 3, "Human Evolution in a Transitional Era (1776–1831)," examines the last half-century of the patrician era. Mild modernization of human evolution appeared in this half-century. Patricians retained a legal monopoly on greyhound ownership and coevolution, but they introduced social changes that presaged more radical changes after 1831. The most important novelty was the formation of coursing clubs, which created elite subpopulations of patricians. Club members referred to their version of coursing as *modern*, and they adopted four features of modernity. They developed local *bureaucracies* (clubs), *standardized* job descriptions (written rules), capitalized on *mass communication* (sporting magazines), and adopted an idea of *progress* through science (breeding). These features of modernity shaped human evolution by creating islands of local similarity in a sea of national variation.

Chapter 4, "Greyhound Evolution and Coevolution in a Transitional Era (1776–1831)," examines the same period as Chapter 3. It focuses on greyhound evolution under the coursing club system and consequent coevolution of human populations. The pattern of evolution in club greyhounds resembled the pattern of evolution in club members: from national variation to islands of local uniformity. Clubs shaped the evolution of greyhound populations by narrowing niches, which led to narrowed variation in traits. Clubs narrowed variation in jobs by standardizing the rules of coursing. Clubs narrowed variation in the habitats by coursing the same estate repeatedly. Human populations coevolved when they developed new memes and behavioral traits, such as claiming that smooth-coated greyhounds of southern clubs were universally superior animals.

Chapter 5, "Modernizing Human Evolution (1831–1900)," introduces the modern era in human–greyhound coevolution. Parliament abolished class-based limits on greyhound use in 1831. This rupture enabled greyhounds to evolve to serve the interests of all classes of people, and enabled people of all classes to evolve to serve the interests of greyhounds. Human evolution modernized when features seen in the transitional decades waxed. The scale of *bureaucratization* and *standardization* grew national. The speed and scale of *mass communication* swelled. The ideology of *progress* expanded from an elite enterprise to members of all classes. Full modernization also flowered because of new features. Before 1831, *capitalism, democracy,* and *industrial infrastructure* played little role in coursing. After 1831, they became integral.

Chapter 6, "Modern Coevolution for Coursing (1831–1900)," examines greyhound evolution and human coevolution in the same period as Chapter 5. Democracy, capitalism, bureaucracy, mass communication, and industrial transportation standardized greyhound niches at the same time they standardized human niches. Greyhound populations evolved when narrowed variation in niches led to narrowed variation in traits. Human populations coevolved when memes about fur length and purity spread. This evolution circled back to shape greyhounds when many breeders selected against long fur and gave up on cross breeding.

Chapter 7, "Modern Coevolution for Shows (1860–1900)," examines the impact of radically new occupations on human and greyhound populations. In the nineteenth century, profit-seeking entrepreneurs created dog shows. Previous greyhound jobs demanded that greyhounds behave in certain ways. Shows required that greyhounds look a certain way. Behavior was irrelevant. Shows rewarded narrow ranges of traits, which were different from traits prized in hunting greyhounds. Show niches were thoroughly modern. *Capitalism, industrial transportation, urbanization, mass communication, democracy,* and *bureaucracy* underpinned show niches. An anti-democratic backlash by patricians led to a ban on cross breeding, which created a new era in coevolution after about 1900.

Chapter 8, "Epilogue," races over the history of greyhounds from 1900 to the present. Greyhound jobs changed in the twentieth and twenty-first centuries, sparking further evolution and coevolution, which will continue so long as people and greyhounds reside on earth.

Notes

1. Francis Galibert et al., "Toward Understanding Dog Evolutionary and Domestication History," *Comptes Rendus Biologies* 334, no. 3 (March 2011): 190–96; Greger Larson et al., "Rethinking Dog Domestication by Integrating Genetics, Archeology, and Biogeography," *Proceedings of the National Academy of Sciences* 109, no. 23 (2012): 8878–83; Arman Ardalan et al., "Comprehensive Study of mtDNA among Southwest Asian Dogs Contradicts Independent Domestication of Wolf, but Implies Dog–Wolf Hybridization," *Ecology and Evolution* 1, no. 3 (2011): 373–85, doi:10.1002/ece3.35; Z.-L. Ding et al., "Origins of Domestic Dog in Southern East Asia is Supported by Analysis of Y-Chromosome DNA," *Heredity* 108, no. 5 (May 2012): 507–14, doi:10.1038/hdy.2011.114; Darcy F. Morey, *Dogs: Domestication and the Development of a Social Bond* (New York: Cambridge University Press, 2010); A. K. Niskanen et al., "MHC Variability Supports Dog Domestication from a Large Number of Wolves: High Diversity in Asia," *Heredity* 110, no. 1 (January 2013): 80–85, doi:10.1038/hdy.2012.67; Nikolai D. Ovodov et al., "A 33,000-Year-Old Incipient Dog from the Altai Mountains of Siberia: Evidence of the Earliest Domestication Disrupted by the Last Glacial Maximum," *PLoS ONE* 6, no. 7 (July 28, 2011): e22821, doi:10.1371/journal.pone.0022821; O. Thalmann et al., "Complete Mitochondrial Genomes of Ancient Canids Suggest a European Origin of Domestic Dogs," *Science* 342, no. 6160 (November 15, 2013): 871–74, doi:10.1126/science.1243650.
2. Heidi G. Parker, "Genomic Analyses of Modern Dog Breeds," *Mammalian Genome* 23, no. 1–2 (2012): 19–27; Joshua M. Akey et al., "Tracking Footprints of Artificial Selection in the Dog Genome," *Proceedings of the National Academy of Sciences* 107, no. 3 (January 19, 2010): 1160–65, doi:10.1073/pnas.0909918107; Heidi G. Parker, Abigail L. Shearin, and Elaine A. Ostrander, "Man's Best Friend Becomes Biology's Best in Show: Genome Analyses in the Domestic Dog," *Annual Review of Genetics* 44 (2010): 309–36, doi:10.1146/annurev-genet-102808-115200; Aaron K. Wong et al., "A Comprehensive Linkage Map of the Dog Genome," *Genetics* 184, no. 2 (February 1, 2010): 595–605, doi:10.1534/genetics.109.106831; Kerstin Lindblad-Toh et al., "Genome Sequence, Comparative Analysis and Haplotype Structure of the Domestic Dog," *Nature* 438, no. 7069 (December 8, 2005): 803–19; Heidi G. Parker et al., "Genetic Structure of the Purebred Domestic Dog," *Science* 304, no. 5674 (2004): 1160–64.
3. Douglas J. Futuyma and Montgomery Slatkin, *Coevolution* (Sunderland: Sinauer, 1983); Edmund Russell, "Coevolutionary History," *The American Historical Review* 119, no. 5 (December 1, 2014): 1514–28.
4. Charles Darwin, *The Origin of Species by Means of Natural Selection or the Preservation of Favoured Races in the Struggle for Life*, 6th edn. (London: Odhams Press, 1872), 31 (emphasis added).
5. Paul R. Ehrlich and Peter H. Raven, "Butterflies and Plants: A Study in Coevolution," *Evolution* 18 (1964): 586–608; Darwin, *Origin of Species*, 109.
6. Darwin, *Origin of Species*, 31 (emphasis added).

7. Reviewed in Eric R. Pianka, *Evolutionary Ecology*, 6th edn. (San Francisco: Addison Wesley Longman, 2000), 268–93.

8. G. Evelyn Hutchinson conceived of niches as having many dimensions. Each resource was a *dimension* on a graph. One could graph one dimension, such as water quantity, on the x-axis of a graph. A second resource, such as food, could be graphed on the y-axis. Graphing the overlap between the amount of water and food a greyhound needed produces a quadrangle – the niche for greyhounds. One could graph a third resource, temperature, on the z-axis. The overlap in tolerable ranges produces a box or volume. We could define four, five, and more niche dimensions up to n, even if we cannot draw them. G. E. Hutchinson, "Concluding Remarks," *Cold Spring Harbor Symposium on Quantitative Biology* 22 (1957): 415–27.

9. Cynthia A. Branigan, *The Reign of the Greyhound: A Popular History of the Oldest Family of Dogs* (Hoboken: Howell, 1997), 49.

10. Ernst Mayr, *One Long Argument: Charles Darwin and the Genesis of Modern Evolutionary Thought* (Cambridge, MA: Harvard University Press, 1991), 40–42.

11. Mayr, *One Long Argument*, 40–42.

12. Edmund Russell, *Evolutionary History: Uniting History and Biology to Understand Life on Earth* (New York: Cambridge University Press, 2011); Edmund Russell, "Evolutionary History: Prospectus for a New Field," *Environmental History* 8, no. 2 (2003): 204–28; Russell, "Coevolutionary History"; Sam White, "From Globalized Pig Breeds to Capitalist Pigs: A Study in Animal Cultures and Evolutionary History," *Environmental History* 16, no. 1 (2011): 94–120; Donald Worster, "Historians and Nature," *American Scholar*, Spring (2010), http://theamericanscholar.org/; Christian W. Simon, "Evolutionary History: Trends in Contemporary History of the Historiography of Environment," *Storia Della Storiografia* 47, no. 1 (2005): 90–112; Christophe Bonneuil and François Hochereau, "Gouverner le 'progrès génétique,'" *Annales. Histoire, Sciences Sociales* 63, no. 6 (2008): 1305–40; Edmund Russell, "Introduction: The Garden in the Machine: Toward an Evolutionary History of Technology," in *Industrializing Organisms: Introducing Evolutionary History*, ed. Susan R. Schrepfer and Philip Scranton (New York: Routledge, 2004), 1–16; Abraham Gibson, *Feral Animals in the American South: An Evolutionary History* (New York: Cambridge University Press, 2016); Joshua Abram Kercsmar, "Wolves at Heart: How Dog Evolution Shaped Whites' Perceptions of Indians in North America," *Environmental History* 21, no. 3 (July 1, 2016): 516–40.

13. The literature on environmental history is enormous. A few examples include Edmund Russell, "The Strange Career of DDT: Experts, Federal Capacity, and 'Environmentalism' in World War II," *Technology and Culture* 40 (1999): 770–96; Edmund Russell, "'Lost among the Parts per Billion': Ecological Protection at the United States Environmental Protection Agency, 1970–1993," *Environmental History* 2 (1997): 29–51; Edmund Russell, *War and Nature: Fighting Humans and Insects with Chemicals from World War I to Silent Spring* (New York: Cambridge University Press, 2001); J. R. McNeill, *Something New under the Sun: An Environmental History of the Twentieth-Century World*

(New York: W.W. Norton, 2000); J. R. McNeill and Erin Stewart Mauldin, eds., *A Companion to Global Environmental History*, 1st edn. (Wiley-Blackwell, 2012); William Cronon, *Nature's Metropolis: Chicago and the Great West* (New York: W.W. Norton, 1991); Donald Worster, *Nature's Economy: A History of Ecological Ideas* (Cambridge: Cambridge University Press, 1977); Donald Worster, *Dust Bowl: The Southern Plains in the 1930s* (New York: Oxford University Press, 1979); Donald Worster, ed., *The Ends of the Earth: Perspectives on Modern Environmental History* (New York: Cambridge University Press, 1988); Richard White, *The Organic Machine* (New York: Hill and Wang, 1995), 3; Sam White, *The Climate of Rebellion in the Early Modern Ottoman Empire* (New York: Cambridge University Press, 2011); Alan Mikhail, *The Animal in Ottoman Egypt* (New York: Oxford University Press, 2014); Nancy Langston, *Toxic Bodies: Hormone Disruptors and the Legacy of DES* (New Haven: Yale University Press, 2010); Ling Zhang, *The River, the Plain, and the State: An Environmental Drama in Northern Song China, 1048–1128* (New York: Cambridge University Press, 2016); Harriet Ritvo, *The Dawn of Green: Manchester, Thirlmere, and Modern Environmentalism* (Chicago: University of Chicago Press, 2009).

14. Philip Scranton and Susan R. Schrepfer, eds., *Industrializing Organisms: Introducing Evolutionary History* (New York: Routledge, 2004); Ann Norton Greene, *Horses at Work: Harnessing Power in Industrial America* (Cambridge, MA: Harvard University Press, 2008); George Basalla, *The Evolution of Technology* (Cambridge: Cambridge University Press, 1988).

15. Harold Perkin, *The Origins of Modern English Society, 1780–1880* (London: Routledge and Kegan Paul, 1969); J. C. D. Clark, *English Society, 1660–1832: Religion, Ideology, and Politics during the Ancien Regime*, 2nd edn. (Cambridge: Cambridge University Press, 2000); William B. Willcox, *The Age of Aristocracy, 1688–1830* (Lexington: D. C. Heath, 1976); Dror Wahrman, *Imagining the Middle Class: The Political Representation of Class in Britain, c. 1780–1840* (Cambridge/New York: Cambridge University Press, 1995); Frederick C. Dietz, *A Political and Social History of England* (New York: Macmillan, 1932); F. M. L. Thompson, *The Cambridge Social History of Britain, 1750–1950* (Cambridge: Cambridge University Press, 1990); Walter E. Houghton, *The Victorian Frame of Mind, 1830–1870* (New Haven: Yale University Press, 1957); Lytton Strachey, *Eminent Victorians: Cardinal Manning, Florence Nightingale, Dr. Arnold, General Gordon* (New York: G. P. Putnam's Sons, 1918); Iain McCalman, *An Oxford Companion to the Romantic Age* (New York: Oxford University Press, 1999); Keith Robbins, *Nineteenth-Century Britain: Integration and Diversity* (New York: Clarendon Press, 1988); G. S. R. Kitson Clark, *The Making of Victorian England* (Cambridge: Harvard University Press, 1962); John W. Dodds, *The Age of Paradox: A Biography of England, 1841–1851* (New York, Rinehart, 1952); Norman McCord and Bill Purdue, *British History 1815–1914*, 2nd edn. (New York: Oxford University Press, 2007); Robert W. Malcolmson, *Popular Recreations in English Society, 1700–1850* (New York: Cambridge University Press, 1973); Kingsley Bryce Smellie, *Great Britain since 1688: A Modern History* (Ann Arbor: University of Michigan Press, 1962); R. K. Webb, *Modern*

England: From the Eighteenth Century to the Present (New York: Dodd, Mead, 1968); Lacey Baldwin Smith, *A History of England*, 4th edn. (Lexington: D. C. Heath, 1983).

16. Erica Fudge, *Animal* (London: Reaktion, 2002); Erica Fudge, ed., *Renaissance Beasts: Of Animals, Humans, and Other Wonderful Creatures* (Urbana: University of Illinois Press, 2004); Erica Fudge, *Pets* (Durham, GBR: Acumen, 2008); Harriet Ritvo, *The Platypus and Mermaid, and Other Figments of the Classifying Imagination* (Cambridge, MA: Harvard University Press, 1997); Harriet Ritvo, *The Animal Estate: The English and Other Creatures in the Victorian Age* (Cambridge, MA: Harvard University Press, 1987); Harriet Ritvo, "Pride and Pedigree: The Evolution of the Victorian Dog Fancy," *Victorian Studies* 29, no. 2 (January 1, 1986): 227–53; Harriet Ritvo, *Noble Cows and Hybrid Zebras: Essays on Animals and History* (Charlottesville: University of Virginia Press, 2010); Mary Henninger-Voss, *Animals in Human Histories: The Mirror of Nature and Culture* (Rochester: University of Rochester Press, 2003); Angela N. H. Creager and William Chester Jordan, *The Animal/Human Boundary: Historical Perspectives* (Rochester: University of Rochester Press, 2003); Bruce Thomas Boehrer, ed., *A Cultural History of Animals in the Renaissance* (Oxford: Berg, 2011); Boria Sax, *Animals in the Third Reich: Pets, Scapegoats, and the Holocaust* (New York: Continuum, 2000); Dorothee Brantz, ed., *Beastly Natures: Animals, Humans, and the Study of History* (Charlottesville: University of Virginia Press, 2010); Stephen Budiansky, *The Covenant of the Wild: Why Animals Chose Domestication* (New York: William Morrow, 1992); Hannah Velten, *Beastly London: A History of Animals in the City* (London: Reaktion Books, 2013); Aaron Gross and Anne Vallely, eds., *Animals and the Human Imagination: A Companion to Animal Studies* (New York: Columbia University Press, 2012); Brian Harrison, "Animals and the State in Nineteenth-Century England," *The English Historical Review* 88, no. 349 (October 1, 1973): 786–820; Linda Kalof, ed., *A Cultural History of Animals in Antiquity* (Oxford: Berg, 2011); Linda Kalof and Amy J. Fitzgerald, *The Animals Reader: The Essential Classic and Contemporary Writings* (Oxford; New York: Berg, 2007); Kathleen Kete, ed., *A Cultural History of Animals in the Age of Empire* (Oxford: Berg, 2011); Kathleen Kete, *The Beast in the Boudoir: Petkeeping in Nineteenth-Century Paris* (Berkeley: University of California Press, 1994); Alan Mikhail, "Unleashing the Beast: Animals, Energy, and the Economy of Labor in Ottoman Egypt," *The American Historical Review* 118, no. 2 (2013): 317–48; Margo DeMello, *Animals and Society: An Introduction to Human-Animal Studies* (New York: Columbia University Press, 2012); Arien Mack, ed., *Humans and Other Animals* (Columbus: Ohio State University Press, 1999); Randy Malamud, ed., *A Cultural History of Animals in the Modern Age* (Oxford: Berg, 2011); Margaret E. Derry, *Bred for Perfection: Shorthorn Cattle, Collies, and Arabian Horses since 1800* (Baltimore: Johns Hopkins University Press, 2003); Donna J. Haraway, *When Species Meet* (Minneapolis: University of Minnesota Press, 2008); Velten, *Beastly London*; Mikhail, *The Animal in Ottoman Egypt*.

17. Ritvo, "Pride and Pedigree"; Ritvo, *The Animal Estate*; Philip Howell, *At Home and Astray: The Domestic Dog in Victorian Britain* (Charlottesville: University of

Virginia Press, 2015); Kete, *The Beast in the Boudoir*; James Serpell, ed., *The Domestic Dog: Its Evolution, Behaviour and Interactions with People* (New York: Cambridge University Press, 1996); Neil Pemberton and Michael Worboys, *Mad Dogs and Englishmen: Rabies in Britain 1830–2000* (New York: Palgrave Macmillan, 2007); Katharine MacDonogh, *Reigning Cats and Dogs* (New York: St. Martin's Press, 1999).

18. Emma Griffin, *England's Revelry: A History of Popular Sports and Pastimes, 1660–1830* (Oxford: Oxford University Press, 2005); Emma Griffin, *Blood Sport: Hunting in Britain since 1066* (New Haven/London: Yale University Press, 2007); Norman Baker, "Going to the Dogs – Hostility to Greyhound Racing in Britain: Puritanism, Socialism, and Pragmaticism," *Journal of Sport History* 23, no. 2 (1996): 97–119; John Lowerson, *Sport and the English Middle Classes, 1870–1914* (Manchester: Manchester University Press, 1995); Mark Clapson, *A Bit of a Flutter: Popular Gambling and English Society, c. 1823–1961* (Manchester: Manchester University Press, 1992); Pascal Delheye, *Routledge Research in Sports History: Making Sport History: Disciplines, Identities, and the Historiography of Sport* (New York: Routledge, 2014); Paul Christesen, *Sport and Democracy in the Ancient and Modern Worlds* (Cambridge/New York: Cambridge University Press, 2012); Allen Guttmann, *Women's Sports: A History* (New York: Columbia University Press, 1991); Allen Guttmann, *Japanese Sports: A History* (Honolulu: University of Hawai'i Press, 2001); David M. K. Sheinin, ed., *Sports Culture in Latin American History* (Pittsburgh: University of Pittsburgh Press, 2015).

19. S. R. Palumbi, "Humans as the World's Greatest Evolutionary Force," *Science* 293 (2001): 1786–90; Stephen R. Palumbi, *Evolution Explosion: How Humans Cause Rapid Evolutionary Change* (New York: W.W. Norton, 2001); Stephanie M. Carlson et al., "Four Decades of Opposing Natural and Human-Induced Artificial Selection Acting on Windermere Pike (*Esox lucius*)," *Ecology Letters* 10 (2007): 512–21; P. Handford, G. Bell, and T. Reimchen, "A Gillnet Fishery Considered as an Experiment in Artificial Selection," *Journal of Fisheries Research Board of Canada* 34 (1977): 954–61; Akey et al., "Tracking Footprints of Artificial Selection in the Dog Genome"; Yan Li et al., "Artificial Selection on Brain-Expressed Genes during the Domestication of Dog," *Molecular Biology and Evolution*, May 8, 2013, doi:10.1093/molbev/mst088; J. A. Hutchings and D. J. Fraser, "The Nature of Fisheries- and Farming-Induced Evolution," *Molecular Ecology* 17, no. 1 (2008): 294–313, doi:10.1111/j.1365-294X.2007.03485.x; Christian Jorgensen et al., "Managing Evolving Fish Stocks," *Science* 318, no. 5854 (2007): 1247–48; Richard Law, "Fishing, Selection, and Phenotypic Evolution," *ICES Journal of Marine Scientists* 57 (2000): 659–68; Matthew R. Walsh et al., "Maladaptive Changes in Multiple Traits Caused by Fishing: Impediments to Population Recovery," *Ecology Letters* 9 (2006): 142–48; Eve Abe, "Tusklessness amongst the Queen Elizabeth National Park Elephants, Uganda," *Pachyderm* 22 (1996): 46–47; H. Jachmann, P. S. M. Berry, and H. Imae, "Tusklessness in African Elephants: A Future Trend," *African Journal of Ecology* 33 (1995): 230–35; Anna M. Whitehouse,

"Tusklessness in the Elephant Population of the Addo Elephant National Park, South Africa," *Journal of the Zoological Society of London* 257 (2002): 249–54; David W. Coltman et al., "Undesirable Evolutionary Consequences of Trophy Hunting," *Nature* 426 (December 11): 283–92.

20. William H. Durham, *Coevolution: Genes, Culture, and Human Diversity* (Stanford: Stanford University Press, 1991); Robert Boyd and Peter J. Richerson, *Not by Genes Alone: How Culture Transformed Human Evolution* (Chicago: University of Chicago Press, 2005); Robert Boyd and Peter J. Richerson, *The Origin and Evolution of Cultures* (New York: Oxford University Press, 2005); Luigi Luca Cavalli-Sforza and Marcus W. Feldman, *Cultural Transmission and Evolution: A Quantitative Approach* (Princeton: Princeton University Press, 1981); Eric J. Richards, "Inherited Epigenetic Variation – Revisiting Soft Inheritance," *Nature Reviews Genetics* 7 (2006): 395–401; Kate Distin, *Cultural Evolution* (New York: Cambridge University Press, 2010); Peter J. Richerson and Morten H. Christiansen, *Cultural Evolution: Science, Technology, Language, and Religion* (Cambridge: MIT Press, 2013); Paul R. Ehrlich, "Cultural Evolution and the Human Predicament," *Trends in Ecology & Evolution* 24, no. 8 (August 1, 2009): 409–12, doi:10.1016/j.tree.2009.03.015; J. Hinshaw, "Karl Marx and Charles Darwin: Towards an Evolutionary History of Labor," *Journal of Social, Evolutionary and Cultural Psychology* 2 (2008): 260–80; Charles J. Lumsden and Edward O. Wilson, *Genes, Mind, and Culture: The Coevolutionary Process* (Cambridge, MA: Harvard University Press, 1981); Eva Jablonka and Marion J. Lamb, *Evolution in Four Dimensions* (Cambridge: MIT Press, 2006); Sarah A. Tishkoff et al., "Convergent Adaptation of Human Lactase Persistence in Africa and Europe," *Nature Genetics* 39, no. 1 (2007): 31–40; Pascale Gerbault et al., "Evolution of Lactase Persistence: An Example of Human Niche Construction," *Philosophical Transactions of the Royal Society B: Biological Sciences* 366, no. 1566 (March 27, 2011): 863–77; T. Bersaglieri et al., "Genetic Signatures of Strong Recent Positive Selection at the Lactase Gene," *American Journal of Human Genetics* 74, no. 6 (2004): 1111–20; N. S. Enattah et al., "Independent Introduction of Two Lactase-Persistence Alleles into Human Populations Reflects Different History of Adaptation to Milk Culture," *American Journal of Human Genetics* 82, no. 1 (2008): 57–72; N. S. Enattah et al., "Evidence of Still-Ongoing Convergence Evolution of the Lactase Persistence T-13910 Alleles in Humans," *American Journal of Human Genetics* 81, no. 3 (2007): 615–25; F. Imtiaz et al., "The T/G 13915 Variant Upstream of the Lactase Gene (LCT) Is the Founder Allele of Lactase Persistence in an Urban Saudi Population," *Journal of Medical Genetics* 44, no. 10 (2007): e89; Sean Myles et al., "Genetic Structure and Domestication History of the Grape," *Proceedings of the National Academy of Sciences* 108, no. 9 (March 1, 2011): 3530–35, doi:10.1073/pnas.1009363108; Kevin N. Laland, John Odling-Smee, and Sean Myles, "How Culture Shaped the Human Genome: Bringing Genetics and the Human Sciences Together," *Nature Reviews Genetics* 11 (2010): 137–48.

21. K. N. Laland, F. J. Odling-Smee, and M. W. Feldman, "Evolutionary Consequences of Niche Construction and Their Implications for Ecology,"

Proceedings of the National Academy of Sciences 96, no. 18 (August 31, 1999): 10242–47, doi:10.1073/pnas.96.18.10242; Mikhail Lipatov, Melissa J. Brown, and Marcus W. Feldman, "The Influence of Social Niche on Cultural Niche Construction: Modelling Changes in Belief about Marriage Form in Taiwan," *Philosophical Transactions of the Royal Society B: Biological Sciences* 366, no. 1566 (March 27, 2011): 901–17, doi:10.1098/rstb.2010.0303; K. N. Laland, J. Odling-Smee, and M. W. Feldman, "Cultural Niche Construction and Human Evolution," *Journal of Evolutionary Biology* 14, no. 1 (2001): 22–33; Elhanan Borenstein, Jeremy Kendal, and Marcus Feldman, "Cultural Niche Construction in a Metapopulation," *Theoretical Population Biology* 70, no. 1 (August 2006): 92–104; F. J. Odling-Smee, "Niche Construction, Genetic Evolution and Cultural Change," *Behavioural Processes* 35, no. 1–3 (December 1995): 195–205, doi:10.1016/0376-6357(95)00055-0; Gerbault et al., "Evolution of Lactase Persistence"; Kevin Laland et al., "Does Evolutionary Theory Need a Rethink?," *Nature* 514, no. 7521 (October 8, 2014): 161–64, doi:10.1038/514161a; Peter Rowley-Conwy and Robert Layton, "Foraging and Farming as Niche Construction: Stable and Unstable Adaptations," *Philosophical Transactions of the Royal Society B: Biological Sciences* 366, no. 1566 (2011): 849–62; Bruce D. Smith, "General Patterns of Niche Construction and the Management of 'Wild' Plant and Animal Resources by Small-Scale Pre-Industrial Societies," *Philosophical Transactions of the Royal Society B: Biological Sciences* 366, no. 1566 (2011): 836–48, doi:10.1098/rstb.2010.0253; Bruce D. Smith, "Niche Construction and the Behavioral Context of Plant and Animal Domestication," *Evolutionary Anthropology: Issues, News, and Reviews* 16, no. 5 (2007): 188–199, doi:10.1002/evan.20135; Bruce D. Smith, "Resource Resilience, Human Niche Construction, and the Long-Term Sustainability of Pre-Columbian Subsistence Economies in the Mississippi River Valley Corridor," *Journal of Ethnobiology* 29, no. 2 (September 1, 2009): 167–83, doi:10.2993/0278-0771-29.2.167; Nicole L. Boivin et al., "Ecological Consequences of Human Niche Construction: Examining Long-Term Anthropogenic Shaping of Global Species Distributions," *Proceedings of the National Academy of Sciences* 113, no. 23 (June 7, 2016): 6388–96, doi:10.1073/pnas.1525200113; Maurits W. Ertsen, Christof Mauch, and Edmund Russell, eds., *Molding the Planet: Human Niche Construction at Work* (Munich: Rachel Carson Center, 2016).

2

PATRICIAN COEVOLUTION
(1200–1776)

This chapter offers an overview of human–greyhound coevolution in England from 1200 to 1776. The year 1200 is important because it marked the first time greyhounds appeared in written records. The year 1776 is important because it saw the formation of the first coursing club, which initiated a new era in human–greyhound coevolution.

The first two sections of the chapter describe the main canine and human populations of interest in this book: greyhounds and owners. Greyhounds were dogs called greyhounds by the people around them. We know greyhounds lived in England around 1200, but we do not know their ancestors. Greyhounds could have descended from dogs in England or from recent immigrants. Between 1200 and 1831, the primary human population that coevolved with greyhounds was patricians – royals, nobles, and large landowners (gentry). Only patricians could legally own greyhounds. Patricians held a legal monopoly on hunting, and greyhounds were hunting dogs, so rulers restricted greyhound ownership to limit poaching. A secondary coevolving population was kennel servants, who did the hard work of training and caring for greyhounds.

The third section examines the impact of greyhounds on human cultural evolution between 1200 and 1776. Greyhounds did not force people to behave in any specific way. They did create the opportunity for people to behave in certain ways, and patricians took advantage of many of them. Patricians developed complex rituals (behaviors based on memes) for hunting and coursing with greyhounds. These rituals helped patricians advance their interests as a class and as individuals. Greyhounds advanced class interests by symbolizing the line separating political and economic elites from everyone else. Participating in greyhound sports – hunting and coursing – helped patricians build class identity. Greyhounds advanced individual goals of patricians by enabling them to put food on the table, sell meat and fur on the market, and create an elite fraternity within elite classes. Greyhounds also shaped human behavior by exacting prices for desired behaviors. Servants performed most of these exacted behaviors, which including feeding, watering, and training greyhounds.

The fourth section focuses on greyhound niches (job–habitat combinations) and traits. Greyhounds as a whole performed a variety of jobs in a variety of habitats, but individual greyhounds did not. They performed specific jobs in specific habitats. Each species of prey created a different job description for greyhounds. Greyhounds performing the same job (such as hare hunting) in different habitats needed different traits. Greyhounds were packages of physical and behavioral traits adapted to specific niches.

The overall trend in greyhound and human traits was from wider to narrower variation. The primary reason was narrowing of the job dimension of niches. In the medieval period, people and greyhounds hunted and coursed half a dozen species of prey. Each prey species, and each method of pursuit, created a different job description for people and greyhounds. By the eighteenth century, the range of prey had contracted to hares and rabbits. The range of behavioral traits of people, and the range of physical and behavioral traits of greyhounds, narrowed to those used in hunting and coursing lagomorphs.[1]

The fifth section examines the techniques used to adapt greyhounds to niches. Breeders used well-developed techniques to breed greyhounds with the traits they wanted. They believed that environmental variables, as well as parentage, affected the traits of offspring. I call this approach *environmental breeding*. We no longer embrace all elements of environmental breeding, but environmental breeders did develop greyhounds with desired traits.

Overall, the chapter tells the story of coevolution. Greyhounds made it possible for patricians to hunt. Patricians evolved by developing complex hunting and coursing rituals. These rituals defined the jobs performed by greyhounds. Patricians adapted greyhounds to these jobs. This back and forth, with each changing in response to the other, was coevolution.

Origin of Greyhounds

The origin of greyhounds is unclear. If we use a social and linguistic definition of the breed – greyhounds were the dogs called greyhounds by the people living with them – greyhounds seem to have originated in England in the Middle Ages. Some authors have suggested that the laws of Canute (who reigned 1016–1035) proved the presence of greyhounds

in Britain during the Norse period.[2] One such law states that only aristocrats could use greyhounds. The commonly cited laws of Canute were,
however, forged in the twelfth century to justify Norman hunting laws.
The only law Canute apparently issued about hunting consisted of one
sentence that did not mention greyhounds: "And let every man forego my
hunting, wherever I wish to have it free from trespass, under penalty of
the full fine."[3]

One of the earliest records of greyhounds dates from around 1200 CE,
when a treatise on Anglo-Saxon law referred to "The dog, which the
English call *greihund*."[4] The origin of *grei* in *greihund* is mysterious.
It differs from the first half of today's synonyms for *greyhound* in
Germanic languages, such as *Windhund* in German and *windhond* in
Dutch. These names mean, literally (and unsurprisingly), *windhound*.
Wind seems an apt word to apply to a breed famous for its speed.[5]
English speakers sped in a different direction when naming dogs that
ran like the wind. No one knows why. *The Oxford English Dictionary* nomi-
nates words from several languages – Old Icelandic, German, Old
English, Middle English, modern English, and Latin – as roots of *grey* in
greyhound. Candidates include the color *grey*, *Greece* (where greyhounds
originated, according to some), and words meaning *leprosy*, *a kind of fur*,
or *infirm*. The dictionary highlights uncertainty by sprinkling qualifiers
throughout the discussion of candidate roots, including *apparently*, *very
doubtful*, *perhaps*, *alleged*, and *probably*.[6]

Other sources offer other hypotheses for the origin of *grey*. In a 1792
sporting dictionary, William Osbaldiston noted that *grey* may derive from
gre (an abbreviation of *degree*) "because among all dogs they are the most
principal, having the chiefest place, and being surely and absolutely the
best of the gentle kind of hounds."[7] (Here, *gentle* did not mean kind or
well behaved. It meant high-ranking and suitable for gentlemen.) Other
authors noted that *grey* was a medieval and early modern word for *badger*,
so badger-hunting dogs might have been called greyhounds.[8] A painting
accompanying Gaston Phébus's medieval *Le Livre de Chasse* shows long-
snouted dogs attacking a badger.[9] *Le Livre de Chasse* was a French book,
but the English could have used dogs against greys (badgers), too.
Another possibility is that *grey* came from *great*, meaning large. (See
Figure 2.1.) Whatever the origin of *gre*, it seems likely that greyhounds,
defined as dogs called by that name by those around them, originated in
England. They were probably the first population known by that name.

The origin of the second half the breed name – *hund*, later *hound* –
seems clear. *Hund* was a Germanic and Old English word for *dog*; it

Of the *GRAY-HOUND*, with a narration of all strong and great hunting *DOGS*.

Figure 2.1 Gray-Hound in 1658. Before the nineteenth century, English people saw dogs primarily as packages of behaviors that performed specific jobs for specific groups of people. Like other employees, they needed tools (physical traits) to do their jobs. Greyhounds were hunting dogs with sizes scaled to the size of their prey. Large greyhounds chased red deer (elk), small greyhounds caught rabbits, and intermediate size greyhounds chased prey of intermediate sizes. *Gray-hound 1658*, in Edward Topsell, *The History of Four-footed Beasts and Serpents Woodcuts* (London: G. Sawbridge, T. Williams, and T. Johnson, 1658), Special Collections, University of Houston Libraries, accessed March 7, 2016, http://digital.lib.uh.edu/collection/p15195coll18/item/117. Used with permission.

evolved into *hound*.[10] By the sixteenth century, *hound* referred to hunting dogs in particular.[11]

The appearance of *greihund* in print around 1200 coincided with the emergence of a distinct, English identity among elites in Britain. After the

Norman invasion in 1066 CE, Anglo-Norman elites saw themselves as belonging to both England and Normandy. They spoke French. King John (reigned 1199–1216) sparked a split between England and France. The rupture reduced the incentive among elites to speak French, and use of English grew in the thirteenth and fourteenth centuries. In 1362, Parliament ordered legal proceedings to use English because so few people understood French.[12] A royal edict soon dictated that patricians would use greyhounds, under their English name, as tools of class identity and discrimination. Richard II limited greyhound keeping to elites in 1389 because butchers, shoemakers, and tailors were using them to hunt. Parliament followed Richard II's lead and limited the keeping of greyhounds (under the English name) to patricians (aristocrats and the gentry).

Greyhounds descended from other dogs, but we do not know which. The history of dogs began with the domestication of wolves perhaps 15,000 years ago in Eurasia. An unknown line of descent, in which history and biology intertwined, led from the first domesticates to greyhounds in England. Dogs probably immigrated to England around 10,000 years ago, but no skulls from England in that era have the long snout we associate with greyhounds. Ancient art shows long-snouted dogs running around the Mediterranean in the Roman era, but no skulls in England from that period have this feature.[13] Even if dogs with long snouts and greyhound-like bodies lived in England before 1200 CE, it would not prove greyhounds descended from them. The best tool we have to determine ancestry at the moment is genetic analysis, but geneticists have not compared the genomes of ancient and living dogs.[14]

Several scenarios for the ancestry of greyhounds are plausible. One is that an English breed was renamed *greihund* around 1200. A second is that the English created a new breed with distinctive traits, dubbed *greihund*, from other breeds in England. A third is that the English (or someone else) created greihunds by crossing dogs from England and elsewhere. A fourth is that greihund ancestors were recent immigrants from another country.

The strongest candidates for immigrants around 1200 would be dogs from Normandy. Hunting dogs (including some that looked like greyhounds) were common on the continent. Hunting practices, and surely hunting dogs, crossed the English Channel with Anglo-Norman elites.[15] If greihund ancestors were French immigrants, however, it is curious that their French name failed to board the boat or lost its way in Britain. The names of other breeds bespeak their French roots. *Terriers* (dogs that dig into the earth, *terre*) are examples.[16] Today's French translation for *greyhound* is *lévrier*. It comes from *lièvre*, meaning *hare*, which ties the dog's name to its occupation.[17] English greyhounds may have descended, at least in part, from French hunting dogs, but *greihund* did not descend from *lévrier*. *Greihund* appears to be an English coinage.

In sum, *greihunds* were a population of dogs in England around 1200 with traits distinctive enough to merit their own name. We do not know their immediate ancestors (their distant ancestors were wolves). The appearance of *greihund* coincided with a cross-Channel rupture in the Anglo-Norman elite. As a distinct English identity developed among elites, they used dogs with a distinct English name as a tool for defining and distinguishing classes of people. Beginning around 1200, then, greyhounds comprised an identifiable population of dogs.

Greyhound Owners

Like all dog breeds, greyhounds existed only because a particular group of people wanted them to exist. And as with all dog breeds, the traits of greyhounds reflected the desires of that particular group of people. People employed dogs to perform specific jobs, and breed traits enabled dogs to carry out their job descriptions. For greyhounds, the relevant group of people was patricians. Patricians employed greyhounds as hunting dogs, coursing dogs, and symbols of elite status. (See Figure 2.2.) The traits of greyhounds enabled them to fulfill their duties in these occupations.

The occupation that created the most jobs for greyhounds was hunting. Patricians embraced hunting as a birthright. In "the noble Arte of Venerie" (1575), George Gascoigne expressed the belief that God ordained that nobles, and only nobles, should hunt:

> ... it is a *Noble sport,*
> *To recreate the minds of Men, in good and godly sort,*
> *A sport for Noble peeres, a sport for gentle bloods,*
> The paine I leave for servants such, as beate the bushie woods,
> To make their masters sport. *Then let the Lords rejoyce,*
> *Let gentlemen beholde the glee, and take thereof the choyce.*
> For my part (being one) I just needs say my minde,
> *That Hunting was ordeyned first, for Men of Noble kinde.*
> And unto them therefore, I recommend the same
> As exercise that best becomes, their worthy noble name.[18]

Figure 2.2 Coat of Arms of King Henry VII (1485–1509). Greyhounds symbolized such high status that one appeared in Henry VII's coat of arms from 1504. Coat of Arms of King Henry VII (1485–1509), UK National Archives, Catalogue Reference: E33/1, Date: 1504. Reproduced by permission.

The idea that specific breeds of dogs performed specific jobs for specific classes of people was a commonplace in England. In the sixteenth century, the Swiss naturalist Konrad Gesner wrote to Johannes Caius for information about English dogs. Caius served as physician to Mary and Edward VI and headed Gonville College, Cambridge (later renamed "Gonville and Caius" in his honor). Caius's reply to Gesner grew into the first book on English dogs. Originally written in Latin, *Of Englishe Dogges* appeared in an English translation in 1576.[19] Caius assigned breeds to divisions based on the class of their employers. Dogs in the first division, gentle breeds, worked for patricians (here *gentle* meant *elite*, as in *gentlemen and gentlewomen*). Most gentle breeds were hunting dogs (harriers, terriers, bloodhounds, gazehounds, greyhounds, leviners, tumblers, setters, water spaniels, and fishers). One was a pet (spaniels gentle). Gentle breeds had some economic benefits, but patricians were willing to employ them at a financial cost because they served political and social purposes.[20]

Dogs in Caius's second and third divisions, in contrast, worked for tradespeople. They provided net economic benefits to owners. Caius listed two breeds in the second division, homely dogs. Sheep dogs worked for shepherds. Mastiffs were a generalist breed, but individual mastiffs held specialized jobs. They worked for business owners (guarding storehouses), butchers (managing cattle), and tinkers (carrying supplies). Dogs in the third division, mongrels, worked as turnspits, dancers, and wappets. Turnspits helped cooks (they walked in wheels mounted on walls in kitchens, which, thanks to belts and pulleys, rotated spits of meat roasting over open fires). Dancers aided entertainers by prancing in time to music. Wappets (small, yapping, house dogs) protected homes from thieves by barking at strangers.[21]

The class system of England, then, helped draw boundaries around human populations that coevolved with specific breeds of dogs. Patricians used their seats on thrones and in Parliament to harden these boundaries. They issued laws that made hunting a patrician monopoly. They criminalized taking of game by anyone else. The same action – pursuing and killing game – was admirable for one class of people and criminal for everyone else. Patricians managed to write this belief into the English language. The English had no universal term for pursuing and taking game. The same actions were *hunting* if done legally and *poaching, destruction,* or *stealing* if done illegally. Class determined belief, action, law, and language.

Class governed human–greyhound interactions, too. Greyhounds were hunting dogs. To prevent poaching, kings and Parliament limited the ownership of hunting dogs (including greyhounds) to the people who could legally hunt. The legal term for the people entitled to hunt and keep hunting dogs was *qualified.* The qualified, and only the qualified, could hunt and keep greyhounds. Rulers made it clear the purpose of qualification was to divide the population by class. As a 1732 legal treatise put it, "Our legislators tell us, that hunting the Hare is a Recreation for Kings and Noblemen; and that destroying the Game by Persons not qualified by Law, is prejudicial to the Nobility and Gentry, and therefore almost in all Reigns, Statutes have been made to preserve the Game from Destruction, by the meaner Sort of People."[22] It is hard to overestimate the degree to which patricians obsessed over hunting, and ownership of hunting dogs, as class monopolies. Between 1500 and 1831, Parliament passed seventy hunting laws – an average of one every five years.[23]

Patricians restricted other hunting dogs to the qualified, too. In 1389, a law permitted only the qualified to keep dogs to take deer, hares, conies, or "other gentleman's game." This restriction remained in effect until 1831. It applied to any kind of dog kept to take game or rabbits, but it had a loophole. Unless caught in the act, people could claim they kept their dogs for purposes other than catching rabbits or killing game. Parliament tried to solve this problem by restricting four breeds to the qualified: greyhounds, setting dogs (used to locate game), coney-dogs, and lurchers.[24] The listing of these four breeds suggests they were favorites of poachers. Greyhounds, and perhaps setting dogs, may have had shapes distinctive enough to recognize on sight, but *coney-dog* was a generic term for dogs that caught rabbits. *Lurcher* was a generic term for dogs used in poaching.

Greyhounds and other breeds were biotechnologies designed for specialized purposes. The game laws illustrated an instrumental way of thinking about greyhounds by listing them with other technologies limited to patricians. The 1671 law allowed only the qualified to keep or use ferrets (which dove into holes to catch rabbits), nets, crossbows, hand guns, hagbuts and demi-hakes (firearms), bows, setting dogs, hays (nets for catching animals), lowbels (bells used to catch birds), hare-pipes (traps for catching hares), gins (devices for catching game, such as nets and traps), snares, and other "engines" for taking game or rabbits.[25]

The English state punished unqualified people caught with hunting dogs, including greyhounds. A man named Hartley (his first name is lost) offers an example. During the reign of King George III (1760–1820), Hartley was convicted of keeping a greyhound. He faced a fine of five pounds or prison for three or four months.[26] He appealed his conviction. The prosecutor, he said, had not proven that his dog was a greyhound. It might be a different breed, such as an Italian greyhound. Nor had the prosecutor proven that Hartley used his dog for an illegal purpose. The law prohibited him from "keeping and using a greyhound to kill and destroy the game." Hartley argued that he might keep his dog to guard his house. The court rejected both arguments. Keeping "the dog of that species generally known [as the greyhound] in this country," the judges concluded, was "*prima facie* evidence of a keeping for the purpose prohibited."[27]

Patricians took it for granted that kings and nobles qualified by birthright. This seemed so obvious that they neglected to write it in laws for centuries. In 1603, someone realized that this entitlement should be added to the law. A new law qualified sons of "any knight, or of any baron of parliament, or of some person of higher degree, or son and heir apparent of any esquire."[28] First custom, then law, placed kings and nobles inside the human population that coevolved with greyhounds.

The tougher question for legislators was who else should hunt and keep greyhounds. The key criterion that emerged was owning large properties. In 1389, Richard II announced that laymen needed to own property worth forty shillings, and clergy needed incomes of ten pounds per year, to keep greyhounds.[29] In 1430, forty shillings was also the requirement to vote for members of Parliament, illustrating the link between membership in the hunting classes and political voice.[30] The same criteria governed admission to the ruling elite and the ranks of the qualified.

Ideas about qualification went hand in hand with ideas about game ownership. Medieval and early modern kings claimed they owned all game in England. This claim enabled them to hunt anywhere, including on land owned by others. Royals granted aristocrats and members of the gentry permission to hunt in specific areas, which helped to build alliances and control the countryside. Some landowners managed deer preserves and hare warrens to keep game populations high. Over time, landowners came to see the animals they protected as something like livestock, rather than as truly wild beasts. They claimed a right to hunt the animals they protected, and they extended this claim to animals more broadly. Queen Elizabeth I acknowledged this extension when she proclaimed that game "belongeth to men of the best sort and condition."[31] A 1607 game law codified the right of the gentry and nobles to hunt animals on their own land. This law implied that individual patricians owned the game on their own property. A 1671 law gave patricians the right to take game anywhere, which implied that patricians, as a class rather than as individuals, owned all the game in England. In theory, laws against trespass limited the damage hunters could do to the land of others. In practice, the weakness of trespass laws discouraged landowners from filing suit.[32]

Because the purpose of qualification was exclusion, patricians raised requirements when inflation allowed too many barbarians inside the gate. The income threshold under Richard II was forty shillings. In 1603, Parliament raised the property requirement to land or tenements worth ten pounds per year, copyholds worth thirty pounds per year, or goods worth two hundred pounds. In 1671, Parliament increased the property qualification to one hundred pounds, and it qualified owners and keepers of game preserves.[33] The 1671 law qualified warren owners and keepers to keep greyhounds to catch rabbits – that is, to manage their livestock.[34] A sporting magazine later defended these increases by claiming Parliament had not acted "owing to any increasing spirit of monopolization in the Legislature, but to the gradual alteration in the value of money, which has decreased."[35] The "spirit of monopolization in the Legislature" may not have increased over time, but it had not decreased, either. Parliament raised the threshold when inflation allowed too many of "the meaner Sort of People" to hunt.

By legislating qualification, Parliament narrowed niches for greyhounds and people. Niches had two main components: jobs and habitats. Qualification laws set boundaries on greyhound niches by limiting greyhound jobs. Greyhounds could not work for anyone they wished. They could work legally only for patricians. They held only jobs patricians wished them to hold. Similarly, qualification laws set boundaries on human niches. People could not hold any job they wanted with greyhounds. Ninety-nine percent of people became criminals the instant they possessed a greyhound. Only patricians and their servants could legally hold greyhound-related jobs. The human niche was narrower than it would have been in a free market.

In sum, English law defined the human population that could legally coevolve with greyhounds. The force driving the law was the English class system. The purpose of qualification was to reserve hunting, and hunting dogs, to the most powerful classes. Some classes – royals and nobles – inherited qualification by title. Others (mainly the gentry) gained qualification through wealth (which was often inherited). When inflation undermined exclusivity, Parliament raised the property requirements for qualification. The state enforced the boundary around greyhound owners through the criminal justice system, which relied on fines and jail terms to keep greyhounds out of the hands of ordinary people. By limiting the job opportunities for people and greyhounds, Parliament created narrower niches for people and greyhounds than a free market would have afforded.

Human Traits and Coevolution

Greyhound owners evolved in response to both dimensions that made up niches. The first dimension was habitat. Social and ecological forces created and changed habitats. When habitats changed, owners adapted. The frequency of ideas (culture, memes) and behaviors (traits) changed in the population of greyhound owners. The population evolved. These kinds of changes are familiar to historians. We call them history.

The second niche dimension was jobs. Greyhounds shaped the evolution of people through two mechanisms that created job titles and duties.

One mechanism was *creating the opportunity* for patricians to have certain jobs (that is, to behave in certain ways). Greyhounds gave patricians the chance to limit ownership to themselves. Greyhounds' ability to chase fleet prey created the opportunity for patricians to hunt and course. People chose to accept these opportunities. Greyhounds created the opportunity for patricians to behave in other ways, too. Patricians could have chosen to eat greyhounds. So far as I know, they did not capitalize on this opportunity.

The other mechanism through which greyhounds shaped human evolution was *exacting prices* for performing jobs. The price of using greyhounds was performing undesired jobs. These included feeding, watering, housing, and cleaning up after greyhounds. Patricians pushed these jobs onto another human population: servants. Behaviors are traits of organisms. Evolution is change in the frequency of traits in populations. Jobs are packages of behavioral traits. So, whenever the frequency of jobs – hunting, coursing, or feeding greyhounds – changed, human populations evolved. Patricians and greyhounds *coevolved* when they repeatedly changed traits in response to each other.

Greyhounds generated economic opportunities for patricians, and people chose to accept them. One economic opportunity and behavior was putting meat on the table. In the medieval and early modern periods, greyhounds chased at least half a dozen species of prey. In 1576, Johannes Caius reported that greyhounds pursued hares, harts (male red deer aged six years or more), bucks (male fallow deer aged five years or more), does (female fallow deer), foxes, wolves, "and other beastes of semblable kinde ordained for the game of hunting."[36] Roe deer and rabbits were "beastes of semblable kinde."[37] Except for wolves and foxes, these animals provided common, popular meats. Recipes for game were standard features of cookbooks.[38] In 1753, the College of Durham's menu included rabbits, hares, and venison on sixteen of twenty-two days.[39]

A second economic opportunity, and resulting behavior, was generating income. Landowners introduced rabbits in the medieval period, and raised them in warrens, to sell meat and fur on the market.[40] The investment was often high. In the eighteenth century, patricians built walls to prevent rabbits from escaping, protect crops, and keep predators (stoats, weasels, cats, and foxes) at bay. The wall enclosing one warren in the Breckland measured eight miles in length.[41] Greyhounds helped harvest rabbits by driving them into nets or catching and killing them.

Greyhounds created social as well as economic opportunities for patricians. Two social opportunities were defining elite class boundaries and reinforcing hierarchy within elites. We have already seen that patricians on the throne and in Parliament used greyhounds to draw boundaries around elites. Greyhounds enhanced class solidarity by making hunting realistic. By chasing game in groups, patricians got to know each other, did each other favors, and developed a sense of community. In the fifteenth century, Edward (Second Duke of York) noted that hunters who helped find game gained a lord's wine and favor.[42] At the same time, greyhounds created the opportunity to reinforce social status. One example was a butchering ritual. The honor of butchering a hunted animal went to the highest-ranking individual in the company. (See Figure 2.3.) The allocation of pieces of carcass reminded individuals of their social positions. The man who dressed a hart received the left shoulder and the forester the right.[43] Hare loins went to the lord.[44]

More subtly, greyhounds created the opportunity to create a meritocratic elite within the elite. Rank or property qualified someone to hunt, but qualification alone did not make one a respected hunter. Aspiring hunters had to master complex rituals, which helped to keep all but the most committed out of the fraternity. Hunters memorized long sequences of cuts to follow in a prescribed order when butchering greyhound prey. When dismembering a hart, for example, the highest-ranking man performed thirty-three steps in order. He put the hart on its horns, cut off the cods (which seems symbolic of the hunter's masculinity), slit the hart from jaws to cods, and so on for thirty more steps.[45] The allocation of meat to greyhounds followed arcane rules. Those that killed deer received the tongue, brain, lungs, small guts, and blood. Those that killed hares received the shoulders, side, head, and all the entrails except the gall.[46]

Patricians used complex terminology, along with complex behaviors, to enhance barriers to entry to the hunting elite. A 1595 edition of the *Boke of St. Alban's* (a hunting manual attributed to Dame Juliana Berners) stressed the importance of mastering specialized terms: "Now in the hunting of the hart being a princely and royall chace, it giveth an exceeding grace unto a Huntsman, to use the termes fit and proper unto the same."[47] The practice of using different words for similar things illustrated this complexity. Two greyhounds made a *brace*; two hounds made a *couple*. *Hound* was a generic term for hunting dogs, including greyhounds. It was illogical to count greyhounds in a different way from other hounds, which was the point. Only members of the hunting

Figure 2.3 A butchering ritual. Greyhounds created the chance for hunters to create social distinctions among themselves. This image shows a hunter handing a knife to a woman, often presumed to be Queen Elizabeth, to slice a dead deer. Complex rules governed the sequence in which animals were divided and the identity of the person doing the dividing. The dogs in the background helped make these rituals possible. The huntsmen in the background are blowing horns, perhaps in one of the patterns in Figure 2.4. George Turbervile, *Turbervile's Book of Hunting* ([1576] London: Clarendon Press, 1908), 133. Scan by Pam LeRow, University of Kansas.

Figure 2.4 Notes to blow on a horn when greyhounds killed deer. Greyhounds created the opportunity for people to erect a complex culture of hunting. Hunters eschewed common terms in favor of abstruse language specific to types, ages, and sexes of animals. The top staff shows the notes to be blown when greyhounds killed deer (including bucks, which were male roe deer aged five years). The bottom staff shows a different set of notes to blow when other kinds of hounds killed a buck. George Turbervile, *Turbervile's Book of Hunting* ([1576] London: Clarendon Press, 1908), 253. Scan by Pam LeRow, University of Kansas.

fraternity understood this complex, counter-intuitive language. *Brace* and *couple* sat on the tip of the iceberg. Three greyhounds made a *leash*; three hounds made *a couple and a half*. One *slipped* greyhounds; one *cast off* hounds. (When Antony says, "Cry 'Havoc,' and let slip the dogs of war" in William Shakespeare's *Julius Caesar*, he implies the dogs of war were greyhounds.) A cord restraining a greyhound was a *leash*; a cord restraining a hound was a *lyame*. Greyhounds wore *collars*; hounds wore *couples*.[48]

Hunters developed complex terminology for greyhound prey, too. A male red deer was a *Calf* in his first year, a *Brocket* in his second, a *Spayad* in his third, a *Stag* in his fourth, a *Great stag* in his fifth, and a *Hart* in his sixth and subsequent years.[49] A young fallow deer was a *Fawn*, and a young roe deer was a *Kid*.[50] Even terms for waste varied by species. The excrement of deer was *Fewmets* or *Femmishing*, of hares *Crotizing* or *Crotels*, of boars *Lesses*, of foxes and other vermin *Fiaants*, and of otters *Spraints*.[51] Complexity extended to notes on hunting horns. Hunters blew one set of notes when greyhounds killed a buck (or other deer) and a different set of notes when other kinds of hounds killed a buck. (See Figure 2.4.)

Greyhounds enabled patricians to adopt coursing behaviors along with hunting behaviors. *Coursing* has had many meanings, including pursuit of hares or deer with greyhounds, pursuit in which greyhounds used only their eyes (not noses) to follow prey, and contests in which greyhounds competed against each other while onlookers gambled on performance. Here, we focus on the last of these. The purpose of hunting was to kill game; the purpose of coursing was to use game animals to test greyhounds against each other while gambling on their performance. The main species pursued in coursing were hare and deer. As in hunting, patricians developed elaborate rituals and terms to govern coursing.

Hare coursing contests usually featured two greyhounds in pursuit of an animal scared up in the field. In 1575, George Gascoigne reported that finders located a hare by walking and beating through a field. When someone spied a hare, he shouted *sa how*. Those holding greyhounds approached, and the group decided which dogs would course the hare. The person who found the hare walked toward it while saying *up puss up* to start it. Once the hare ran, a mounted company rode between the hare and coverts to keep it in the open. The person holding the greyhounds gave the hare a head start (called *law*). The distance of the law depended on the "grounde and countrie where she [the hare] sitteth." The handler released the greyhounds, which chased the hare.[52]

The complexity of coursing rules, like the complexity of hunting traditions, created an elite within the qualified classes. One might think that the first greyhound to kill a hare would win the course, but this would have been simple enough for anyone to understand. Instead, coursers developed rules that were hard to understand and harder to apply. Roughly, the greyhound that turned a hare more often won the contest. Coursers divided turns into categories and developed formulas for weighting them. It was a wonder anyone could determine the winner of a contest, which was the point. Only those who invested the time to master the culture belonged to the coursing fraternity.

Imagine trying to apply the following rules to greyhounds racing at top speed far across the countryside from judges. Under Gascoigne's rules, the greyhound that gave the most *cotes* usually won. "A Cote," Gascoigne explained, "is when a Greyhounde goeth endways by his fellow [greyhound] and giveth the hare a turne." (See Figure 2.5.) If both dogs gave an equal number of cotes, the one that "beareth [kills] the hare shall winne the wager." If neither greyhound gave a cote, the one that turned the hare more often won. Turning meant the hare was "set about" or directed "round about." When a dog caused the hare to change

THE TURN

Figure 2.5 Turning a hare. Titled "The Turn," this image highlights a contrast between wagering and hunting. Wagering rules rewarded greyhounds for changing a hare's course more than for killing it. Among wagering greyhounds, physical and behavioral traits varied because localities offered different prey, topography, soil, vegetation, gambling rules, and interpretations of rules. A large, fast, smooth-coated greyhound might excel in open, flat terrain against straight-running hares but lose to a small, quick-turning, rough-coated greyhound in hilly, brushy country against hares that darted into hedges. Although this image dates from 1892, the emphasis on turning hares in wagering contests dated to the sixteenth century or earlier. Harding Cox and Gerald Lascelles, *Coursing and Falconry* (London: Longmans, Green, and Co., 1892), facing 30. Courtesy of Special Collections, Kenneth Spencer Research Library, University of Kansas Libraries.

directions to a lesser degree, it was a wrench, not a turn. Two wrenches equaled a turn. Two turns equaled a cote. If one greyhound passed the other but failed to turn the hare, it was strypping, not a cote, but two stryppings equaled a cote. If a greyhound should "coast and so come by his fellow, that is no Cote." If neither greyhound managed a turn, the dog "which went foremost throughout the course must winne the wager."[53]

Complex rules governed the behavior of human coursers, too, and their silliness exemplified the degree to which coursers used arbitrary conventions to separate themselves from others. Under George Turbervile's rules from 1576, anyone saying *bear, ape, monkey,* or *hedgehog* would forfeit the match and "be payde with a flippe upon the buttockes in the fielde before he go any furder."[54]

Rules about flipping coursers on the buttocks exemplified the extravagance with which patricians evolved in response to greyhounds. Greyhounds did not force patricians to use them to symbolize elite status, put food on the table, hunt, or course. Greyhounds did not demand that hunters and coursers develop terminology and rituals so complex they beggared understanding. Greyhounds created the opportunity to do these things. Patricians seized these opportunities with enthusiasm. As the poem above noted, nobles hunted by "choyce," which led them to "rejoyce" with "glee." When the frequency of any behavior, such as handing hare loins to lords, rose or fell, the population of patricians evolved.

At the same time, greyhounds sparked evolution in a different human population by exacting prices. Greyhounds did not work for free. They demanded payment in food, water, and shelter. People had to behave in certain ways to meet these needs. Greyhounds exacted certain behaviors. When the frequency of watering or doctoring greyhounds in a given way rose or fell, a human population evolved. But this population was not, for the most part, patricians. It comprised servants who worked for patricians. They fed, watered, sheltered, doctored, trained, and cleaned up after the dogs. Some servants may have found these activities innately pleasurable, but few would have performed them without pay. Gascoigne reminds us that only masochists could have enjoyed some of them. Beating the woods for prey caused servants "paine."[55] Kennel and hunt servants comprised a second human population that coevolved with greyhounds.

Behavioral traits, whether desired or exacted, were inherited. They passed from one individual to the next via memes. Memes are instructions for behavioral traits. They are the means of inheritance in cultural evolution. Genes, which also are instructions for traits, pass bodily from parents to offspring. Memes do not. They pass from one individual to the next through learning. Learning might come through formal or informal instruction. It might come from mimicking behaviors. It can come from books and sheet music. Patricians and servants inherited hunting, coursing, and kenneling memes through instruction, manuals, and mimicry of observed behavior.[56]

In sum, human populations evolved in many ways in response to greyhounds. So far as we know, all this evolution was cultural, not genetic.

One human population, patricians, evolved by one greyhound-generated mechanism: accepting the chance to engage in desired jobs. Patricians responded to this opportunity with glee. They developed memes and behaviors for hunting, coursing, and earning income. These jobs served economic and social purposes, such as enhancing elite solidarity while reinforcing a hierarchy within elites. A second human population, servants, evolved through a second greyhound-generated mechanism: performing the jobs greyhounds demanded. These jobs included feeding, watering, sheltering, and training greyhounds. Patricians and servants inherited memes for these jobs through informal and formal means. Whenever the frequency of memes and behaviors changed, populations evolved.

Greyhound Traits and Evolution

Like human populations, greyhound populations evolved in response to two factors: habitats and jobs. The working habitats of greyhounds were the same as the working habitats of the people interacting with them (e.g., fields and kennels). Greyhounds evolved when their physical and behavioral traits adapted to habitats. Greyhounds also evolved in response to human-generated jobs. People made it possible for greyhounds to hold a variety of jobs, and greyhounds capitalized on the opportunities. Human and greyhound jobs came in pairs, so, for example, human hunting jobs created greyhound hunting jobs. Similarities among greyhound jobs created similarities in body shape. Variation in greyhound jobs led to variation in traits. Because jobs and habitats varied across England, greyhounds in any given period varied. Because jobs and habitats varied over time, greyhounds varied over time. Whenever the frequency of behavioral or physical traits changed in a greyhound population, the population evolved.

The most distinctive trait of greyhounds, highlighted more in the German *Windhund* than in the English *greyhound*, was a behavior required in all greyhound occupations: running like the wind. Speed enabled greyhounds to catch hares, foxes, and deer. Edward, second Duke of York, wrote in *The Master of Game* (1406–1413), "A good greyhound should go so fast that if he be well slipped he should overtake any beast."[57] Johannes Caius (1576) observed that greyhounds were known for their "incredible swiftnesse."[58]

Selection for speed (a behavioral trait) led greyhounds to have certain physical traits – large chests, narrow waists, and long legs – summed up under the heading of shape. Genetic studies support the idea that selection for speed, more than ancestry, led greyhounds to have these traits. After comparing genomes of purebred dogs today, researchers divided breeds into four groups: Asian/ancient breeds, herding breeds, hunting breeds, and mastiff breeds. Dogs with greyhound shapes appeared in three of the four groups. Afghan hounds and salukis belonged to the Asian/Ancient genome group, along with Siberian huskies and Samoyeds. Greyhounds and borzois appeared, surprisingly, in the herding group, along with Belgian sheepdogs and collies. Whippets, Italian greyhounds, and Ibizan hounds belonged to the hunting group. Despite descending from very different ancestors, then, dogs selected for speed converged on greyhound body shapes.[59]

Consistent selection for speed led to a recognizable body shape over centuries. In a 1486 edition of *The Boke of St. Albans*, a poem listed "the properties of a good greyhound."

> Headed like a Snake,
> Necked like a Drake,
> Footed like a Cat,
> Tailed like a Rat,
> Sided like a Breame,
> And chined like a Beame.[60]

The poem used two terms uncommon today. *Breame* means *gadfly*. Gadflies had wasp-like bodies, so "Sided like a Breame" meant greyhounds had large chests and narrow waists. (See Figure 2.1.) *Chined* refers to the shape of a spine. The poem implied that greyhounds had small heads, long necks, small paws, long and smooth tails, and straight backs. Authors in subsequent centuries quoted this poem as an accurate description of the shape of greyhounds in their day, providing evidence of consistency.

Although similar in shape, greyhounds varied within and between periods. Some of the most important variation came in behaviors. In the fifteenth century, Edward (Duke of York) described ten packages of behaviors that greyhounds needed to pursue ten species of prey. Each species of deer, for example, behaved differently. Greyhounds pursuing harts had to follow animals that walked in water, which made following by scent difficult.[61] Greyhounds, men, and horses had to take care to avoid being killed by cornered harts. The danger led to an adage: "after the boar the leech and after the hart the bier."[62] Greyhounds had to beware lest bucks run them over.[63] Greyhounds pursuing roebucks had to run in and out of streams. When exhausted, roebucks immersed themselves in brooks under roots, so greyhounds had to look for the only body part above water, the head.[64]

Smaller prey also called for species-specific behaviors. Greyhounds chasing hares had to twist and turn their way through brush and open areas for a distance of about four miles.[65] Greyhounds chasing rabbits snapped up and killed their prey.[66] Greyhounds chasing foxes also snapped up and killed their prey, but they added a behavior unnecessary with rabbits. Foxes bit greyhound legs, so greyhounds jumped, folded back their forelegs, and landed on foxes with their chests to pin them. Then they seized foxes about the ears and shook them until they killed them or broke their spines.[67] Boars, wolves, badgers, wildcats, and otters demanded other behaviors from greyhounds.[68]

Prey differed in physical traits as well as behaviors, which rewarded physical variation in greyhounds. One of the more obvious variations came in size. At the large end of the prey scale towered monumental red deer (also known as elk), and at the small end cowered dainty rabbits. In between fell hares, foxes, badgers, roe deer, fallow deer, and wolves. As a result, greyhounds varied in size. As Caius (1576) noted, "the bigger [greyhounds] therefore are appoynted to hunt the bigger beasts, and the smaller serve to hunt the smaller accordingly."[69] Great size helped greyhounds pull down red deer, but large greyhounds had so much momentum they hurtled past turning rabbits. Smaller greyhounds changed direction more adroitly, making them superior in rabbit warrens. For prey of intermediate size, patricians used greyhounds of intermediate size.[70]

Variation in hunting practices also encouraged variation in greyhound behavior. Hunters used more than one method to chase the same species of prey. Deer provide an example. In drive hunting (a medieval method also known as "the king's hunt" or "bow and stable hunting"), servants with dogs drove many deer toward pre-positioned archers. Greyhounds in drive hunting acted as herders and avoided killing the deer, which may explain why greyhounds share so many genes with herding dogs. In hunting *par force*, hunters pursued a single deer with dogs wherever the deer led them.[71] Greyhounds in *par force* hunting acted as trackers and often killed the deer.

When patricians changed their methods of hunting, they adapted the physical and behavioral traits of greyhounds to new methods. In the early modern period, most hunters followed hares on foot (though some rode). In the eighteenth century, following on horseback became popular. Pedestrian hunters (especially in enclosed areas) favored stout, relatively slow, rough greyhounds that turned hares in small circles until they caught the hare or the hare escaped. Horseback riders sought long, straight gallops over open country in pursuit of a hare. They wanted greyhounds that ran as fast as racehorses and forced hares to stay on a straight course. Fleet greyhounds had shorter fur and more lithe bodies than greyhounds followed by pedestrians.[72]

Variation in habitats, like variation in prey, encouraged variation in greyhounds. From the fourteenth to eighteenth centuries, topography and agricultural practices created eight farming regimes: wolds and downlands, arable vale lands (fielden or champion), pastoral vale lands, heathland, forests and wood pastures, fells and moorland, marshland, and fenland.[73] Each regime had distinctive features that demanded different traits in greyhounds. Greyhounds that coursed open, grassy plains usually had short, straight coats, which may have helped them shed heat while running three or four miles in a straight line after hares. Greyhounds that coursed enclosed, brushy areas had long, rough, curly coats to protect them from cuts.[74]

Deer coursing exemplified the extent to which breeders tailored grey-hounds to specific niches (job–habitat combinations). The rules for deer coursing varied by prey species and habitat.[75] One habitat was unfenced forests. Contests with red or fallow deer pitted eight to ten greyhounds against each other at a time. The rules for settling bets in forests depended on the deer species. With red deer, the first greyhound to "pinch" (bite) the deer won the wager. With fallow deer, the first grey-hound to pinch and hold the deer won the wager.[76]

Another deer-coursing habitat was paddocks, where coursers used different rules from those employed in forests. Paddocks were fenced areas about a mile long and a quarter-mile wide. Two greyhounds chased deer with the assistance of a third "teaser" greyhound. After a deer gained a head start, a "teaser or mongrel greyhound" drove the deer forward. A slipper released two greyhounds, which pursued the deer toward the far end. If the deer swerved before reaching a certain post, the course was canceled and run again three days later. If a deer swerved after passing the post, the dog nearest the deer won the match. If the deer ran straight past the post, the dog that leaped the ditch first won.[77]

Patricians adapted greyhounds to variation in hare coursing rules as well. Several sets of hare coursing rules floated around Britain in the patrician era, and each valued different behaviors in greyhounds. Thomas, Duke of Norfolk, wrote rules during the reign of Queen

Elizabeth I that proved popular but as perplexing as Gascoigne's.[78] Sets of rules differed enough to reward different behaviors in greyhounds. Even if coursers used the same written rules, variation in interpretation encouraged variation in greyhound behaviors. Sometimes coursers modified rules explicitly. Gervase Markham (1615) noted, "worthy and well knowing Gentlemen, who having the office of the leashe confer'd upon them, have both authoritie and power to make laws therein according to the customes of countries, and the rules of reason."[79] In other cases, vague language invited differences in interpretation. Gascoigne did not define terms, such as *coast*. He did not state the angle that separated a wrench from a turn. Even the meaning of *cote* was unclear. Coursing expert John Henry Walsh reported in the nineteenth century that for hundreds of years *cote* "was enveloped in mystery. No two sets of rules agreed in defining it, and, in fact, no rule before [one issued in the nineteenth century] was at all intelligible."[80]

The range of jobs open to greyhounds narrowed over time, which led to narrowing of greyhound traits. Jobs hunting deer disappeared except for occasional work culling overstocked parks.[81] Wolves went extinct in England by the late medieval period, boars became rare, and foxhounds developed a monopoly on fox hunting.[82] By the eighteenth century, greyhounds worked almost solely catching hares and, occasionally, rabbits. Greyhounds evolved in response to narrowing of job opportunities. Behavioral traits used in hunting nine species of prey drifted (that is, became more or less frequent due to chance rather than selection). Physical traits needed for specific prey, such as large size for deer, probably declined as well. Narrowing prey species to hares did not, however, produce identical job descriptions. Hunting and coursing were different jobs calling for different traits, and rules for coursing varied as well.

Greyhounds lost jobs because patricians lost interest and habitats changed. In the medieval and early modern period, patricians valued deer as a source of meat and status. They raised deer in protected areas known as parks, chases, and forests. Parks were private, fenced lands for deer. Earls, bishops, monasteries, nunneries, minor gentry, colleges, and the crown owned parks, which made deer into semi-domesticated animals in large corrals. Around 1300, England hosted about 3,200 parks. If each averaged 200 acres, parkland would have covered 2 percent of England. Owners relied on parks for venison, other meat, and wood.[83] In contrast, chases were private, unfenced deer preserves.[84] Forests were royal, unfenced preserves, which might or might not have woodlands. Trees, heaths, farms, and villages lay within forests. We owe this sense of *forest* to the Normans. William the Conqueror adored deer and forests, and the crown owned at least twice as many unfenced deer preserves as all other landowners combined. The king owned the deer, but only some of the land, in forests.[85]

Habitats changed in the seventeenth century because the Civil War threw open the metaphorical doors to deer preserves. Opponents of royal and aristocratic privilege, unpaid soldiers, and opportunists rushed in to slaughter deer as fast as they could. The Restoration returned a monarch to power, but efforts to protect deer never returned to pre-war levels.[86] As a passion for scenery surged in the eighteenth century, landowners converted parks to deer-free uses.[87] Roe deer went extinct in England by 1800, except in the far north.[88] Fallow deer lived in parks and forests rather than roaming loose.[89] Decline in the number of prey species reduced the number of jobs open to greyhounds.[90]

Several habitat changes helped rabbit and hare populations to soar when other prey species disappeared, which increased jobs for greyhounds pursuing lagomorphs. One was the enclosure movement. Enclosure of common areas to create private fields generated a need to demarcate parcels of land set aside for a landowner's use, and hedgerows proved popular for doing so. These woody borders, which abutted farm fields rich with food favored by hares and rabbits, created an ideal habitat. Hedges also supplied rabbits and hares with places to hide from predators. A second factor was the introduction of winter fodder. A scarcity of food in wintertime had acted as a brake on rabbit and hare populations. When farmers introduced winter fodder crops (such as vetch) in the seventeenth and eighteenth century, they enabled more rabbits and hares to survive and reproduce. A third factor was a surge in predator control. Interest in hunting small game (such as pheasants, partridges, and hares) drove an increase in efforts to kill predators, such as stoats, weasels, and birds of prey. Rabbits and hares benefited from the reduction of predators even when they were not the intended beneficiaries.[91] A fourth process was protection of warrens for both species. Rabbits entered England as live-stock raised in warrens, and hares hopped into England on their own as wild species after the last ice age, but they both found themselves living in protected warrens in the eighteenth century. In 1781, Peter Beckford maintained a warren of 30 acres, and it provided him with 60 hares a year. He recommended keeping dogs out of the warren (except when starting hares) and setting traps for polecats and stoats.[92]

In sum, two patterns characterized greyhound traits and evolution in the patrician period. The first pattern was variation. The greyhound population as a whole varied because individual greyhounds specialized in specific niches (job–environment combinations). Because jobs and habitats varied, greyhound traits – physical and behavioral – varied in space and time. The second pattern was narrowing of variation. As the range of jobs narrowed, the range of traits needed in greyhounds narrowed. The frequency of certain behavioral and physical traits declined. The greyhound population evolved when the range of variation in traits narrowed.

Environmental Breeding

Patricians tailored greyhounds to niches using well-developed breeding techniques. In much of the patrician period, breeders took a broad approach I call *environmental breeding*. Breeders thought many variables, including the environment, shaped the traits of animals. They considered breeding to be a long process with many steps, including nursing and training of dogs. (In the eighteenth century, elite breeders narrowed the definition of breeding to selective mating of males and females to enhance desired traits. This approach, known as *modern breeding*, is covered in Chapter 3.) Breeders did not breed greyhounds as generalists. Instead, they bred individual greyhounds for specific niches.

The first step in environmental breeding was to determine the traits an individual dog needed for its job and habitat. George Turbervile's manual of 1576 recommended that breeders analyze about forty traits.[93] Both the kind and the number of traits in Turbervile's list were important. The list included two kinds of traits: behavioral and physical. Almost half the traits were behaviors. They included gallantry, lustiness, scenting ability, persistence in following a scent despite noise from the field, reaction to horses, reaction to water, inclination to run at livestock, endurance, speed, tolerance of heat, tolerance of cold, trainability, ability to endure pain, ability to turn, courage, response to the calls and horns of its master, tendency to emulate other dogs, desire to kill prey, and suitability for hunting a variety of prey (some dogs generalized more than others, depending on an owner's preferences). The other half or so were physical traits. They included color, coat pattern, suitability for prey (such as harts versus hares), strength, body size, leg length, weight, head shape, nostril shape, ear shape and thickness, spine shape, haunch shape, thigh shape, ham shape, tail shape, texture of belly hair, moistness of the sole of the foot, claw size, and foot shape.[94]

Selecting for alternate versions of forty traits could have made every greyhound in England unique. If we make the simplifying assumption that each trait (such as coat length) came in two versions (such as long or short), *the number of trait combinations exceeded one trillion* (2^{40} = 1,099,511,627,776). The number of greyhound versions fell short of the maximum because fewer than a trillion greyhounds lived in England (tens of thousands might be a reasonable estimate) and breeders produced multiple greyhounds with similar traits. But few breeders made identical decisions about all traits, so variation was more common than uniformity.

The second step in environmental breeding was selective mating. In addition to looking for the right working traits, breeders chose parents for their breeding traits. A good bitch was strong, well proportioned, and had large flanks. Young studs would produce light whelps, and old studs would father heavy, less gallant whelps. In choosing the stud, breeders considered the long-term impact. They believed every litter from a dam would include one whelp that resembled the father of a bitch's first litter. Breeders timed mating to coincide with the right environmental conditions. Once a bitch came into heat, breeders waited until the full moon passed (and, preferably, until the signs of Gemini and Aquarius appeared) for mating. Mating under the right signs encouraged more males in the litters and protected the offspring from madness.[95] In other words, offspring inherited traits from the heavens as well as from parents.

Subsequent steps reflected the impact of surroundings on the traits of pups. In the third step, raising whelps, Turbervile cautioned that dams (not foster dams) should nurse their pups to ensure they inherited the mother's traits. In the fourth step, culling whelps, some breeders favored the pups that sucked the teats nearest the dam's heart because the blood there was most delicate. Other breeders focused on physical traits when culling, such as hair texture, mouth color, and number of dewclaws. In the fifth step, nursing (here meaning *maturing*, rather than *suckling* or *tending*), Turbervile counseled raising pups in the country, where they would learn to track and roam, rather than in butcher shops, where they could grow heavy and mad from eating too much meat. In the sixth step, kenneling, breeders used diet to tailor greyhounds to prey species. They fed meat to greyhounds destined to chase harts because it would bulk up their bodies, and they used mainly a vegetarian diet for dogs designed to chase hares to keep them lean and fast.[96]

In sum, breeders used well-developed techniques to shape the traits of greyhounds. Whether we embrace all the principles of environmental breeding today is not important. The point is that breeders developed dogs with desired traits. The result was a breed with similarities in some traits and variation in others. Few breeders developed generalist greyhounds. Instead, they tailored individual dogs to specific niches. The fine-tuning was astonishing. By selecting for alternate versions of forty traits, breeders could create a trillion different versions of greyhounds. They did not create this many, but nothing would have stopped them if they tried. No organization policed breeding. Decisions were in the hands of individuals, who manipulated greyhound traits as they wished. By shaping the traits of individual dogs, breeders shaped the evolution of greyhound populations as a whole.

Conclusion

When patricians bred greyhounds, they used evolution to advance their interests as a class and as individuals. Selecting greyhounds to pursue fleet prey produced dogs with a distinctive appearance, which enabled patricians to use the breed for class definition. Adapting greyhounds to specific job–environment combinations enabled individual patricians to pursue varied economic and social goals. Variation in patrician goals encouraged variation among greyhounds. Greyhounds were biotechnologies, breeders were product designers, and breeding was the process of making biotechnologies.

Change in the traits of the greyhound population as a whole was important because it demonstrated the extent to which breeds were historical products, not fixed entities that raced through time unchanged. The traits of greyhounds in 1400 differed from the traits of greyhounds in 1800 because conditions changed. In 1400, patricians thought it was important to protect deer in preserves for economic and social reasons, which fostered deer-chasing jobs, which led breeders to adapt greyhounds to deer-chasing. A political revolution in the seventeenth century attacked deer preserves, reducing the number of deer-chasing jobs for greyhounds. A shift in aesthetic values in the eighteenth century hammered the nail in the coffin of deer-chasing except in a few isolated spots. With no need for deer-chasing traits, breeders stopped selecting for those traits.

Once patricians shaped greyhounds, the traits of greyhounds circled back to shape human experience. Greyhounds had biological needs that

How a Kennell ought to be ſituate and trimmed ſor Houndes.   Chap. 12

Figure 2.6 Patrician investment in greyhounds. George Turbervile's (1576) plan for a kennel portrayed an elaborate, well-constructed kennel with provisions for fresh water and a house-like shelter. George Turbervile, *Turbervile's Book of Hunting* ([1576] London: Clarendon Press, 1908), 26. Scan by Pam LeRow, University of Kansas.

set limits on breeding and placed demands on owners. If patricians could have bred dogs for any trait they wanted, they would have eliminated the need for food, water, and shelter. But they could not, which encouraged people to build kennels, deliver food and water, and treat illness. (See Figure 2.6.) In other aspects of their interaction, greyhounds did not set limits so much as create opportunities for patricians to behave in certain ways. The people described in this chapter did not have to use greyhounds to reach their goals, but they did so in a way that shaped lives of the qualified, the unqualified, and greyhounds.

The upshot of this system was class-based coevolution and niches. Class determined which human populations would coevolve with which classes of dogs. Within classes, occupations determined which human populations would coevolve with which breeds of dogs. Occupations included paid and unpaid labor. Hunting was a human occupation. Hunters coevolved with greyhounds (and other hunting dogs). Because greyhounds made hunting realistic, and because hunting made greyhound jobs realistic, hunters and greyhounds co-constructed niches for each other. Hunter and greyhound niches had similar habitat dimensions. Hunters and greyhounds pursued the same prey in the same landscapes (though they went home to different habitats). The job dimensions of niches for hunters and greyhounds were different but complementary. Servants also coevolved with greyhounds, but they evolved in different ways from patricians. The greyhound-related traits that rose in frequency among servant populations were behaviors that kept greyhounds healthy and helped scare up game. These behaviors were the prices greyhounds exacted in return for making desired human behaviors (hunting) possible. Greyhounds helped patricians and servants alike construct niches, but the niches of the human populations differed.

Notes

1. A number of secondary sources informed my approach to the primary sources used in this chapter, including Emma Griffin, *Blood Sport: Hunting in Britain since 1066* (New Haven; London: Yale University Press, 2007); Arthur W. Coaten, *British Hunting: A Complete History of the National Sport of Great Britain and Ireland from Earliest Records* (London: Sampson Low, Marston & Co, 1909); E. P. Thompson, *Whigs and Hunters: The Origin of the Black Act* (London: Allen Lane, 1975); P. B. Munsche, *Gentlemen and Poachers: The English Game Laws, 1671–1831* (Cambridge: Cambridge University Press, 1981); David Cannadine, *The Decline and Fall of the British Aristocracy* (New Haven: Yale University Press, 1990); Barry Lewis, *Hunting in Britain: From the Ice Age to the Present* (Stroud, Gloucestershire: History Press, 2009); Roger B. Manning, *Hunters and Poachers: A Social and Cultural History of Unlawful Hunting in England, 1485–1640* (Oxford; New York: Clarendon Press; Oxford University Press, 1993); Harriet Ritvo, *The Animal Estate: The English and Other Creatures in the Victorian Age* (Cambridge, MA: Harvard University Press, 1987).

2. Cynthia A. Branigan, *The Reign of the Greyhound: A Popular History of the Oldest Family of Dogs* (Hoboken: Howell, 1997), 75–77; John Henry Walsh, *The Dog in Health and Disease. Comprising the Various Modes of Breaking and Using Him for Hunting, Coursing, Shooting, Etc., and Including the Points or Characteristics of All*

Dogs, Which Are Entirely Rewritten, 3rd edn. (London: Longmans, Green, 1879), 19.

3. Laurence M. Larson, *Canute the Great 995 (circa)-1035 and the Rise of Danish Imperialism during the Viking Age* (New York: G. P. Putnam's Sons, 1912), 279.

4. The treatise was in Latin: "*Canem quem Angli dicunt* greihund," in *Oxford English Dictionary*.

5. *Oxford English Dictionary*.

6. *Oxford English Dictionary*.

7. William Osbaldiston, *The British Sportsman, Or, Nobleman, Gentleman, and Farmer's Dictionary, of Recreation and Amusement* (London: J. Stead, 1792), 366; for a discussion of other theories not included in the *Oxford English Dictionary*, see Hugh Dalziel, *The Greyhound; Its History, Points, Breeding, Rearing, Training, and Running* (London: L. Upcott Gill, 1887), 11–12.

8. Delabere Pritchett Blaine, *An Encyclopaedia of Rural Sports: Or a Complete Account, Historical, Practical, and Descriptive, of Hunting, Shooting, Fishing, Racing, and Other Field Sports and Athletic Amusements of the Present Day* (London: Longman, Orme, Brown, Green and Longmans, 1840), 556.

9. Gaston Phébus, *Le Livre de Chasse de Gaston Phébus* (Paris: Bibliotheque de l'Image, Maison de la Chasse et de la Nature, 2002), 66.

10. *Oxford English Dictionary*.

11. Gervase Markham, *Countrey Contentments, in Two Bookes: The First, Containing the Whole Art of Riding Great Horses in Very Short Time, with the Breeding, Breaking, Dyeting and Ordring of Them, and of Running, Hunting and Ambling Horses, with the Manner How to Use Them in Their Travell. Likewise in Two Newe Treatises the Arts of Hunting, Hawking, Coursing of Grey-Hounds with the Lawes of the Leash, Shooting, Bowling, Tennis, Baloone &c. The Second Intituled, the English Huswife: Containing the Inward and Outward Vertues Which Ought to Be in a Compleate Woman: As Her Physicke, Cookery, Banqueting-Stuffe, Distillation, Perfumes, Wooll, Hemp, Flaxe, Dairies, Brewing, Baking, and All Other Things Belonging to an Houshold. A Worke Very Profitable and Necessary for the Generall Good of This Kingdome* (London: I. B. for R. Iackson, 1615), 4 (emphasis in original).

12. Albert C. Baugh and Thomas Cable, *A History of the English Language*, 5th edn. (Upper Saddle River.: Prentice Hall, 2002), 108–49.

13. R. A. Harcourt, "The Dog in Prehistoric and Early Historic Britain," *Journal of Archaeological Science* 1, no. 2 (June 1974): 151–75.

14. Francis Galibert et al., "Toward Understanding Dog Evolutionary and Domestication History," *Comptes Rendus Biologies* 334, no. 3 (March 2011): 190–96.

15. Phébus, *Le Livre de Chasse de Gaston Phébus*; Branigan, *Reign of the Greyhound*, 21–94.

16. *Oxford English Dictionary*.

17. Phébus, *Le Livre de Chasse de Gaston Phébus*, 24–27, 54, 58–59, 66, 89, 93.

18. George Gascoigne, *The Noble Arte of Venerie or Hunting. VVherein Is Handled and Set out the Vertues, Nature, and Properties of Fiuetene Sundrie Chaces Togither, with the Order and Maner How to Hunte and Kill Euery One of Them. Translated and Collected for the Pleasure of All Noblemen and Gentlemen, out of the Best Approued Authors, Which Haue Written Any Thing concerning the Same: And Reduced into*

Such Order and Proper Termes as Are Vsed Here, in This Noble Realme of England (London: Henry Bynneman, 1575), unpaginated front matter. Emphasis in original.

19. Thomas E. Marston, "Of Englishe Dogges," *The Yale University Library Gazette* 51, no. 1 (July 1, 1976): 18–20.

20. Johannes Caius, *Of Englishe Dogges* ([1576] Amsterdam, New York: Da Capo Press, 1969).

21. Caius, *Of Englishe Dogges.*

22. William Nelson, *The Laws of England concerning the Game of Hunting, Hawking, Fishing and Fowling, Etc.*, 2nd edn. (The Savoy: Richard Chandler, 1732), Preface (unpaginated).

23. Munsche, *Gentlemen and Poachers*, 170–71.

24. Munsche, *Gentlemen and Poachers*, 180–81.

25. Munsche, *Gentlemen and Poachers*, 180–81.

26. Munsche, *Gentlemen and Poachers*, 180–82.

27. Richard Burn and William Woodfall, *The Justice of the Peace, and Parish Officer*, 20th edn., vol. 2 (London: A. Strahan, 1805), 417–18. Emphasis in original.

28. Munsche, *Gentlemen and Poachers*, 180.

29. Nelson, *The Laws of England concerning the Game of Hunting, Hawking, Fishing and Fowling, Etc.*, 2nd edn. (unpaginated); Munsche, *Gentlemen and Poachers*, 170–71, 180; Griffin, *Blood Sport*, 62.

30. Frederick C. Dietz, *A Political and Social History of England* (New York: Macmillan, 1932), 494.

31. Munsche, *Gentlemen and Poachers*, 10–11.

32. Munsche, *Gentlemen and Poachers*, 12–13.

33. Munsche, *Gentlemen and Poachers*, 180–81.

34. Munsche, *Gentlemen and Poachers*, 180–81.

35. Anonymous, "Compendium of the Game Laws," *Sporting Magazine* 9, Oct. (1821): 9–14, see 9.

36. Caius, *Of Englishe Dogges*, 9–10.

37. Gascoigne, *Noble Arte of Venerie or Hunting*, 142–44, 244–45.

38. Anonymous, *A Propre New Booke of Cokery Declaryng What Maner of Meates Bee Best in Ceason for All Tymes of Ye Yere and How Thes Ought to Bee Dressed and Serued at the Table Bothe for Fleshe Daies and Fisshe Daies: With a Newe Addicion, Veri Necessarye for All Them That Delighteth in Cokery*, Early English Books, 1475–1640/1773:01 (London: Richard Lant and Richarde Bankes, 1545); John Murrell, *Murrels Tvvo Books of Cookerie and Carving*, Early English Books, 1641–1700/2051:08 (London: M. F[lesher] for Iohn Marriot, 1641); John Thacker, *The Art of Cookery Containing above Six Hundred and Fifty of the Most Approv'd Receipts Published under the Following Heads ...*, 2nd edn. (London: J. Richardson, 1762).

39. Thacker, *Art of Cookery*, unpaginated at end of book.

40. John Sheail, *Rabbits and Their History* (Newton Abbot: David and Charles, 1971), 35–47.

41. Sheail, *Rabbits and Their History*, 35–47.

42. Edward, Second Duke of York, *The Master of Game* ([1406–1413] London: Chatto and Windus, 1909), 8, 13.

43. Juliana Barnes and Gervase Markham, *The Gentlemans Academie, Or, the Booke of S. Albans: Containing Three Most Exact and Excellent Bookes: The First of Hawking, the Second of All the Proper Termes of Hunting, and the Last of Armorie: All Compiled by Juliana Barnes, in the Yere from the Incarnation of Christ 1486, and Now Reduced into a Better Method, by G. M.* (London: Humfrey Lownes, 1595), 34–35.

44. Juliana Barnes (Berners) and William Gryndall, *Hawking, Hunting, Fouling, and Fishing, with the True Measures of Blowing* (London: Adam Islip, 1596), unpaginated ("Of the Hare" and "The Reward for the Hounds").

45. Barnes and Markham, *Gentlemans Academie*, 34–35.

46. Barnes and Markham, *Gentlemans Academie*, 34–35.

47. Barnes and Markham, *Gentlemans Academie*, 34.

48. Gascoigne, *Noble Arte of Venerie or Hunting*, 240.

49. Barnes and Markham, *Gentlemans Academie*, 30.

50. Gascoigne, *Noble Arte of Venerie or Hunting*, 240.

51. Nicholas Cox, *The Gentleman's Recreation, in Four Parts; (Viz.) Hunting, Hawking, Fowling, Fishing. Collected from Ancient and Modern Authors Forrein and Domestick, and Rectified by the Experience of the Most Skilfull Artists of These Times* (London: E. Flesher, 1674), 4.

52. Gascoigne, *Noble Arte of Venerie or Hunting*, 245–46.

53. Gascoigne, *Noble Arte of Venerie or Hunting*, 246–47. Defining "beareth" as killing is in George Turbervile, *Turbervile's Booke of Hunting* ([1576] London: Clarendon Press, 1908), 248.

54. Turbervile, *Turbervile's Booke of Hunting*, 249.

55. Gascoigne, *Noble Arte of Venerie or Hunting*.

56. Gascoigne, *Noble Arte of Venerie or Hunting*; Barnes (Berners) and Gryndall, *Hawking, Hunting, Fouling, and Fishing, with the True Measures of Blowing*; Edward, Second Duke of York, *Master of Game*.

57. Edward, Second Duke of York, *Master of Game*, 115.

58. Caius, *Of Englishe Dogges*, 9.

59. Elaine A. Ostrander and Robert K. Wayne, "The Canine Genome," *Genome Research* 15, no. 12 (December 1, 2005): 1706–16.

60. Her name has also been spelled Barnes and Bernes. Much has been speculated about Berners and her personal history, but little is known. The introduction to an 1800 facsimile of *The Boke of St. Albans* summed up knowledge about her in a way that holds true today. It noted, "She probably lived at the beginning of the fifteenth century, and she possibly compiled from existing MSS some rhymes on Hunting." William Blades and Juliana Berners, *The Boke of Saint Albans* (London: E. Stock, 1800), 13; Rachel Hands, "Juliana Berners and The Boke of St. Albans," *The Review of English Studies* 18, no. 72 (November 1, 1967): 373–86.

61. Edward, Second Duke of York, *Master of Game*, 33.

62. Edward, Second Duke of York, *Master of Game*, 23.

63. Edward, Second Duke of York, *Master of Game*, 39.

64. Edward, Second Duke of York, *Master of Game*, 43–44.

65. Edward, Second Duke of York, *Master of Game*, 1–13.
66. Giles Jacob, *The Compleat Sportsman in Three Parts* (London: Eliz. Nutt, 1718), 70–71.
67. Gascoigne, *Noble Arte of Venerie or Hunting*, 248.
68. Edward, Second Duke of York, *Master of Game*, v.
69. Caius, *Of Englishe Dogges*, 10.
70. Markham, *Countrey Contentments*, 99.
71. Griffin, *Blood Sport*, 50–55.
72. Henry Thomas Alken, *The National Sports of Great Britain: Fifty Engravings with Descriptions* ([1825] New York: D. Appleton, 1903), coursing section (unpaginated).
73. Francis Pryor, *The Making of the British Landscape: How We Have Transformed the Land, from Prehistory to Today* (London: Allen Lane, 2010), 382.
74. D., "Coursing in the North of England and Fox-Hunting in Scotland," *Annals of Sporting and Fancy Gazette* 1, no. 4 (1822): 235–36, see 236; Caius, *Of Englishe Dogges*, 10; Osbaldiston, *British Sportsman*, 367.
75. They may have gambled on contests with roe deer, too, but I have not found a record of it.
76. Gascoigne, *Noble Arte of Venerie or Hunting*, 245.
77. Blaine, *An Encyclopaedia of Rural Sports [1840]*, 582–83; Gascoigne, *Noble Arte of Venerie or Hunting*, 245.
78. Harding Cox and Gerald Lascelles, *Coursing and Falconry* (London: Longmans, Green, and Company, 1892), 4–5.
79. Markham, *Countrey Contentements*, 106.
80. J. H. Walsh, *Manual of British Rural Sports: Comprising Shooting, Hunting, Coursing, Fishing, Hawking, Racing, Boating, Pedestrianism, and the Various Rural Games and Amusements of Great Britain* (London: G. Routledge, 1856), 212.
81. William Taplin, *The Sportsman's Cabinet; Or, a Correct Delineation of the Various Dogs Used in the Sports of the Field: Including the Canine Race in General. Consisting of a Series of Engravings of Every Distinct Breed ... Illustrated by a Comprehensive, Historical, and Systematic Description of the Different Species; with a Review of the Various Diseases to Which They Are Subject, and the Most Approved and Efficacious Modes of Treatment and Cure. To Which Is Added, a Scientific Disquisition upon the Distemper, Canine Madness, and the Hydrophobia*, vol. 1 (London: J. Cundee, 1803), 31.
82. Oliver Rackham, *The History of the Countryside* (London: Phoenix Giant, 1997), 34–37.
83. Rackham, *The History of the Countryside*, 122–29.
84. Rackham, *The History of the Countryside*, 39, 129–39.
85. Rackham, *The History of the Countryside*, 39, 129–39.
86. Griffin, *Blood Sport*, 97–107.
87. Rackham, *The History of the Countryside*, 122–29.
88. University of Michigan, *Animal Diversity Web*, accessed August 12, 2013, http://animaldiversity.ummz.umich.edu/; Rackham, *The History of the Countryside*, 39–40.
89. Rackham, *The History of the Countryside*, 49.

90. Rackham, *The History of the Countryside*, 39, 129–39.
91. Sheail, *Rabbits and Their History*, 110, 132–37.
92. Peter Beckford, *Thoughts on Hunting in a Series of Familiar Letters to a Friend* ([1781] New York: Derrydale Press, 2000), 105.
93. Turbervile, *Turbervile's Booke of Hunting*, "The Contentes of this Booke" (unpaginated).
94. Turbervile, *Turbervile's Booke of Hunting*, 4–15.
95. Turbervile, *Turbervile's Booke of Hunting*, 16–18.
96. Turbervile, *Turbervile's Booke of Hunting*, 25–26.

3

HUMAN EVOLUTION IN
A TRANSITIONAL ERA (1776–1831)

This chapter focuses on ways in which subpopulations of patricians evolved during a period of rapid social change. The subpopulations comprised elites in coursing clubs. Clubs shaped the evolution of human populations by narrowing niches, which led to narrowed variation in behavioral traits. Clubs narrowed niches by standardizing job descriptions for people. They did so by adopting formal rules governing behavior of members while coursing and socializing. Clubs also standardized habitats. Each club coursed the same estate repeatedly, so habitats remained constant. With standardized jobs and habitats, niches for club members narrowed.

Human populations evolved when they adapted to narrowed niches. When club members followed standard rules for behavior while coursing and socializing, variation in behavioral traits of club members narrowed. Human populations adapted to standardization in habitats as well as in job descriptions. Club members behaved in similar ways while coursing a given estate (e.g., by positioning themselves in similar places to watch). Human populations evolved when variation in behavioral traits narrowed in response to habitat standardization.

Meme transmission facilitated narrowing of behavioral traits. Club members learned the rules (memes) governing behavior. Important memes included rules for coursing, rules for socializing, and ideas about breeding. The rate and scale of meme transmission increased in the transitional era. Two of the most important reasons were increased bureaucracy (the rise of clubs) and increased communication (the rise of a sporting press). Clubs made it easier to share memes by writing rules. Once in writing, rules could be spread through the post and the new sporting press. Sporting magazines and books published information from coursing clubs, including rules. When members of one club read about practices of another club, they inherited memes. Information sharing and shared membership encouraged a sense that members of elite clubs belonged to a fraternity. Clubs created islands of local uniformity in human populations. Exchange of memes among clubs enhanced similarities in behaviors among club members separated in space.

Larger forces created an environment favoring the spread of certain memes and behaviors. Key memes in this regard were beliefs that club members, club greyhounds, and club breeding methods were superior to other people, dogs, and breeding methods. The period from 1776 to 1831 saw economic, political, and social developments that challenged the status of landed elites. With the idea of inherited superiority under threat, aristocrats and the landed gentry created exclusive coursing clubs that reinforced inherited privilege.

With these changes, club members modernized their evolution in modest ways. Coursing club members referred to their version of coursing as *modern*, and they adopted four features of modernity in the transitional decades. They developed local *bureaucracies* (clubs), *standardized* job descriptions (written rules), capitalized on *mass communication* (sporting magazines), and adopted an idea of *progress* through science (breeding). These features of modernity shaped courser evolution by creating islands of local uniformity in a sea of national variation. Compared to events after 1831, however, these changes were weak versions of modernity. Clubs were local bureaucracies, rules were standardized locally, magazines moved at a stately pace compared to the telegraphic news that followed, and their ideology of progress was constrained (it barred everyone but patricians from participating).

Creating New Human Populations

Aristocrats had good reason to feel nervous between 1776 and 1831. One reason was political ferment. In 1776, pesky colonials on the other side of the Atlantic declared their independence from England. To justify rejection of rule by an inherited monarch, the upstarts claimed an "equal station to which the Laws of Nature and of Nature's God entitle them."[1] In the subsequent decade, commoners across the narrow English Channel overthrew the aristocracy and monarchy. Elite French heads, accustomed to ruling the body politic, could not rule even their own bodies after the guillotine finished its work. What would stop democratic ideas from inspiring commoners in England?

Economic change was also in the air. Adam Smith tried to understand these changes in a massive book titled the *Wealth of Nations*, which he published in 1776. Smith breathed life into the claim that ordinary merchants, more than government rulers, knew how to run the economy. Their collective decisions, embodied in markets, would allocate resources well if left alone. A third source of change was technology. Textile manufacturers in the north introduced new machines that replaced labor and powered the rise of industry. In 1776, James Watt developed a new steam engine that generated more power than earlier models. Steam engines soon powered the machines of industrialization. Change was afoot.

Rapid change became the norm. The English population grew 52 percent in the second half of the eighteenth century. Between 1700 and 1801, the number of people making a living outside agriculture jumped from 240,000 to three million. Industrialization increased population and wealth in the northern part of the country. The French Revolution terrified English patricians and spawned clubs dedicated to fighting republicans and levelers. In 1816–1817, disorder led to suspension of *habeus corpus* and the passage of a seditious meetings bill. Calls for reform of Parliament grew louder. The Tories, who controlled Parliament from 1783 to 1830, had a large stake in defending the status quo.[2]

Amidst these tossing seas, an eccentric Norfolk noble built an island of reassurance. He came from the Walpole family, which had been part of the landed gentry in Norfolk since the eleventh century. One member of the family was Whig Prime Minister Robert Walpole (1676–1745). Robert became the first Lord Orford upon his resignation from government in 1742. Robert's grandnephew, George Walpole (1730–1791), became the third Lord Orford in 1751 (hereafter, Lord Orford). The lord enjoyed a profligacy of titles, including Baron of Houghton, Baron Clinton and Say, ranger and keeper of Saint James's and Hyde Park, lord lieutenant for the county of Norfolk and the city of Norwich, militia colonel, high steward of Great Yarmouth, and lord of the bedchamber to King George II.[3]

To this abundance of titles, Lord Orford offered a shortage of sense. He developed a reputation for eccentricity, profligacy, and, eventually, insanity.[4] He spent without limit. Mired in debt, he sold Houghton Hall's collection of paintings, which great uncle Robert Walpole had built, to Catherine the Great of Russia in 1779.[5] Catherine placed the paintings in the Hermitage in St. Petersburg (where some remain).[6] If anyone wanted to challenge the notion that aristocrats were inherently superior beings, Lord Orford would supply example one.

Lord Orford did one thing well. He lacked the character traits that supposedly made aristocrats superior, such as judgment, reliability, moral fiber, and managerial skill. Where he excelled was in flaunting the symbols of aristocratic superiority. Nothing symbolized the divide between patricians and everyone else better than greyhounds and hunting. In addition, hunting had long offered a way to create an elite within the elite. Traditionally, individual patricians earned membership in this informal elite through merit. They mastered arcane hunting terms and practices.

Lord Orford hit upon a simpler way to create an elite within the elite while ensuring he qualified for membership. He created his own exclusive coursing club. In 1776, he founded the Swaffham Coursing Society in Norfolk. The club organized coursing matches for its members. Orford ensured exclusivity by limiting membership to himself and twenty-five men he chose as members.[7] Bereft of most of his senses by the end of his life, Orford had enough sense to die a martyr to coursing. According to legend, the lord was sick when his favorite dog, Czarina, was competing in a match. Orford left his bed, mounted his piebald pony, and rode to the match. When Czarina won, the lord fell from his pony and died. Orford may have died in the saddle, or he may have toppled and died upon hitting the ground, but either way coursers loved the symbolism of dying while watching a coursing match.[8]

Swaffham attracted other aristocrats who, like Orford, were distinguished by their lack of distinction in their ostensible duty: running England. After Lord Orford's death, Lord Rivers (George Pitt, 1751–1828) became, in the words of a coursing manual, "the great patron of emulative coursing."[9] The son of a man with the same name (George Pitt, 1721–1803, the first Baron Rivers) and Penelope (daughter of a baronet), the younger George succeeded to title upon his father's death in 1803. Pitt moved in fashionable circles as a young man, visited the king at Windsor, and became Lord of His Majesty's Bedchamber. He represented Dorset in Parliament from 1774 to 1790. If he ever said a word in Parliament, or if he cast a vote between 1783 and 1790, no record of these actions survives. Pitt's fame came from Swaffham. As Lord Rivers, he joined Swaffham in 1813. By the time of his death in 1828, he was the only courser to have won five cups from that meeting.[10]

Orford inspired other patricians to found exclusive coursing clubs. Some founders belonged to the aristocracy. In 1780, Lord Orford's friend, Lord Craven, founded the Ashdown Park Coursing Meeting at Lambourn, Berkshire. Other founders came from the gentry. In 1781, a Colonel Thornton and a Major Topham created the Malton club in Yorkshire.[11] By 1828, at least seventeen clubs had formed.[12] Like Swaffham, new clubs guarded exclusivity by keeping memberships small.

Newmarket limited the members to twenty-six, Letcombe Bowers and Altcar to twenty-four, and Ashdown to twenty.[13] Dog writer Hugh Dalziel reflected in 1887, "The old clubs were, in accordance with the spirit of the times, rigidly exclusive. The votaries of the leash of that period determined that, in coursing at least, 'the toe of the peasant should not come so near the heel of the courser as to gall his kibe [skin sore].'"[14]

Compared to other events of 1776 – Jefferson's writing the Declaration of Independence, Smith's publishing *Wealth of Nations*, and Watt's developing a new steam engine – founding Swaffham Coursing Society was trivial. But to greyhound coursers, it was momentous. They toasted Lord Orford as the "father" of their sport long after his death.[15] Orford did not, in fact, invent coursing. It had been around for centuries. Orford invented club coursing. The sport did not need clubs. Coursers continued to course outside club settings. The key advantage of clubs was membership itself. Coursers referred to club contests, and sometimes to clubs themselves, as *meets* or *meetings,* which reflected their role in bringing members together.[16] Clubs offered a simple way to create exclusive islands of inherited privilege at a time when waves of social change mounted.

Clubs created new human (sub-)populations. The boundary dividing the new human populations from everyone else was club membership. These human populations coevolved with greyhounds. Greyhounds created the opportunity for people to behave in certain ways, and people accepted the opportunity. Greyhounds had a suite of traits (coursing skills) that enabled people to adopt behaviors (creating clubs and limiting membership) that formed new populations (coursing clubs) reliant on those greyhound traits. The human populations did not form solely in response to greyhounds. They formed primarily in response to social and personal incentives, such as protecting status in an era of social change. But the new human populations formed partly in response to greyhounds. Men could not have founded coursing clubs without coursing dogs. Greyhounds affected the formation of human club populations.

Memes, Behavior, and Human Evolution

Coursing clubs evolved in different directions from parent populations of coursers. Formation of clubs was a sampling process. Because club members were small subsets of the larger English coursing population, the clubs could not contain all the variation in the larger population. Surviving records make it hard, however, to know all the ways the new populations differed from the parent population. Clearer are the ways the new human populations evolved distinctive traits. Creating and joining clubs were new behaviors seen in club members but not in other coursers. The frequency of a behavior (club joining) was 100 percent in club members and 0 percent in other coursers. Because the frequency of a behavioral trait in the new human populations differed in the new versus parent populations, the new populations evolved.

Coursing clubs immediately set about evolving more distinctive behavioral traits. They poured enormous effort into creating memes to govern behavior of members, which changed the frequency of behavioral traits in club populations. Clubs formalized many memes in written rules. Some of the most important focused on policing population boundaries.[17] People who wanted to join Swaffham could not nominate themselves. Candidates had to be nominated by a current member. Members voted on nominees, and they blackballed candidates they disliked.[18] Memes reinforced social exclusion with physical exclusion. Rules barred outsiders from Swaffham events except when introduced by a member. Members could introduce one friend but no more.[19] Along with memes governing human–human interactions, clubs adopted memes governing human–dog interactions. Orford limited the number of Swaffham members to the number of letters of the alphabet so each member could be assigned a unique letter.[20] Names of members' greyhounds had to begin with assigned letters.[21] Orford claimed C, so the names of his greyhounds (such as Czarina) began with C.

Other memes governed the scheduling, management, and attendance at coursing contests. Outside of clubs, variation in coursing behavior was the norm. Coursers scheduled matches when they wished, they chose judges using whatever method they wished, and no organization compelled an individual to enter a contest. Clubs countered variation with standardization. Swaffham rules dictated the schedule for contests (the second Monday in November and the first Monday in February), and the methods for choosing judges, stewards, and assistants.[22] Swaffham demanded that members compete in events. In early rules, missing two meetings without a good excuse enabled thirteen members to vote the truant out of the club. Later rules made expulsion automatic for anyone missing two meetings.[23] No one could plead ignorance of meeting dates because they appeared in the rules.[24] Clubs enhanced commitment by forcing members to compete. If a member arrived without a greyhound, he had to pay a one guinea fine to the treasurer.[25]

Clubs standardized memes governing the methods of coursing matches as well as scheduling and attendance. Outside of clubs, traditions varied by region and locality. Individuals modified rules, and chose contest officials, as they wished. Although standardized locally, jobs and environments varied nationally because club rules and estates differed. Thomas Goodlake said in 1828, "It frequently happens, that the principle on which courses are decided vary [sic] in different countries and over different grounds."[26] Clubs standardized memes with written rules governing all club matches. In contrast to variation outside clubs, uniformity in coursing memes was the norm within clubs. Most clubs adopted rules resembling those of Turbervile and Thomas of Norfolk. In a typical match, beaters started a hare, a handler released two greyhounds, a judge on horseback evaluated the performance of the greyhounds, and the judge named a winner at the end. Rules rewarded turning the hare more than killing it. Gambling was a key part of club culture. Some – perhaps all – clubs required owners of competing dogs to bet with each other.[27]

The direction of evolution in coursing clubs, then, was toward narrowed variation compared to the parent population of coursers. The purpose of rules was to narrow variation in behaviors. It is easy to deduce pre-rule variation from rules. Rules governing selection of contest officials tell us that other coursers used a variety of practices to select officials. Rules requiring betting on matches tell us some coursers wanted to bet on matches and others did not. The betting rule reduced variation in behavior. The rule enabling clubs to vote truant members out of the club tells us some members attended meets and others did not. The replacement of that rule with a harsher rule – automatic expulsion for truancy – suggests that variation remained high despite the first rule. Expulsion eliminated individuals with a behavioral trait (skipping matches) from the population. The club population evolved when the frequency of a new behavioral trait (expelling truants automatically) rose and the frequency of another behavioral trait (voting truants out of the club) declined. Most likely, the frequency of another trait (truancy from contests) declined as well.

Clubs narrowed both aspects of niches. One aspect was jobs. The new job title was member of a specific club (e.g., member of Swaffham). The rules of the club defined occupational duties. Members had to show up for coursing contests, bet on matches in which they competed, and introduce at most one guest to the club. Rules first enabled, then forced, clubs to fire "employees" (members) who failed to perform their jobs (by skipping contests). Standardized job descriptions (written rules) narrowed the niche of club members compared to the niches of coursers outside clubs, who retained flexibility in performing their jobs as they wished.

Clubs also narrowed the second aspect of niches: habitat. Outside clubs, coursers competed in a variety of habitats. They coursed their own estates, each of which was unique. Each club narrowed variation in habitats by coursing one estate repeatedly. Clubs relied on large land-owners, often club founders, to supply their competition grounds. Some clubs took their names from the estates they coursed. In the late 1700s, the Ashdown Coursing Meeting coursed Ashdown Park, which belonged to the club's founder, Lord Craven.[28]

Club coursing encouraged temporal uniformity in habitats. Clubs expected landowners to keep hare populations high if they wanted to host club contests. When hare populations declined, some estates enclosed warrens and employed gamekeepers. If a landowner lost interest or ran low of funds for hare habitat preservation, decline in hares led coursing to suffer. Lord Craven's passion for coursing waned in the late eighteenth century. His efforts to preserve hares lapsed, and by 1804 the hares on his Ashdown estate disappeared. This habitat change led the Ashdown club to adopt a new, standard habitat. From 1799 to 1804, the Ashdown meeting coursed Barton Manor, which belonged to the Earl of Aylesbury. The earl protected hares with an enclosed warren. The club returned to Ashdown Park in 1814, after Lord Craven resumed efforts to preserve hares.[29]

The development of a new meme for coursing, championship contests, pushed the traits of club populations further from the larger population of coursers.[30] The records examined for this study offered no examples in which coursing matches outside clubs were organized to produce an over-all champion. Informal meets comprised matches, each of which produced a winner and a loser. Clubs introduced contests in which one dog emerged as the champion of a group of greyhounds. Championships relied on a series of knockout rounds. In each match, two dogs competed against each other. The winning dog advanced. The loser dropped out. The dog that won all its matches became the champion. The number of entrants was usually two raised to some power (typically eight, sixteen, thirty-two, or sixty-four dogs), which eliminated the need for byes. In club coursing's early years, a club might organize one championship per year.[31] Over time, the popularity of championships increased.[32] Club populations evolved when the frequency of championship-related behaviors increased over time.

A second meme piggybacked atop the championship meme. The piggyback meme said clubs should award prizes to champions, which elevated the symbolic importance of the contests. Some championships were sweepstakes that rewarded the winner with money staked by all competitors. Other championships awarded symbolic prizes. These included silver cups, plates, and dog collars. Some championships awarded money and symbolic prizes.[33] At an 1821 contest, coursers at the Louth meeting competed for a Cup, Louth Sweepstakes, Withcall Sweepstakes, and Tathwell Sweepstakes. The Tathwell Sweepstakes and the Cup each required knockout rounds spread over four days.[34] Club populations evolved with respect to prize-awarding behavior at the same time they evolved with respect to championship behavior.

The first two memes increased the frequency of a third meme. It defined the purpose of coursing as winning championships. The idea of winning matches was not new. Coursers outside clubs tried to win matches, too, although coursers did not always equate the purpose of coursing with winning. Many men coursed hares because they enjoyed the thrill of following greyhounds on horseback. This mode of coursing, later called private coursing, often involved only greyhounds owned by the courser. Even if one greyhound performed better than the other, the same man came out ahead because he owned both dogs.[35] The meme in private coursing was that the purpose of coursing was entertainment (and sometimes food on the table), so we can call it the *entertainment meme*. In private matches, men sometimes bet and sometimes did not. In clubs, in contrast, men had to bet that their dogs would win. These rules enforced the meme that equated the purpose of coursing with winning matches, making the meme more common in clubs than among other courser populations. Owners wagered on every match, elevating the significance of victory and defeat. The meme that the purpose of coursing was winning championships was a new meme that only coursers inside clubs could adopt because only they could compete in championships. We can call it the *victory meme*. The frequency of this meme outside clubs was zero.

If viewed from space, clubs looked like islands of local uniformity in a sea of variation in human populations. Most coursers in England continued to follow the individualistic practices of previous centuries. Each patrician set his own rules on his own estate. He chose to course or not on a given date. He chose to bet on a contest or not. He assigned greyhounds whatever names he wished. He could course for fun or to win a bet. Club populations, in contrast, developed memes to minimize variation in human behavior. Members had to attend coursing meetings. They had to bet on contests. They had to give their dogs names that began with the same letter. They followed standard rules to determine winners of coursing contests. They came to equate the purpose of coursing with victory, especially in championships.

Meme Transmission

Memes passed among club members through learning. Within clubs, new members read and mastered written rules. They learned other memes through experience and informal means, such as song lyrics. An example is a 1796 song, "The Coursing Club." It prescribed rules for drinking during wintertime social gatherings, when coursing halted because hares were scarce. The lyrics analogized drinking to riding horses after coursing greyhounds:

> Well mounted with Wine, ev'ry Glass is our Steed,
> And the Spurs from our Heels are transferr'd to the Head.[36]

The song prescribed that members drink whenever the chair offered a toast. If members refused, they had to pay a fine – the same mechanism clubs used to force members to bet on coursing matches:

> When the Chair starts the Toast, should the Chace we decline,
> No Victim Defaulter escapes without Fine.[37]

The effect of the memes in the song was to narrow the range of variation in social behavior of club members compared to the ways they would have behaved if left to their own preferences.

Memes spread between clubs as well as within clubs. One reason was shared membership. The Ashdown club made members of Swaffham, Newmarket, and Malton honorary members with reciprocal privileges. Malton did the same with Ashdown, Amesbury, and Deptford Inn.[38] Swaffham made the importance of the club network clear in the way it honored Lord Orford after his death. The club created an annual competition for a silver cup in Orford's memory and invited "any member of the Lincolnshire, Yorkshire, Wiltshire, and the Berkshire coursing Societies" to enter the competition.[39] Lord Rivers belonged to the Swaffham, Ashdown, Newmarket, Beacon Hill, and Ilsley clubs.[40] Multiple memberships, reciprocal privileges, and joint coursing contests enabled coursers to share memes (rules, traditions) with each other face to face.

Meme transmission among clubs accelerated thanks to the growth of sporting books. Books about sports were nothing new. Turbervile transmitted memes about coursing behavior in the sixteenth century. In the transitional decades, however, the rate at which sporting books appeared accelerated. In the late eighteenth century, Peter Beckford's *Thoughts on Hunting* (1781) and William Osbaldiston's *The British Sportsman* (1792) added to the sporting canine literature.[41] Additional books on rural sports in general appeared in the early nineteenth century.[42]

More striking in the early nineteenth century was the growth of books focused on sporting dogs, greyhounds, and coursing. In 1803–1804, William Taplin published *The Sportsman's Cabinet: A Correct Delineation of the Various Dogs Used in the Sports of the Field: Including the Canine Race in General*. Coursing clubs helped to create demand for the book. Taplin dedicated it "To the Ladies Patronesses, Vice Patronesses, and Members of the Swaffham, Ashdown-Park, Bradwell, and Flixton Coursing Societies."[43] An anonymous *A Treatise on Greyhounds* (1816), Thomas Goodlake's *The Courser's Manual or Stud-Book* (1828), and Thomas Thacker's *The Courser's Companion* (1829) followed.[44] In 1831, William Dansey published a translation of *Arrian on Coursing: The Cynegeticus of the Younger Xenophon*.[45] Even more than Taplin's book, coursing books thrived thanks to a desire among club members to learn memes from other coursing clubs. The publication of an ancient Greek text seemed to suggest a desire of patricians to justify their status by anchoring it in antiquity.[46]

A novel means of transmitting memes came with the rise of sporting magazines. The first sporting periodical, *The Sporting Magazine* (1793), covered coursing, horse racing, pedestrianism, pugilism, hunting, whist, shooting, and archery. Its first issue included rules from the Swaffham Coursing Society and a song about a hare chase.[47] Imitators followed, including *Sporting Repository*, *Annals of Sporting and Fancy Gazette*, and *Bell's Life in London*. News of club contests filled pages and attracted subscribers. Magazines publicized the exploits of coursers and informed them of coursing events outside their own regions.

By reporting contest results, sporting magazines boosted the frequency of the meme that equated the purpose of coursing with winning matches and championships. The reports named owners as well as greyhounds, which enabled local contests to affect a man's national reputation. In 1822, for example, a sporting magazine published the following results from the Newmarket meeting.

- Lord Rivers's black bitch Rhoda beat Mr. H. Redhead's black dog York.
- Lord Rivers's black bitch Riddle beat Lord Maynard's black bitch Key.
- Mr. Northey's black bitch Nutshell beat Lord Maynard's black bitch Kettle.
- Mr. Scott's black and white bitch Ida beat Mr. Redhead's brown dog Link Boy.[48]

These results introduced meritocracy into the evaluation of men who inherited different social ranks. Nobles defeated the gentry, nobles defeated nobles, the gentry defeated nobles, and the gentry defeated the gentry. Men gained status from belonging to a coursing club, but meritocratic competition created a hierarchy within the elite. A man's reputation derived partly from his dog's ability to win matches and championships.

Efficient meme transmission enabled club populations to evolve similar traits. Each club was self-governing, thus able to choose its own memes and behaviors, but clubs chose to mimic each other's traits. They adopted similar rules governing membership and coursing. Taken individually, clubs created islands of local uniformity. Taken as a group, clubs created an archipelago of islands (human populations) with similar, but not identical, traits.

Modernization

In the early nineteenth century, members and publicists referred to club coursing as *modern*.[49] They used the term mainly in the sense of *recent* and *improved*, but they introduced four features we now associate with modernity: bureaucracies, standardization, mass communication, and an ideology of progress. Clubs were local *bureaucracies*. They were formal organizations governed by written rules. The rules created organizational structures with defined roles (such as coursing officials). Individuals rotated through the roles, so the bureaucracy, rather than individuals, defined the roles. Clubs *standardized* rules for behavior while coursing and socializing. They issued the rules in writing to ensure members knew and obeyed them. Clubs capitalized on *mass communication* to spread their ideas. They relied on sporting magazines to transmit information about clubs and coursing. Clubs believed they *improved* the sport of coursing by sponsoring regular matches, standardizing rules, and uniting elite sportsmen.

All of these changes modernized evolution because they shaped the frequency of memes and behaviors in club populations. When people conformed to the rules of local bureaucracies, they behaved differently from the way they did before clubs arose. When they read sporting maga-zines and adopted rules and practices from other clubs, they inherited memes that changed the frequency of behavior. When they embraced the meme that club coursing created progress, and when they voiced that belief, they evolved in ways they could not before the rise of clubs.

The modernization carried out by patricians between 1776 and 1831 was a mild version of what would follow. Clubs were small, local bureau-cracies, not national behemoths. Clubs standardized job descriptions and environments on a local scale, not a national one. The press linked coursers at scattered clubs, but magazines appeared at a pace slower than newspapers and telegraphs would soon accomplish. Nevertheless, these changes convinced coursers they had updated their sport enough by the 1820s to call it modern.

Conclusion

In 1776–1831, clubs created a transition between the age of aristocracy and the age of modernity by adopting modest versions of modernity and eschewing other aspects of later modernity. Clubs avoided democracy, urbanization, and capitalism. Club members excluded all but a small elite within the elite rather than welcoming all comers, sported in rural areas rather than cities, and eschewed commercial breeding rather than put-ting dogs out for stud. In adopting infant versions of four features of modernity, however, they planted the seeds of change that would trans-form coursing more thoroughly in subsequent decades. *They started to modernize evolution.* Democracy, urbanization, and capitalism joined stron-ger versions of bureaucracies, standardization, mass communication, and belief in progress to transform the coursing world after 1831.

Notes

1. John Hancock [and fifty-five others], "Declaration of Independence in Congress, July 4, 1776," in *A People and a Nation: A History of the United States,* by Mary Beth Norton et al., 4th edition (Boston: Houghton Mifflin, 1994), Appendix A-7.
2. Frederick C. Dietz, *A Political and Social History of England* (New York: Macmillan, 1932), 431–509.
3. Anonymous, *The English Peerage; Or, a View of the Ancient and Present State of the English Nobility,* vol. 1 (London: T. Spilsbury and Son, 1790), 329–33.

4. Paul Langford, "Walpole, Horatio, Fourth Earl of Orford (1717–1797)," in *Oxford Dictionary of National Biography*, online edition May 2011, 2004, www .oxforddnb.com/view/article/28596.

5. Frank Herrmann, "Christie, James (1730–1803)," in *Oxford Dictionary of National Biography* (Oxford: Oxford University Press, 2004), www .oxforddnb.com/view/article/5362.

6. Anna Porter, "Houghton Revisited: Walpole Masterpieces from the Hermitage," *Queen's Quarterly* 120, no. 4 (2013): 544–55.

7. Thomas Goodlake, *The Courser's Manual or Stud-Book* (Liverpool: Geo. B. Whittaker and Jos. Booker, 1828), xiii.

8. Goodlake, *Courser's Manual [1828]*, xv.

9. Goodlake, *Courser's Manual [1828]*, xvi.

10. *The Annual Biography and Obituary of 1828*, vol. 13 (London: Longman, Rees, Orme, Brown, and Green, 1829), 465–66; Mary Drummond, "Pitt, George (1751–1828), of Strathfieldsaye, Hants.," *The History of Parliament*, accessed September 20, 2014, www.historyofparliamentonline.org/volume/1754 -1790/member/pitt-george-1751-1828; Goodlake, *Courser's Manual [1828]*, xvi.

11. Goodlake, *Courser's Manual [1828]*, xv.

12. Delabere Pritchett Blaine, *An Encyclopaedia of Rural Sports: Or a Complete Account, Historical, Practical, and Descriptive, of Hunting, Shooting, Fishing, Racing, and Other Field Sports and Athletic Amusements of the Present Day* (London: Longman, Orme, Brown, Green and Longmans, 1840), 586–88.

13. Blaine, *An Encyclopaedia of Rural Sports [1840]*, 586–88.

14. Hugh Dalziel, *The Greyhound; Its History, Points, Breeding, Rearing, Training, and Running* (London: L. Upcott Gill, 1887), 41.

15. Goodlake, *Courser's Manual [1828]*, xv.

16. Anonymous, "Swaffham Coursing Meeting," *Sporting Magazine* 13, October (1798): 41–43.

17. Anonymous, "Swaffham Coursing Meeting."

18. William Taplin, *The Sportsman's Cabinet; Or, a Correct Delineation of the Various Dogs Used in the Sports of the Field: Including the Canine Race in General. Consisting of a Series of Engravings of Every Distinct Breed ... Illustrated by a Comprehensive, Historical, and Systematic Description of the Different Species; with a Review of the Various Diseases to Which They Are Subject, and the Most Approved and Efficacious Modes of Treatment and Cure. To Which Is Added, a Scientific Disquisition upon the Distemper, Canine Madness, and the Hydrophobia*, vol. 1 (London: J. Cundee, 1803), 34–35.

19. Goodlake, *Courser's Manual [1828]*, xxxi.

20. Goodlake, *Courser's Manual [1828]*, xiii.

21. Taplin, *Sportsman's Cabinet*, 34–35.

22. Anonymous, "Swaffham Coursing Meeting."

23. Goodlake, *Courser's Manual [1828]*, xxxi.

24. Taplin, *Sportsman's Cabinet*, 34–35.

25. Anonymous, "Coursing (with an Engraving)," *Sporting Repository* 1, no. 3 (1822): 231–39.

26. Goodlake, *Courser's Manual [1828]*, xx.

27. Anonymous, *A Treatise on Greyhounds, with Observations on the Treatment and Disorders of Them* (London: [n.p.], 1816), 61–63.

28. John H. Walsh, *The Coursing Calendar for the Spring Season 1871 Containing Returns of All the Public Courses Run in Great Britain and Ireland* (London: Horace Cox, 1871), 105.

29. Walsh, *Coursing Calendar [1871]*, 105.

30. It is possible coursers used championships before the club era, but my research found no mention of them, including in a search of Google Books for "coursing sweepstakes" from 1500 to 1900 (search conducted September 21, 2014).

31. Harding Cox and Gerald Lascelles, *Coursing and Falconry* (London: Longmans, Green, and Company, 1892), 161–62.

32. Anonymous, "Coursing Meetings," *Sporting Magazine* 9, November (1821): 77–82.

33. Blaine, *An Encyclopaedia of Rural Sports [1840]*, 586.

34. Anonymous, "Coursing Meetings."

35. Henry Thomas Alken, *The National Sports of Great Britain: Fifty Engravings with Descriptions* ([1825] New York: D. Appleton, 1903).

36. The Author of The Louth Coursers, *The Coursing Club* (London: [n.p.], 1796).

37. The Author of The Louth Coursers, *Coursing Club*.

38. Goodlake, *Courser's Manual [1828]*, xxxix, xlvii.

39. Anonymous, "Swaffham Coursing Society: The Silver Cup," *Sporting Magazine* 1 (1793): 39–41.

40. *The Annual Biography and Obituary of 1828*, 13: 465–66; Drummond, "Pitt, George (1751–1828), of Strathfieldsaye, Hants."; Goodlake, *Courser's Manual [1828]*, xvi.

41. Peter Beckford, *Thoughts on Hunting in a Series of Familiar Letters to a Friend* ([1781] New York: Derrydale Press, 2000); William Osbaldiston, *The British Sportsman, Or, Nobleman, Gentleman, and Farmer's Dictionary, of Recreation and Amusement* (London: J. Stead, 1792).

42. T. H. Needham, *The Complete Sportsman: A Compendious View of the Ancient and Modern Chase . . . With Every Instruction and Information Relative to the Diversions of the Field* (London [?]: W. Simpkin and R. Marshall, 1817).

43. Taplin, *Sportsman's Cabinet*, 1803, 1: dedication page (no number). The dedication went on to include fox hunters. William Taplin, *The Sportsman's Cabinet, or Correct Delineation of the Dogs Used in the Sports of the Field: Including the Canine Race in General*, vol. 2 (London: J. Cundee, 1804).

44. Anonymous, *A Treatise on Greyhounds, with Observations on the Treatment and Disorders of Them*; Goodlake, *Courser's Manual [1828]*; Thomas Thacker, *The Courser's Companion; Or, a Practical Treatise on the Laws of the Leash; with the Defects of the Old Laws Considered; and a New Code, with Notes of Explanation, by an Experienced Courser* (Derby: Thomas Richardson, 1829).

45. Arrian, *Arrian on Coursing: The Cynegeticus of the Younger Xenophon, Translated from the Greek, with Classical and Practical Annotations, and a Brief Sketch of the Life and Writings of the Author. To Which Is Added an Appendix, Containing Some*

Account of the Canes Venatici of Classical Antiquity, trans. William Dansey (London: J. Bohn, 1831).

46. I thank John McNeill for this insight.

47. Anonymous, "Swaffham Coursing Society: The Silver Cup"; Anonymous, "Cynegeticos; or, The Pleasures of Hare-Hunting, A Song," *Sporting Magazine,* 1 (1793): 46–47.

48. Anonymous, "Coursing," *Sporting Repository* 1, no. 3 (1822): 231–39.

49. Needham, *Complete Sportsman.*

4

GREYHOUND EVOLUTION AND COEVOLUTION IN A TRANSITIONAL ERA (1776–1831)

Club members did more than modernize their own evolution in the decades between 1776 and 1831. They also modernized the evolution of greyhounds. As with human evolution, the modernization of greyhound evolution was a mild and partial version of what would follow after 1831. But it was important because it planted seeds that would come to full flower after 1831. This chapter focuses on populations of greyhounds owned by coursing club members. These populations excluded most greyhounds, who continued to work on estates of their owners in owner-defined jobs.

The pattern of evolution in club greyhounds resembled the pattern of evolution in club members: from national variation to islands of local uniformity amidst a national sea of variation. Clubs shaped the evolution of greyhound populations by narrowing niches, which led to narrowed variation in traits. Clubs narrowed variation in the job dimensions of niches by standardizing, on a local scale, the rules of coursing. The same standardization of rules that shaped the behavior of club members also shaped the duties of club greyhounds. Clubs narrowed variation in the habitat dimensions of niches by coursing the same estate repeatedly. With standardized jobs and habitats, niches for club greyhounds narrowed.

Members adapted greyhounds to narrow club niches through a combination of methodical and unconscious selection. They used methodical selection with the conscious intent to shape the traits of future generations of greyhounds. Among other things, they selectively mated greyhounds with bulldogs and Italian greyhounds to enhance specific traits in greyhound populations. Members and breeders adapted greyhounds through unconscious selection when they killed dogs that performed poorly.

In addition to adapting dogs to niches, people adapted to dogs (creating coevolution). They did so when they chose to capitalize on

opportunities created by dogs. Bulldogs created opportunities by display-
ing desirable traits and mating with greyhounds. In the population of
club members, the frequency of cross breeding greyhounds with bulldogs
increased. Human populations coevolved with canine populations.

Human populations further evolved in response to changes in greyhound traits and broader social forces. Several memes arose or increased
in frequency. These memes included a narrowing of the definition of
breeding from environmental breeding to selective mating, belief that
selective mating improved greyhounds in a universal sense, belief that
smooth greyhounds were superior to rough greyhounds, and equation of
improvement with modernization. The sporting press helped to spread
these memes.

The narrowing of breeding from environmental breeding to selective
mating reflected an enhanced concern with inherited superiority.
Under environmental breeding, the excellence of greyhounds derived
partly from parents and partly from environments. Narrowing the definition of breeding to selective mating made ancestry alone the determi-
nant of excellence. The growth of elite breeding in farm animals
nurtured memes equating club breeding with superiority, progress,
and modernity.

Another factor encouraging spread of memes about superiority was
blindness to evidence. Club members claimed that selective mating created universally superior greyhounds. Southern English clubs trumpeted
this claim most loudly. In fact, club breeding produced greyhounds that
excelled in local or regional habitats. Greyhounds seemed to improve
because they got better at coursing in local clubs. When the best dogs in
one habitat competed in other habitats, however, they lost to local dogs.
Superiority was not a universal trait. Superiority was a product of the fit
between the traits of a dog and the niche in which it worked. Some club
breeders mistook adaptation to narrow club niches for universal superiority. Many club members resisted the southern English meme that
clamed universal superiority for smooth southern greyhounds. They
developed at least five other varieties (populations of greyhounds)
adapted to local niches (jobs and habitats).

Jobs, Breeding, and Evolution of Smooth Greyhounds

Club coursing prompted evolution in greyhound populations by narrowing variation in niches and traits on a local scale. By standardizing coursing rules, clubs standardized the job descriptions of greyhounds.

By coursing the same estate repeatedly, clubs standardized the habitats of greyhounds. Breeders tailored greyhounds to these narrowed niches, which encouraged local uniformity. Because clubs coursed in a variety of habitats, however, club populations of greyhounds varied on a national scale.

Club memes determined the job descriptions of club greyhounds. One of the most important was the victory meme, which equating the purpose of coursing with winning. This meme narrowed the job description of club greyhound populations compared to those of other greyhound populations. Outside clubs, the job of some greyhounds was to lead owners on long gallops across the countryside, and the job description of others was to win matches. In the greyhound population of England as a whole, jobs varied. Inside club populations, the job description narrowed to winning matches and championships.

The victory meme led club coursers to equate greyhound quality with winning championships. When Thomas Goodlake introduced *The Courser's Manual or Stud-Book* in 1828, he divided greyhounds into two classes. Class I greyhounds had taken first or second place in club championships (cups, sweepstakes, and plates). Class II greyhounds had competed unsuccessfully for cups but had identifiable parents. Goodlake could not have been clearer. Greyhounds that won championships were first-class dogs. Greyhounds that lost championships were second-class dogs.[1]

The victory meme called for different greyhound traits than some memes outside clubs. Because of the entertainment meme, coursers outside clubs often prized endurance, long careers, and stupidity in greyhounds. They liked endurance because it enabled greyhounds to pursue hares for miles without falter. This trait enabled coursers to achieve their goal of galloping long distances on horseback. Private coursers valued long careers in greyhounds because they wanted to be entertained by high-performing dogs for years. They liked stupidity in greyhounds because it meant instinct ruled behavior. Stupid greyhounds would pursue hares without fail because instinct told them to do so. These traits came with tradeoffs. The price of endurance and long careers was reduced speed. The price of stupidity was a limited ability of a greyhound to make its own decisions about how to chase hares. The victory meme called for greyhounds with different traits. Club coursers valued speed over endurance because the first greyhound to reach a hare could rack up points faster than a laggard. They valued speed over long careers because winning a championship was top priority. They appreciated intelligence because smart greyhounds could figure out how to outwit competitors and hares. And they wanted courage, by which they meant a fierce drive to course hares in any conditions.

Lord Orford, who had trouble with many aspects of life but was an inspired breeder, gained fame for adapting greyhounds to the victory meme through cross breeding. He appears not to have looked outside greyhound populations for speed. Greyhounds were the fastest dogs around, so selecting for speed meant breeding from the fastest greyhounds. This part of his methods was conventional. Orford looked to other breeds for other traits, and he introduced them to greyhounds through cross breeding. Breeders used crosses long before Orford, so this practice too was conventional. The idea contemporaries considered novel and eccentric was crossing greyhounds with bulldogs to improve courage.[2] Thanks to the courage gained from bulldogs, a sportsman's guide explained, "the well-bred greyhound will rather expire than relinquish the chase."[3] Orford mated greyhounds with lurchers (poachers' dogs) to increase intelligence.[4] He crossed greyhounds with Italian greyhounds to make their form lighter and movement quicker. Other breeders adopted Orford's memes to breed greyhounds with similar traits.[5]

Coursers considered Orford's crossbreeding a stunning success because his dogs fulfilled the club members' goal of victory. The idea that the bulldog cross produced superior greyhounds became a meme spread in the sporting literature. In 1817, T. H. Needham thought it was common knowledge that "the present highly-improved race of greyhounds, owe their superiority to the acute perception and persevering sprit of the Earl of Orford." The lord's breeding had produced "the best greyhounds, which, up to this period, had ever been seen."[6] In 1822, *Sporting Repository* described Orford's dogs as "the finest greyhounds ever seen."[7] Another magazine called Orford's dogs "the best greyhounds in the world."[8] Orford's favorite, Czarina, won forty-seven matches without a loss. Orford's crosses also led to famous champions Jupiter and Claret.[9] Orford's success became part of the larger breeding literature. When an 1810 treatise on livestock discussed cross breeding, it noted, "It is a well-known fact, that Lord Orford improved his greyhounds by a cross with the bulldog."[10]

Orford's methods shaped the physical traits of greyhounds along with behavioral traits, which created a meme that associated quality with a certain appearance. It is unclear how much appearance guided Orford's breeding goals, but his greyhounds looked distinctive. *Sporting Repository* summed up the traits of Orford's greyhounds as "the small ear, the rat-tail, the skin sleek and smooth, without hair; together with that innate courage, as to die on the field rather than relinquish the chase."[11] The sporting press spread the meme that equated sleekness and short fur with excellence. In 1825, Henry Alken published a book of fifty engravings of sporting scenes, including six of coursing. His engravings showed only smooth greyhounds, which, he said, had replaced coarse (long-furred) greyhounds over the previous fifty or sixty years (that is, during the club era). Now breeders aimed "entirely for fineness, symmetry and speed; being assimilated, as nearly as possible, to the race horse, their rival in that qualification." The spread of this meme shaped the evolution of club greyhounds. It drove the frequency of short fur up and the frequency of long fur down. The "old coarse breed of Greyhounds has gradually disappeared," Alken reported.[12] (See cover image and Figures 4.1 and 4.2.)

Figure 4.1 Smooth greyhounds and open landscapes. During the patrician club era, coursers in open country bred smooth-coated greyhounds with endurance, speed to run in front of horses, and the practice of relying entirely on sight. Although short coats and failure to use scent were suboptimal traits in regions with more hedges and brush, breeders of smooth greyhounds claimed their dogs were universally superior. Henry Alken, *The National Sports of Great Britain* ([1825] New York: D. Appleton, 1903), Coursing – Plate IV, Picking Up, NE960 . A4 1825. Special Collections, University of Virginia, Charlottesville, VA.

IRISH GREYHOUND.

Figure 4.2 Rough greyhounds. Greyhounds with long hair suited country with woody vegetation. Their rough coats protected against cuts as they forced their way through hedges after prey, and willingness to use scent was valuable when prey ducked out of sight. Although superior in their own environments, rough greyhounds in the nineteenth century found themselves stigmatized as inferior by coursers from clubs in open landscapes who prized smooth greyhounds. Dog writers and natural historians in the late eighteenth and early nineteenth centuries classified long-snouted dogs with rough coats under many names, including greyhounds, rough greyhounds, Irish greyhounds, Irish wolf-dogs, Scotch greyhounds, and lurchers. Sometimes they lumped dogs with different names into one breed with multiple jobs, and sometimes they split them into separate breeds with specialized jobs. Those who believed that Irish greyhounds formed a separate breed that specialized in wolf killing, such as the author of the book that published this engraving, suggested that the breed had become rare because of wolf extirpation. William Taplin, *The Sportsman's Cabinet; or, A Correct Delineation of the Various Dogs Used in the Sports of the Field: Including the Canine Race in General. Consisting of a Series of Engravings of Every Distinct Breed ... To Which Is Added, a Scientific Disquisition upon the Distemper, Canine Madness, and the Hydrophobia* (London: J. Cundee, 1804), after 98. SF428.5 .T36 1803 v.2. Special Collections, University of Virginia, Charlottesville, VA.

By publishing prints, sporting magazines helped club coursers spread the idea that smooth greyhounds were superior and *modern*. In 1822, *Sporting Repository* described southern greyhounds as smooth, beautiful, high-bred, modern, and improved. It included an image of two of these dogs by Henry Alken. The magazine described the image as "a correct engraving" of "the most elegant and beautiful of the canine race."[13] (See Figure 4.3.) The use of images for greyhounds built on a tradition of the eighteenth century in which patricians dedicated to livestock breeding and field sports created a market for paintings of themselves and their animals. Only the wealthy could afford originals, but many people could buy prints and see them in periodicals. Several thousand sporting prints appeared between 1775 and 1850.[14] Henry Alken was one of the most prolific sporting illustrators of the nineteenth century.[15]

Memes about greyhound breeding spread rapidly partly because they were elements of a larger discourse about animal improvement that a club courser helped to promote. Coursing club members were landowners, many of whom raised livestock. In the eighteenth and nineteenth centuries, a passion for improving livestock through breeding developed. A member of the Swaffham Coursing Society, Sir John Sebright (1767–1846), was one of the leaders of this movement. The seventh in a line of baronets, he inherited his father's title and estates in 1794. He served in Parliament from 1807 to 1834, where he supported the Whigs, religious tolerance, and Parliamentary reform.[16] Sebright's passion for improving government seems of a piece with his passion for improving animals. Other large landowners, such as Francis Russell, Duke of Bedford (1785–1802), and Thomas Coke, First Earl of Leicester (1754–1842), experimented with selective mating to make rapid changes in breeds. These amateur breeders patronized professional breeders as well. The most famous of the latter was Robert Bakewell, a tenant farmer who bred sheep and cattle. Sebright observed the work of these amateur and professional breeders, and he carried out his own experiments on birds and dogs.[17]

Animal breeding was, in turn, part of a larger agricultural improvement movement. Led by large landowners, agricultural improvers introduced new crops, added fertilizers, drained wetlands, and enclosed common areas to create private fields. Developments in markets, transportation, and credit helped the process. As a result, the period from the seventeenth to nineteenth centuries has been called the British Agricultural Revolution.[18]

GREYHOUNDS.

Figure 4.3 Coursing meet in 1822. Coursing clubs organized meets and other social activities that helped patrician men socialize with each other. The tents in the background flagged this meet as an organized event with numerous participants. The article accompanying this engraving described these smooth-coated Southern greyhounds as "the most elegant and beautiful of the canine race" and denigrated

In 1809, Sebright attempted to systematize breeding principles – that is, to spread standardized memes about progress through breeding. He wrote an influential essay, *The Art of Improving the Breeds of Domestic Animals*, as a letter to Sir Joseph Banks (1743–1820), president of the Royal Society. The essay reached a wide audience when a London publisher issued it as a book. Sebright and Banks were part of the Enlightenment project to improve the world through knowledge and mastery of nature. As Sebright put it, breeding succeeded "when any desired quality has been increased by art, beyond what that quality was in the same breed, in a state of nature."[19]

One key meme equated breeding with selective mating, a narrower job description for breeders than under environmental breeding. Sebright defined "the art of breeding" as "the selection of males and females, intended to breed together, in reference to each other's merits and defects."[20] This narrow definition contrasted with a broader concept in earlier centuries, when breeders considered control of environments and training to be part of breeding. The new breeders thought the environment played a small role in determining traits. Sebright criticized growers who believed that the quality of wool derived from the environment in which sheep lived. "The fineness of the fleece," he argued, "like every other property of all kinds, may be improved by selection in breeding . . . Climate, food, and soil, have certainly some effect upon the quality of wool, but not so much as is generally supposed."[21] Sebright believed breeders needed to select parents carefully to develop a breed with improved traits, and then to continue selective mating to preserve these traits. Without this effort, a breed would revert to "a state of nature, or perhaps defects will arrive, which did not exist when the breed was in its natural state."[22]

Two big questions faced the new breeders.[23] The first was whether to crossbreed (mate individuals from different breeds). Some breeders favored this strategy to introduce new traits. They believed Bakewell,

---

Caption for Figure 4.3 (cont.)

rougher-coated northern dogs as "partaking much of the lurcher." The open countryside pictured here and in Figure 4.2 made it realistic to use smooth greyhounds. Henry Alken engraving in Anonymous, "Coursing (with an Engraving)," *Sporting Repository* 1, no. 3, 1822: facing 231. Reproduced with the permission of the Pennsylvania State University Libraries.

who kept his techniques secret, used this method.[24] Others argued against it. Sebright tried it and found the results disappointing. "I do not," he counseled, "approve of mixing two distinct breeds ... The first cross frequently produces a tolerable animal, but it is a breed that cannot be continued."[25] The second question was whether to *breed in and in* (that is, to mate close relatives, such as parents and children). Earlier generations thought breeding in and in (later called *inbreeding*) led to weak animals. Sebright credited Bakewell with "destroying the absurd prejudice" against mating relatives.[26] The idea behind inbreeding was that, once a breeder had individuals with desired traits, mating close relatives would perpetuate those traits. Some breeders claimed success from breeding in and in, but most breeders thought the practice dangerous. Sebright tried it with strong spaniels and found it led to "weak and diminutive lap-dogs."[27] Sebright favored moderation. He concluded, "animals must degenerate, by being long bred from the same family, without the intermixture of any other blood, or from being what is technically called, *bred in-and-in*."[28]

In addition to selective mating, coursers practiced culling – though the latter practice rarely enjoyed the spotlight shone on selective mating. Breeders used rules of thumb to *select* (their word) the best individuals in a litter. In 1816, many greyhound breeders kept only the lightest members of a litter in the belief they would grow into the "most active and speedy" adults.[29] As dogs aged, selection shifted from physical traits to behavior. As an 1822 account put it, if a greyhound "should manifest a disposition to *run foul*, or meet the hare, he is immediately set aside or destroyed."[30] Another publicist of improved breeding, John Wilkinson, generalized this point in 1820. In herds of improved animals, he pointed out, quality varied among individuals. So, in addition to judicious selection of parents, breeders had to discard the worst progeny so they could not pass their traits to the next generation.[31] Wilkinson credited the nobility and gentry with advancing breeding in two ways. First, they experimented with breeding and, when they succeeded, made the results known to the public. Second, they sponsored livestock exhibitions, which spread knowledge of breeding to a wide audience.[32]

Memes about improvement, modernity, and science went hand in hand. In 1816, a treatise on greyhounds noted, "It is the *modern* opinion at Newmarket, that the training of the greyhound may be reduced to the same *scientific* rules as that of the racehorse."[33] A guide to livestock breeding in 1823 said the book offered "the most *scientific* instructions."[34] Here, *science* meant formal principles that enabled people to manipulate nature for human benefit.[35] Breeders believed science produced progress. In his 1828 studbook, Goodlake included more than championship losers in his list of second-class dogs. Class II also included "eminent Stallions, Brood Bitches, and Racers of old times, not included in Class I."[36] In assigning "old time" competitors to Class II, Goodlake reflected the belief that coursers had improved greyhounds through breeding.

Club breeders argued that their methods produced universally superior greyhounds, and publicists repeated this claim. Goodlake's list of first-class dogs, club champions, created the impression that these dogs were a national elite. Their similarities, Goodlake implied, outweighed their differences. Goodlake wanted to credit elite traits to elite parentage, which led him to search for pedigrees. The idea of inherited, universal superiority must have appealed to men who justified their rank on the same basis.[37] Goodlake credited the members of Swaffham, Ashdown, and Malton with "improving the breed of greyhounds" and creating coursing's "present fashionable popularity from one end of the kingdom to the other."[38]

The claim that clubs produced the best greyhounds in the country rested on a fallacy. By design, coursing clubs were small, exclusive, and unrepresentative. Members owned a small portion of the greyhounds in the land. Some champions in Goodlake's list of first-class greyhounds triumphed in fields as small as eight dogs. Saying the best of eight dogs was one of the best dogs in the land was like picking eight students from a school of a thousand pupils, having the eight run a foot race, and naming the winner the best runner in the school. Questioning the assumption that club greyhounds were superior was, however, unlikely to catch on among aristocrats who believed they were superior to everyone else.

Elite breeders pointed to Lord Orford's greyhounds as their central example of universal superiority through selective mating. Orford's dogs, such as Czarina, were remarkably successful. Some descendants of Orford's dogs excelled as well, which seemed to offer proof of inherited superiority.[39] Orford's Claret was a key example. He sired a litter with three dogs – Snowball, Sylvia, and Major – that won every match they ran. Snowball won more than forty matches and ten large pieces of silver plate.[40]

Winning on multiple estates enhanced Snowball's reputation for universal superiority. Sir Walter Scott vaunted Snowball's excellence in multiple environments in a poem.

> Who knows not Snowball? He whose race renowned
> Is still victorious on each coursing ground:
> Swaffham, Newmarket, and the Roman camp.[41]

These arguments had flaws. One was the implication that Snowball's progeny excelled in all environments. Swaffham, Newmarket, and Roman Camp (presumably the one in Norfolk) did not comprise a representative sample of coursing habitats. All three offered open environments that rewarded similar traits in greyhounds. Better tests of universal superiority came when Orford's dogs competed in different habitats. When one of his best Norfolk dogs competed in Berkshire, it lost to a local dog. Observers thought the outcome would have been reversed if the contest had taken place in Norfolk. The test repeated itself after Lord Orford died. Colonel Thornton of Thornville Royal, Yorkshire, bought Orford's dogs at auction. Superior in Norfolk, Orford's breed proved inferior on the wolds of Yorkshire. Yorkshire hares turned quickly on sides of hills, and Norfolk greyhounds shot past them. The hares escaped.[42]

These results suggest that Orford and his ilk did not breed universally superior dogs. They bred greyhounds that excelled in a narrow niche. The job dimension of the niche was narrow because clubs standardized rules of coursing. The habitat dimension of the niche was narrow because each club competed on one estate. Orford's dogs excelled in their home niches, and in similar niches, but not in other niches. When they competed in hilly Yorkshire, a trait that helped them win in Norfolk (large size, which seemed to improve endurance on long, straight runs in open country) proved a detriment (bulk created too much momentum to follow quick-turning hares on hillsides). Rough greyhounds remained superior in the north. In 1822, a sporting magazine noted that rough northern greyhounds were "the best adapted for the country in which they run, as the tender coat of the high-bred greyhound is not so well calculated to resist the bushes and brambles" of northern England.[43]

A focus on selective mating as the source of excellence, to the exclusion of population size, was another flaw in the reasoning of Orford and his followers. It is possible that selective mating was correlated with, rather than the cause of, success in coursing. Most coursers owned a few greyhounds. If one chose a small number of individuals (say, five) from a sample of 100 varied greyhounds, it was impossible for those five to capture the full variation in traits in the parent population. Because more greyhounds clustered in the middle of the bell curve of coursing ability, coursers with five dogs (5 percent of the greyhound population) would be most likely to own middling coursers. The chance they would have the few best dogs at the high end of the scale of coursing ability was small. If they owned fifty greyhounds (50 percent of the population), they would be much more likely to have one of the best dogs in the population.

Kennel sizes varied in the way just described. Lord Orford, Lord Rivers, and other successful nobles had much larger kennels than other coursers.[44] Lord Orford raised fifty brace of greyhounds at a time. Keeping large numbers of dogs, and increasing variation among them through cross breeding, increased the likelihood of an outlier at the tip of the high tail of a normal distribution of quality.[45] Large kennels required a lot of money. When Lord Rivers retired, he sold his fifty-seven greyhounds for a little more than a thousand pounds.[46] In 2014, the equivalent value would be about 72,000 pounds.[47] Wealth, and its impact on kennel size, might have had a bigger impact on success than selective mating.

Yet another flaw in the focus on selective mating was the exclusion of other variables, such as training and diet. William Osbaldiston (1792) stressed the importance of diet when he recommended, "If you design your greyhound for a wager, then give him his diet-bread as follows." A complex recipe called for combining wheat, dried oatmeal, liquorice, anise seeds, egg whites, and beef. Steps included grinding, beating, kneading, baking, and soaking of ingredients.[48] Providing such a diet usually meant paying servants to do the work. Here, too, a large purse might have a bigger impact than selective mating alone.

Greyhound breeders in the transitional era showed little enthusiasm for a meme popular among horse breeders: public pedigrees. In 1791, publication of *An Introduction to the General Stud Book* for horses helped inspire the studbook genre.[49] In 1822, a herd book for shorthorn cattle appeared.[50] Despite these examples, Thomas Goodlake met with middling success in obtaining pedigrees for greyhounds for his 1828 *Courser's Manual or Stud-Book*. Goodlake found some owners had no interest in pedigrees. Of the thirty-six dogs on the first page of Class I greyhounds (Active through Beauty), only about half (seventeen) included the names and owners of at least one parent.[51] The other half had no information on ancestry.

The lack of interest is puzzling for two reasons. First, historians have argued that patricians embraced livestock pedigrees to bolster their own social status. Human and animal pedigrees reinforced the idea of inherited superiority, which helped justify a social order with aristocrats and the gentry at the top.[52] It is unclear why greyhounds, which long symbolized elite status, should be different. It is possible that the success of Lord Orford, who used low-status breeds (bulldogs and lurchers) to improve greyhounds, undermined the argument for inherited superiority too much for comfort. Second, livestock breeders promoted the idea that one should study several generations of ancestors before breeding from an animal. If a long line of ancestors had a desired trait, it increased the odds that the individual's offspring would inherit it.[53] Again, it is unclear why greyhounds should be different. It is possible that Goodlake happened to poll coursers when a fondness for pedigrees was spreading but had not yet become universal. By publishing his studbook, Goodlake helped to stimulate future interest in pedigrees.

Club greyhounds evolved rapidly in the transitional era by becoming more uniform than, and having different traits from, other greyhound populations. One of the main drivers for narrowing of variation was narrowing of job descriptions. Outside of clubs, job duties included winning matches and entertainment, which encouraged variation in greyhound traits. Club coursers focused on winning, which narrowed breeding goals. Breeders selected for greyhound behavioral traits that maximized the odds of victory. They changed traits rapidly through cross breeding with bulldogs, lurchers, and Italian greyhounds. Human populations evolved in response to these changes in greyhound traits. Coursers concluded that Orford's greyhounds and breeding methods were superior to older versions, and they adopted the view that the sleek shape and short fur of Orford's greyhounds were signs of quality. Because people shaped greyhound traits, and greyhound traits shaped the frequency of a meme in human populations, human and greyhound populations coevolved. Coevolution circled back to shape greyhounds. The frequency of greyhounds with smooth coats rose, so the club population evolved further.

Memes Targeting Rough Greyhounds

Populations of club greyhounds evolved when the frequency of smooth greyhounds rose, which meant the frequency of rough greyhounds fell. As we saw, the frequency of rough dogs declined because many coursers favored smooth greyhounds. But that was only part of the story. The other part was that some coursing clubs drove out rough greyhounds. In the early nineteenth century, the Derbyshire coursing club barred rough dogs from competition. The Swaffham Coursing Society went further and wrote rough greyhounds out of the breed. It adopted a rule reading, "No rough haired dog to be deemed a greyhound."[54]

These rules prompted evolution in human populations. The Derbyshire and Swaffham memes were new. Records examined for this study found no examples of barring rough greyhounds from coursing contests before the rise of clubs. Books had, for centuries, noted that the greyhound breed included rough and smooth individuals. The pre-club meme was that coat length was an adaptation to habitat. Smooth greyhounds were superior in open country and inferior in rough terrain. Rough greyhounds were superior in brushy country and inferior in open country. The imposition of rules barring rough dogs from clubs suggests that some members of Derbyshire and Swaffham retained this meme. The purpose of rules was to replace that meme with new memes. The two clubs chose different memes to reach the same goal of barring rough dogs from contests. Derbyshire adopted a meme that made rough greyhounds ineligible for contests. Swaffham adopted a meme that converted rough dogs from greyhounds into some other (unspecified) breed. Memes about coat length changed within clubs, so populations of club members evolved.

Clubs banned rough dogs on the grounds they were inferior to smooth dogs. If this was the reason, the club rules seemed unnecessary. Clubs had well-developed systems, championships, for comparing the virtues of greyhounds. If rough dogs were inferior, members using them would have lost contests. They would have replaced rough dogs with better, smooth dogs. Rough greyhounds would have disappeared from clubs. This reality forces us to look for reasons other than coursing performance to explain the drive to banish rough greyhounds.

Several social forces converged to create a welcoming environment for memes targeting rough greyhounds. One was regional bias. The most prestigious clubs were in the south (along with a couple in Yorkshire). In his 1825 book on English sports, Henry Alken wrote, "The great English *Coursing-Meetings*, and matches with the greyhounds, are held annually at *Newmarket*, *Swaffham* in *Norfolk*, and *Flixton* in *Yorkshire*."[55] Southern and midland English people tended to see themselves as superior to northerners, so it was a small step to see northern coursing and greyhounds (which were often rough) as inferior.[56] In 1822, a sporting magazine claimed that coursers in the south, midlands, and Yorkshire practiced coursing "in much greater perfection than in other parts of England, but particularly in the north."[57] The magazine contradicted itself by crediting Yorkshire, a northern county, with "perfection" while denigrating coursing "in the north." The reason might be that the two most important Yorkshire clubs, Malton and Flixton, coursed in country that resembled the open south more than the rough, mountainous north. Both clubs nestled in the Vale of Pickering, a low, flat area. Smooth greyhounds did well in the vale, so it was easy to lump Malton and Flixton dogs with southern dogs. In general, the south of England offered open habitat, which favored smooth dogs, and the north of England rough (brushy) habitat, which favored rough dogs.

The ideology of improvement joined regional bias in helping anti-rough memes to spread. The new wave of elite livestock breeders claimed to improve animals, which implied superiority over other, "unimproved" animals. Members of southern clubs, with Lord Orford in the vanguard, adopted this view. They advertised themselves as the leading improvers of greyhounds because they used selective mating to change traits rapidly. The most "improved" greyhounds happened to be smooth dogs because southern coursers lived in open areas, but southerners believed they created universally superior dogs. In 1822, a sporting magazine said the "modern highly improved greyhound[s]" of southern England were "smooth, beautiful, high-bred dogs." Greyhounds in the north were "rough-haired animals."[58]

The superiority of rough greyhounds in rough environments forced critics to find memes that disparaged them for traits other than coursing ability. Critics settled on ancestry and aesthetics. In 1816, *A Treatise on Greyhounds* noted that "the rough-haired greyhound is generally stigmatised by the sportsman as a species of mongrel, and undoubtedly has not often that perfect symmetry, which makes the high-bred greyhound so beautiful."[59] The 1822 article that credited rough greyhounds with superiority in the north also criticized them for "impurity of the blood."[60] It was a curious argument because the author noted that "the high-bred smooth greyhound" descended from Orford's greyhound–bulldog cross. If the author were consistent, he would have slammed southern and northern greyhounds alike for mongrelism. One suspects he began with the assumption of southern superiority, which blinded him to a double standard.

National bias encouraged memes targeting rough greyhounds. Some English people regarded the Irish and Highland Scots as inferior and uncivilized brutes, and they extended this way of thinking to Irish and Scottish dogs.[61] Greyhounds in Ireland and Scotland often had rough coats, which suited the challenging conditions in which they worked. (See Figure 4.2.) As the popularity of smooth greyhounds grew in elite clubs, some coursers began to see (a) smooth dogs as *English* greyhounds and (b) rough dogs as *Irish, Scottish, Gaelic,* or *Celtic* greyhounds. National prejudice helps to explain why the 1822 article (discussed above) criticized northern, but not southern, greyhounds for mongrelism. The author suggested that the rough greyhound "in all probability, is descended, in some measure, from the Irish wolf-dog,–perhaps a cross between it and the common lurcher."[62] It was not mongrelism per se, then, but the cross with an Irish dog and lurcher that seemed to bother the critic.

The English rarely felt the need for a meme applying a national adjective to their greyhounds before the nineteenth century. To them, the greyhounds in England were the standard, and dogs from other countries needed to be distinguished. A book referred to *Irish greyhounds* as early as 1590.[63] *Italian greyhound* became popular in the eighteenth century. In 1792, Ralph Beilby described "The Scottish Highland Greyhound, or Wolf-Dog." It was large, powerful, strong, muscular, and fierce-looking. Its hair was harsh, wiry, reddish, and mixed with white.[64] Thomas Brown described the *Scotch greyhound* in 1829 as similar to the "common" greyhound in all ways except that it was larger and had wiry hair. Brown recounted seeing Scotch greyhounds in mountainous Northern Ireland, where small farmers and peasants used them to catch hares. Common English greyhounds lacked the strength to pursue those hares.[65]

Travel and imperialism helped foster a meme that attached *English* to *greyhound.* The term *English greyhound* may have appeared in print for the first time in a 1711 analysis of trade with India. The author described an English greyhound as a good present for a Chinese person.[66] In 1828, two books compared the coat of a lynx in India to that of an English greyhound.[67] The same year, a travel account described an antelope-coursing contest in Persia between an English greyhound named Venus and an Arabian dog named Butcher. Venus ran faster than Butcher, but Butcher's superior endurance enabled him to perform better near the end of a long chase. In the end, the antelope escaped from both dogs.[68]

The trend toward smoother greyhounds, coupled with the superiority that people from southern England felt toward their northern neighbors, encouraged a meme that progressive evolution resulted in superior smooth greyhounds. The meme associated rough, uncivilized dogs with rough, uncivilized, Gaelic people. It linked smooth, civilized greyhounds with refined, civilized, English people.[69] In 1822, *The Sporting Repository* reported that greyhounds in earlier eras had to be strong and hardy because they coursed wolves, foxes, and deer. But as civilization drove ferocious animals extinct, coursing "assumed a different form, and kept pace, as it were, with the progress of other improvements." These changes led to the "modern highly improved greyhound," which was "unquestionably the most elegant and beautiful of the canine race."[70]

Class conflict facilitated memes that targeted rough greyhounds. Greyhounds in the north were "rough-haired animals, partaking much of the lurcher," claimed a sporting magazine.[71] When an author calling himself the Suffolk Sportsman attacked rough greyhounds in 1825, he charged that multi-colored and brindled greyhounds were, at best, "lurchers rectified." (Suffolk was a southern county, putting the Suffolk Sportsman in the region that favored smooth greyhounds.) *Lurcher* was a job title – poacher's dog. The root word, *lurch*, meant *lurking* and *stealing* (two behaviors associated with poaching).[72] Lurchers varied in ancestry and appearance, but many looked like rough greyhounds. (See Figures 4.4 and 4.5.) Before 1831, the law prohibited everyone but patricians from owning lurchers as well as greyhounds.[73]

The meme underpinning limits on lurcher and greyhound ownership was the same for both dogs – to preserve hunting as a patrician monopoly. The Suffolk Sportsman criticized rough greyhounds for *lurching*, a behavior associated with lurchers and poaching. He said rough greyhounds liked to go for the kill, which led them to run directly for hares at the edge of coverts and snap them up rather than waiting for them to get into the open for a long chase. (This behavior was, in fact, useful for poachers.) Rough greyhounds also would lie back to let the lead dog turn a hare, and then snap up the hare. This behavior, also called lurching, made rough greyhounds "usurpers of title."[74] (Some smooth greyhounds lurched, and some rough greyhounds did not, so a double standard was at work.) Because greyhounds did not have titles, this language suggests that the author's real concern was the status of human aristocrats.

Laws (which were memes) that restricted hunting and greyhounds to patricians became symbols of the status quo for defenders and opponents alike. Patricians defended the game laws as vital to the nation because they kept England's most capable citizens in the countryside. Critics attacked the game laws as illogical (no one owned wild animals), harmful to tenants (the law stopped tenants from killing animals that ate their crops), invidious (the same action was legal for some people but not for others), a threat to order (the laws made criminals out of ordinary people), and ineffective (poachers and vendors carried on a brisk trade in game).[75] Poachers and their dogs, lurchers, symbolized the conflict over the game laws for individuals on both sides. By equating rough

Figure 4.4 Lurcher. This dog looks like a rough greyhound, but the author called it a lurcher. The division between greyhounds and lurchers was legal more than biological. Greyhounds were dogs patricians used to hunt animals legally. Lurchers were dogs poachers used to kill animals illegally. Many looked like rough greyhounds, and breeders sometimes crossed greyhounds with shepherds' dogs to manufacture them. As controversy raged over the game laws in the early nineteenth century, some patricians redefined rough greyhounds as lurchers and banned them from club meetings. William Taplin, *The Sportsman's Cabinet; or, A Correct Delineation of the Various Dogs Used in the Sports of the Field: Including the Canine Race in General. Consisting of a Series of Engravings of Every Distinct Breed ... To Which Is Added, a Scientific Disquisition upon the Distemper, Canine Madness, and the Hydrophobia* (London: J. Cundee, 1804), after 102. SF428.5 .T36 1803 v.2. Special Collections, University of Virginia, Charlottesville, VA.

greyhounds with lurchers and banning them, patrician coursers flagged their worry about threats to class privilege.

Natural historians, who relied on dog writers for data, adopted coursers' memes on greyhound classification. Like coursing clubs, they drew no distinction between smooth and rough greyhounds before 1800. In 1771, Thomas Pennant identified two or three greyhounds, depending

POACHERS.

Figure 4.5 Poachers and lurcher. The dog in this engraving (titled "Poachers") looks more like a smooth (if stocky) greyhound than the lurcher in Figure 4.4, but the engraver identified it as a lurcher. *Lurcher* was a job title (poacher's dog) more than the name of a distinct biological population. To patricians, lurchers symbolized violation of the game laws and elite hunting privileges. Dog writers and natural historians in the eighteenth and nineteenth centuries divided dogs into breeds – such as greyhounds, rough greyhounds, and lurchers – that in reality lived in overlapping populations. Henry Alken, *The National Sports of Great Britain* ([1825] New York: D. Appleton, 1903), Poachers, NE960 .A4 1825. Special Collections, University of Virginia, Charlottesville, VA.

on how one counted. The two were the Irish Gre-Hound and the Common Gre-Hound. He described Irish Gre-Hounds as scarce wolf hunters of great size and strength. He did not describe the duties of Common Gre-Hounds, but he broke them into two varieties. Italian Gre-Hounds were small and smooth. Oriental Gre-Hounds were tall, slender, and possessed of long hairs on the tail.[76] The Comte de Buffon saw less difference among breeds. In 1792, he argued that the large Dane, the Irish greyhound, and the common greyhound, "though they appear different at the first sight, are nevertheless the same dog." Buffon considered the large Dane to be "no more than a plump Irish greyhound; and the common greyhound is only the Irish greyhound, rendered more thin and delicate by care; for there is not more difference between these three dogs than between a Dutchman, a Frenchman, and an Italian."[77]

After 1800, when southern coursers separated rough greyhounds from smooth greyhounds, natural historians followed suit. An 1802 English version of Linnaeus's *Systema Naturae* classified six types of greyhounds – Greyhound, Irish Greyhound, Turkish Greyhound, Common Greyhound, Rough Greyhound, and Italian Greyhound. The Greyhound had a long head, robust snout, small ears, long, stout legs, and a long, slender body. The Irish Greyhound and Turkish Greyhound were the size of Mastiffs. Irish Greyhounds had narrowing snouts. Common Greyhounds and Rough Greyhounds were the size of wolves. The only difference between the two was that Rough Greyhounds had long, curled hair. Italian Greyhounds were "less" (smaller) and had tapering snouts.[78] The Baron Cuvier agreed that six kinds of greyhounds roamed the earth, including smooth and rough greyhounds, but his six differed from those in *Systema Naturae*. In 1827, Cuvier gave the Common Greyhound a Latin binomial (*Canis Grajus*, L.). He identified the other five varieties by geography. The large (up to four feet high) Irish Greyhound had become rare because its job, extirpating wolves from Ireland, was complete. The Scotch Greyhound (also known as the Wiry-haired Greyhound) had long, curling, stiff hair. The other two were the Russian Greyhound and the Turkish Greyhound.[79]

The dominant memes for classifying rough and smooth greyhounds, then, reflected social trends more than biological realities. For centuries, the English considered dogs of all coat lengths to be valuable, high-status greyhounds. In the early nineteenth century, some coursers declared smooth greyhounds superior to their rough relatives. Smooth greyhounds came to symbolize progressive, southern, English patricians. Rough greyhounds came to symbolize poachers and backward, northern, working, Irish, and Scottish people. Some of the biases that fed into the divergence, such as a feeling of southern English superiority over northerners and "Gaels," had deep roots.

The divergence appeared in the early nineteenth century, rather than sooner, because several social trends converged. The ideology of improvement through breeding provided a rationale for claiming superiority for smooth greyhounds, the growth of industry and population in the north threatened the inherited status of southern patricians, the French Revolution terrified patricians, advocates of democracy and justice attacked the game laws and patrician privilege, and disorder sparked a political clampdown on groups and individuals that threatened the status quo. Rough, northern greyhounds symbolized the human threats facing southern patricians, and smooth greyhounds symbolized the ostensible superiority of southern patricians and their ability to improve the world.

Regional Populations of Greyhounds

Southern coursers and sporting magazines argued that superior, smooth greyhounds were sweeping rough greyhounds away on a national scale. In fact, national variation persisted throughout the transitional period. This variation falsified two claims: the claim that smooth greyhounds were universally superior, and the claim of national standardization. National variation in greyhounds persisted because habitats varied across England.

Many aspects of habitats varied. As discussed, openness or brushiness affected the frequency of coat lengths. That trait was important because southern coursers claimed short coats correlated with other superior traits. Other aspects of habitats included topography (hilliness versus flatness), soil texture (hardness versus softness), land use (plowed versus unplowed land), drainage (ditched versus ditch-free fields), and hare traits (running straight, fast, and far versus turning frequently). These habitat aspects combined in many, complex ways (open landscapes were hilly in some places and flat in others). Each combination of habitat aspects called for a different package of physical and behavioral traits in greyhounds.

The leading greyhound expert of the nineteenth century, John Henry Walsh, believed regional differences in habitats created six regional varieties of British greyhounds, each with different traits. Walsh implied he was describing club greyhounds. His data suggest a regional bias in sporting magazines, which promoted the meme that smooth southern greyhounds were universally superior. It appears a countervailing meme, that no one package of traits was superior in all environments, dominated many clubs. In each club, members tailored greyhounds to local niches (job–habitat combinations), not to national standards. Human and greyhound populations across England evolved less than the southern supremacists claimed. Variation in memes and packages of greyhound traits continued on a national scale.

It is important to describe each variety and its habitat in moderate detail for several reasons. First, this detail highlights the degree to which breeders saw important variations in habitats, such as soil texture, that are easy for us to overlook today. Second, the variations in habitat led to important differences in greyhound populations that are easy for us to miss. Many of us would notice general similarities, but not subtle differences, among greyhounds. Walsh identified differences in chest depth and shoulder musculature that would be too subtle for many of us to see. Third, the variations in habitat included variation in hares as well as land and plants. The variation in hares had to do with hare behavior more than appearance. Some ran straight and others turned frequently. Fourth, breeders tailored behaviors, as well as physical traits, to habitats. These behaviors were traits just as much as physical traits, but they are impossible to see in images of standing greyhounds from the period.

Walsh called one population of greyhounds Newmarket. The open, flat, grassy terrain around Newmarket favored the same trait in greyhounds as in the area's famous horses – speed. Newmarket greyhounds had deep chests, well-bent thighs and hocks, muscular shoulders, and straight forelegs because, breeders believed, these traits contributed to speed. But, Walsh believed, Newmarket breeders sacrificed three traits to maximize speed. One was intelligence. In their quest for sleek heads, breeders selected for skulls too small to accommodate a brain of adequate size. The second was turning ability. Newmarket greyhounds circled in broad sweeps to keep their speed high, rather than stopping and starting in a new direction. This trait suited fast hares, but not those that turned frequently. The third was endurance. Newmarket greyhounds excelled in short to moderate length courses because they reached hares quickly, but slower dogs with more endurance often defeated them in longer courses. Newmarket greyhounds did well in places with similar landscapes and hares – Essex, Surrey, Cambridgeshire, Suffolk, Norfolk, Bedfordshire, Huntingdonshire, and Lincolnshire.[80]

A second population, Lancashire greyhounds, competed in flat, soft, peaty, plowed, reclaimed land divided by ditches. This landscape favored speed, but greyhounds needed more endurance than in Newmarket because the soft soil demanded more effort per stride. Because they struck the ground less often, long-striding greyhounds had an advantage in Lancashire. The soft soil offered two advantages – it rarely lamed greyhounds, and large dogs turned more easily than on harder turf. Even so, selection for speed over endurance left Lancashire greyhounds unable to pursue far-running hares. Lancashire greyhounds looked like Newmarket greyhounds, but tended to be larger, have shorter necks, and suffer from even smaller brains. The last trait was ironic because, as Walsh put it, Lancashire's ditches increased the need for "tact and cleverness to avoid mistakes at those impediments to the course."[81]

A third population, Yorkshire greyhounds, showed great size and speed. They needed less endurance than dogs from Newmarket or Lancashire because covert-bred Yorkshire hares usually darted back into cover rather than setting off on long runs. The need to work coverts made "cleverness" second in importance after speed. Walsh described Yorkshire greyhounds as looking coarse, "ragged hipped and useful, rather than level or elegant." Some Yorkshire greyhounds lived near the borders of Scotland, where "it becomes intermixed with that blood." Yorkshire offered several landscapes, ranging from fine turf at Malton to flinty, sandy hills at Market Weighton.[82]

Scotland supplied the fourth and fifth populations. Several strains combined to form smooth Scotch greyhounds, with English ancestors playing a larger role than Scotch. The most important trait was speed. These dogs usually showed quickness, cleverness, hardy constitutions, ability to stop and restart after turns, and less endurance than some other varieties.[83] Another population, rough Scotch greyhounds, had rough coats, great size, good but not great speed, good turning skill, ability to bear cold and hardship, and slowness out of turns.[84]

Wiltshire greyhounds made up the sixth population. Walsh considered this variety more distinctive than any of the five others. Wiltshire hares, especially those at Amesbury and the Marlborough Downs, behaved differently from hares elsewhere. They ran far, which made endurance more important than the speed that was the first criterion in other regions. Wiltshire breeders first selected for endurance, and then added as much speed as they could. Wiltshire hares turned in ways that gave them "the power of throwing out even the best worker in a style quite different to the Lancashire and Yorkshire" hares. These turns forced Wiltshire greyhounds to stop, turn, and resume running. The ability to do these maneuvers gave Wiltshire greyhounds an advantage over faster dogs from other regions when competing in their own habitat. Wiltshire greyhounds often were "small, stout, and terrier-like." Although cultivated, the land in Wiltshire lacked fences, which enabled hares and greyhounds to run far, which increased the need for endurance. The region's flinty soils "punished" greyhounds, making "stoutness" an essential trait.[85]

In sum, the pattern of evolution in club populations of greyhounds in the transitional era was toward local uniformity while national variation persisted. Local uniformity derived from narrowing of niches by clubs. Both job descriptions and habitats narrowed on a local scale. Islands of greyhound uniformity emerged. On a national scale, variation among club greyhounds persisted because variation in niches persisted. Breeders adapted greyhounds to local job–habitat combinations. Because local combinations varied on a national scale, greyhounds varied on a national scale. Walsh identified six local varieties of greyhounds in the early nineteenth century. These varieties differed in behavioral traits as well as physical traits. Varieties were packages of physical and behavioral traits adapted to local conditions.

Modernization

As with human evolution, clubs modernized the evolution of greyhounds in the period from 1776 to 1831. This modernization involved small versions of the same forces that shaped human evolution in the same period. First, clubs used local *bureaucracies* to promulgate written rules defining the occupational duties of greyhounds. Second, clubs *standardized* coursing rules and the habitats in which greyhounds worked. Third, clubs capitalized on *mass communication* to spread memes about greyhound job descriptions (coursing rules) and breeding. Fourth, they claimed to *improve* greyhounds through breeding. (See Figure 4.6.)

As with human evolution in the same period, other features of modernity played little role. These features included democracy, urbanization, and capitalism. Laws continued to limit greyhound ownership to a small number of elites, greyhounds worked in rural areas, and commercial breeding had little impact on their traits. Modernization in the transitional decades between the patrician era and modernity meant

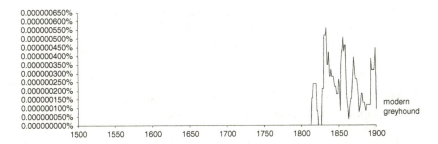

Figure 4.6 Rise of modern greyhounds. This graph shows the frequency with which the phrase "modern greyhound" appeared in British books. Coursers and breeders began describing their sport and greyhounds as modern in the 1820s. Google Books Ngram Viewer, https://books .google.com/ngrams, searched British literature, February 25, 2014, screen shot enhanced by Pam LeRow.

narrowing of traits on a local scale. Outside clubs, breeders adapted greyhounds to varied jobs and environments.

Conclusion

Club members and club greyhounds coevolved in the transitional decades. Greyhounds affected human behavior by creating the opportunity to found clubs around hare coursing. People responded to the opportunity by founding clubs and standardizing greyhound jobs and habitats on a local scale. These changes in the human sphere circled back to reshape greyhounds. Lord Orford led the way by crossing greyhounds with bulldogs and other breeds to suit his estate and his club's rules. His smooth greyhounds spread to other clubs in open country. These modified greyhound traits spiraled back to shape human ideas and behaviors. Club coursers in the south concluded that their smooth greyhounds were universally superior, which led them to denigrate rough greyhounds as inferior. Some clubs barred rough dogs, which narrowed local greyhound traits. The existence of smooth and rough greyhounds enabled people to use both as symbols in a broad social struggle between southern patricians and members of other groups during decades of rapid change.

For greyhound populations, the overall pattern was from variation to local uniformity in traits. Because habitats differed among regions, national variation persisted among populations of club greyhounds. Variation continued in greyhounds that worked outside clubs, too. Clubs were islands of local uniformity in a sea of variation. After 1831, the full forces of modernity would accelerate trends seen in mild forms during the transitional decades.

Notes

1. Thomas Goodlake, *The Courser's Manual or Stud-Book* (Liverpool: Geo. B. Whittaker and Jos. Booker, 1828), v–vii, lxxvii.
2. Goodlake, *Courser's Manual [1828]*, xiv.
3. T. H. Needham, *The Complete Sportsman: A Compendious View of the Ancient and Modern Chase . . . With Every Instruction and Information Relative to the Diversions of the Field* (London [?]: W. Simpkin and R. Marshall, 1817), 137–38.
4. Delabere Pritchett Blaine, *An Encyclopaedia of Rural Sports: Or a Complete Account, Historical, Practical, and Descriptive, of Hunting, Shooting, Fishing, Racing, and Other Field Sports and Athletic Amusements of the Present Day* (London: Longman, Orme, Brown, Green and Longmans, 1840), 584.

5. John Scott, *The Sportsman's Repository: Comprising a Series of Highly Finished Engravings, Representing the Horse and the Dog, in All Their Varieties* (London: Henry G. Bohn, 1845), 89.

6. Needham, *Complete Sportsman*, 137–38.

7. Anonymous, "Coursing," *Sporting Repository* 1, no. 1 (1822): 31–33, see 31.

8. D., "Coursing in the North of England and Fox-Hunting in Scotland," *Annals of Sporting and Fancy Gazette* 1, no. 4 (1822): 235–36.

9. Blaine, *An Encyclopaedia of Rural Sports [1840]*, 584.

10. Richard Parkinson, *Treatise on the Breeding and Management of Livestock*, vol. 1 (London: Cadell and Davies, 1810), xx.

11. Anonymous, "Coursing," 31–33, see 31.

12. Henry Thomas Alken, *The National Sports of Great Britain: Fifty Engravings with Descriptions* ([1825] New York: D. Appleton, 1903), "Coursing" (unpaginated).

13. Anonymous, "Coursing (with an Engraving)," *Sporting Repository* 1, no. 3 (1822): 231–239, see facing 231 and 231.

14. Judy Egerton, *British Sporting Paintings: The Paul Mellon Collection in the Virginia Museum of Fine Arts* (Richmond; Seattle: Virginia Museum of Fine Arts; University of Washington Press, 1985), x–xii, 16; Alken, *National Sports of Great Britain*; Henry Thomas Alken, *Scraps from The Sketch Book of Henry Alken, Engraved by Himself, Containing Forty-Two Plates* (London: Thomas M'Lean, 1821).

15. Alken, *Sketch Book*; Alken, *National Sports of Great Britain*.

16. D. R. Fisher, "Sebright, Sir John, Seventh Baronet (1767–1846)," in *Oxford Dictionary of National Biography* (Oxford: Oxford University Press, 2004), www .oxforddnb.com/view/article/24997.

17. John Sebright, *The Art of Improving the Breeds of Domestic Animals* (London: John Harding, 1809), 4, 13.

18. Jonathan David Chambers and G. E. Mingay, *The Agricultural Revolution, 1750–1880* (New York: Schocken Books, 1966).

19. Sebright, *The Art of Improving the Breeds of Domestic Animals*, 5–6.

20. Sebright, *The Art of Improving the Breeds of Domestic Animals*, 5.

21. Sebright, *The Art of Improving the Breeds of Domestic Animals*, 24–25.

22. Sebright, *The Art of Improving the Breeds of Domestic Animals*, 6.

23. Anonymous, *Remarks on Live Stock and Relative Subjects* (Edinburgh: Archibald Constable, 1806).

24. Parkinson, *Breeding and Management*, xx–xxi; R. W. Dickson, *An Improved System of Management of Live Stock and Cattle; or a Practical Guide to the Perfecting and Improvement of the Several Breeds and Varieties of Agricultural Stock, and Domestic Animals*, vol. 1 (London: Thomas Kelly, 1823), 15.

25. Sebright, *The Art of Improving the Breeds of Domestic Animals*, 17–18; John Wilkinson, *Remarks on the Improvement of Cattle, Etc. in a Letter to Sir John Saunders Sebright, Bart. M. D.* (Nottingham: H. Barnett, 1820), 43.

26. Sebright, *The Art of Improving the Breeds of Domestic Animals*, 10.

27. Sebright, *The Art of Improving the Breeds of Domestic Animals*, 8–13.

28. Sebright, *The Art of Improving the Breeds of Domestic Animals*, 5–6, 8.

29. Anonymous, *A Treatise on Greyhounds, with Observations on the Treatment and Disorders of Them* (London: [n.p.], 1816), 60.

30. D., "Coursing in the North of England and Fox-Hunting in Scotland," 235.

31. Wilkinson, *Remarks on the Improvement of Cattle, Etc. in a Letter to Sir John Saunders Sebright, Bart. M. D.*, 4.

32. Wilkinson, *Remarks on the Improvement of Cattle, Etc. in a Letter to Sir John Saunders Sebright, Bart. M. D.*, 66.

33. Anonymous, *A Treatise on Greyhounds, with Observations on the Treatment and Disorders of Them*, 64. Emphasis added.

34. Dickson, *A Complete System of Improved Live Stock and Cattle Management, Or, The Practical Guide to Gentlemen, Store-Masters, Farmers, and Other Keepers of Stock*, 1: in full subtitle.

35. Carolyn Merchant, *The Death of Nature: Women, Ecology, and the Scientific Revolution* (San Francisco: Harper & Row, 1980).

36. Goodlake, *Courser's Manual [1828]*, v–vii, lxxvii.

37. Harriet Ritvo, "Pride and Pedigree: The Evolution of the Victorian Dog Fancy," *Victorian Studies* 29, no. 2 (January 1, 1986): 227–53.

38. Goodlake, *Courser's Manual [1828]*, xvi.

39. Anonymous, *A Treatise on Greyhounds, with Observations on the Treatment and Disorders of Them*, 55–57.

40. Blaine, *An Encyclopaedia of Rural Sports [1840]*, 584–85.

41. Sir Walter Scott, *The Poetical Works of Sir Walter Scott*, ed. John Dennis, vol. 5 (London: G. Bell & Sons, 1892), 427.

42. Blaine, *An Encyclopaedia of Rural Sports [1840]*, 584–85.

43. D., "Coursing in the North of England and Fox-Hunting in Scotland."

44. J. H. Walsh, *Manual of British Rural Sports: Comprising Shooting, Hunting, Coursing, Fishing, Hawking, Racing, Boating, Pedestrianism, and the Various Rural Games and Amusements of Great Britain* (London: G. Routledge, 1856), 152.

45. Goodlake, *Courser's Manual [1828]*, xiv.

46. Goodlake, *Courser's Manual [1828]*, xvii.

47. Calculated using the Web site Measuring Worth, www.measuringworth.com, viewed September 24, 2014.

48. William Osbaldiston, *The British Sportsman, Or, Nobleman, Gentleman, and Farmer's Dictionary, of Recreation and Amusement* (London: J. Stead, 1792), 367–68.

49. J. Weatherby, *An Introduction to a General Stud-Book: Containing (with Few Exceptions) the Pedigree of Every Horse, Mare, &c. of Note, That Has Appeared on the Turf for the Last Fifty Years, with Many of an Earlier Date; Together with a Short Account of the Most Noted Arabians, Barbs, &c. Connected Therewith* (London: H. Reynell, 1791).

50. Margaret E. Derry, *Bred for Perfection: Shorthorn Cattle, Collies, and Arabian Horses since 1800* (Baltimore: Johns Hopkins University Press, 2003), 20.

51. Goodlake, *Courser's Manual [1828]*, vi, 2.

52. Harriet Ritvo, *The Animal Estate: The English and Other Creatures in the Victorian Age* (Cambridge, MA: Harvard University Press, 1987).

53. Sebright, *The Art of Improving the Breeds of Domestic Animals*, 9.

54. Goodlake, *Courser's Manual [1828]*, xxxi, lii. Swaffham's ban on rough dogs did not appear in its rules published in 1798. Anonymous, "Swaffham Coursing Meeting," *Sporting Magazine* 13, no. October (1798): 41–43.

55. Alken, *National Sports of Great Britain*, "Coursing" (unpaginated). Emphasis in original.

56. Helen M. Jewell, *The North–South Divide: The Origins of Northern Consciousness in England* (Manchester: Manchester University Press, 1994).

57. D., "Coursing in the North of England and Fox-Hunting in Scotland," 235–36, see 235.

58. Anonymous, "Coursing (with an Engraving)."

59. Anonymous, *A Treatise on Greyhounds, with Observations on the Treatment and Disorders of Them*, 54.

60. D., "Coursing in the North of England and Fox-Hunting in Scotland."

61. Peter Fleming, Anthony Gross, and J. R. Lander, *Regionalism and Revision: The Crown and Its Provinces in England, 1200–1650* (London; Rio Grande, Ohio: Hambledon Press, 1998).

62. D., "Coursing in the North of England and Fox-Hunting in Scotland," 235–36, see 236.

63. Philip Sidney, *The Countesse of Pembrokes Arcadia* ([1590] Cambridge: Cambridge University Press, 1912), 517.

64. Ralph Beilby, *A General History of Quadrupeds. The Figures Engraved on Wood by T. Bewick*, 3rd edn. (Newcastle upon Tyne: S. Hodgson, R. Beilby, & T. Bewick, 1792), 312.

65. Thomas Brown, *Biographical Sketches and Authentic Anecdotes of Dogs* (Edinburgh: Oliver and Boyd, 1829), 119–20.

66. Charles Lockyer, *An Account of the Trade in India: Containing Rules for Good Government in Trade, Price Courants, and Tables: With Descriptions of Fort St. George, Acheen, Malacca, Condore, Canton, Anjengo, Muskat, Gombroon, Surat, Goa, Carwar, Telichery, Panola, Calicut, the Cape of Good-Hope, and St. Helena*... (Cornhill: Samuel Crouch, 1711), 187.

67. Reginald Heber, *Narrative of a Journey through the Upper Provinces of India: From Calcutta to Bombay, 1824–1825, (with Notes upon Ceylon,) an Account of a Journey to Madras and the Southern Provinces, 1826, and Letters Written in India*, 4th edn., vol. 1 (Philadelphia: John Murray, 1828), 62; Anonymous, *The Modern Traveller. A Popular Description, Geographical, Historical, and Topographical, of the Various Countries of the Globe. India*, vol. 3 (London: James Duncan, 1828), 110.

68. Anonymous, *Sketches of Persia, from the Journals of a Traveller in the East*, vol. 1 (London: John Murray, 1828), 38.

69. Nicholas P. Canny, "The Ideology of English Colonization: From Ireland to America," *The William and Mary Quarterly*, Third Series, 30, no. 4 (October 1, 1973): 575–98, doi:10.2307/1918596.

70. Anonymous, "Coursing (with an Engraving)."

71. Anonymous, "Coursing (with an Engraving)."

72. *Oxford English Dictionary.*

73. P. B. Munsche, *Gentlemen and Poachers: The English Game Laws, 1671–1831* (Cambridge: Cambridge University Press, 1981), 182–83; William Taplin, *The Sportsman's Cabinet, or Correct Delineation of the Dogs Used in the Sports of the Field: Including the Canine Race in General*, vol. 2 (London: J. Cundee, 1804), 102.

74. Quoted in Blaine, *An Encyclopaedia of Rural Sports [1840]*, 568.

75. Munsche, *Gentlemen and Poachers*, 132–58; House of Commons, "Report from the Select Committee on the Laws Related to Game 1823 (260)," *Parliamentary Papers* IV (1823): 107–53; House of Lords, "Game Laws," *Parliamentary Debates* XVI (1827): 680–92; George Bankes, *Reconsiderations of Certain Proposed Alterations of the Game Laws* (London: J. Hatchard, 1825); Brown, *Biographical Sketches and Authentic Anecdotes of Dogs*, 569.

76. Thomas Pennant, *Synopsis of Quadrupeds* (Chester: J. Monk, 1771), 146.

77. Georges Louis Leclerc, Comte de Buffon, *Barr's Buffon. Buffon's Natural History. Containing a Theory of the Earth, a General History of Man, of the Brute Creation, and of Vegetables, Minerals, &c. From the French. With Notes by the Translator*, vol. 5 (London: J.S. Barr, 1792), 321.

78. Charles Linné, *System of Nature through the Three Grand Kingdoms of Animals, Vegetables, and Minerals*, vol. 1 (London: Lackington, Allen, 1802), 42.

79. Georges Cuvier and Edward Griffith, *The Animal Kingdom Arranged in Conformity with Its Organization*, vol. 2 (London: G. B. Whittaker, 1827), 328–30.

80. Walsh, *Manual of British Rural Sports [1856]*, 163–64. Walsh offered a similar list in John Henry Walsh, *The Greyhound: Being a Treatise on the Art of Breeding, Rearing, and Training Greyhounds for Public Running* (London: Longman, Brown, Green & Longmans, 1853), 202–27. Although these books appeared in the 1850s, Walsh explicitly described varieties of earlier decades.

81. Walsh, *Manual of British Rural Sports [1856]*, 164–65.

82. Walsh, *Manual of British Rural Sports [1856]*, 165–66.

83. Walsh, *Manual of British Rural Sports [1856]*, 166.

84. Walsh, *Manual of British Rural Sports [1856]*, 166–67.

85. Walsh, *Manual of British Rural Sports [1856]*, 167–68.

5

MODERNIZING HUMAN EVOLUTION (1831–1900)

This chapter examines how human populations modernized their evolution between 1831 and 1900. We saw that patrician coursers modernized their evolution, in a small way, in the transitional decades between 1776 and 1831. They created local *bureaucracies* by forming clubs, *standardized* job descriptions by adopting written rules for club members, capitalized on *mass communication* in the form of sporting magazines, and embraced an ideology of *progress* through scientific breeding. These changes narrowed variation in courser memes and behavior on local scales. Club populations evolved when they adopted new memes and narrowed variation in behavioral traits on a local scale.

After 1831, coursers fully modernized their evolution. The catalyst was political. Parliament democratized greyhound ownership in 1831. All classes of people, especially the middle classes, rushed into coursing. Other populations, who did not necessarily own greyhounds, also evolved in response to greyhounds. These populations included innkeepers, railroad managers, bookmakers, and publishers. Radical change in the identity of human populations who coevolved with greyhounds, coupled with broader social changes, opened the door to the full forces of modernity.

Full modernization came partly when the four features seen in the transitional decades grew into larger, more powerful forces. The scale of *bureaucratization* and *standardization* grew from local to national with the formation of the National Coursing Club and the spread of its rules. The speed and scale of *mass communication* swelled with telegraphic news. The ideology of *progress* expanded from an elite enterprise to members of all classes. The middle classes, in particular, embraced the idea of improvement through selective mating of greyhounds.

Full modernization also flowered because of the introduction of new features. In the transitional decades before 1831, *capitalism, democracy,* and *industrial infrastructure* played little role in coursing. After 1831, they became integral. Capitalism entered coursing in the form of profit-oriented entrepreneurs. Entrepreneurial innkeepers founded coursing contests to increase business for their pubs and hotels. Entrepreneurial greyhound breeders profited by offering dogs at stud for a fee. Entrepreneurial bookmakers profited by taking wagers on the outcome of coursing contests. Entrepreneurial impresarios organized coursing contests in enclosed spaces, which enabled them to charge admission.

By lifting class-based limits on greyhound ownership, Parliament democratized greyhound ownership. The middle classes took up coursing. They defeated aristocrats in open coursing contests, which falsified the centuries-old claim of aristocratic superiority over other classes. The working classes became part of the coursing community, sometimes by competing and often by attending and wagering on contests. Coursing became mass entertainment. Industrial infrastructure, in the form of railroads, facilitated the nationalization and popularization of coursing by carrying coursers, greyhounds, spectators, and bookmakers to contests. Industrial communication, in the form of telegraphs, accelerated the spread of memes and news.

These changes shaped the evolution of human populations by creating new populations, new memes, and new traits. The new human populations comprised members of the middle and working classes who became coursers or participated in related activities, such as sponsoring contests and gambling. Greyhounds suddenly had new human populations, with different traits from patricians, with whom to coevolve. New memes told profit-seeking entrepreneurs how to organize contests, offer studs for fees, and take bets on the outcome of contests. Other memes explained how the middle classes could compete in coursing, the working classes could attend and bet on matches, and railroads could offer trains to contests. These memes shaped behavioral traits when people chose to follow their instructions. Human populations evolved when the frequency of new behaviors, based on new memes, increased.

Human populations also evolved by narrowing variation on a national scale. In the transitional decades before 1831, club coursers narrowed variation on a local scale. They adapted to local niches, which standardized jobs and habitats on a local scale. National variation persisted, even among elite clubs. After 1831, coursers and their allies narrowed variation on a national scale by adapting themselves to standardized, national niches. The National Coursing Club and its rules standardized job descriptions. The de facto national coursing championship, the Waterloo Cup, standardized the habitat for testing greyhounds. Coursers across the land adapted their behaviors to Waterloo standards. Variation persisted as well, but the practice of having coursers everywhere adapt to a single contest on a single estate was new.

Populations of patrician coursers responded in multiple ways to the new, democratic populations of coursers and spectators. Some patricians decided to stay the course. They kept their clubs exclusive, reinforcing their islands of privilege as democracy sloshed around them. Some patricians embraced the new coursers. They joined democratic coursing clubs and offered their estates for democratic coursing contests. Some patricians retired from public coursing after being thumped by the middle classes. Some patricians developed new memes to denigrate democratized activities. Before 1831, patricians called the killing of hares with greyhounds *hare hunting*, which they considered one of the highest pursuits of men. At that time, only patricians could hunt hares legally. After 1831, patricians introduced a new meme that redefined the killing of hares with greyhounds as *pot-hunting*, which they considered low and unsporting. They narrowed greyhound *sport* to hare coursing matches, in which killing hares was secondary to the performance of greyhounds. Once hare killing lost its aristocratic privilege and symbolism, patricians used it to demonize other classes. Patrician coursers evolved in response to democratic coursers by reducing the frequency of coursing behaviors.

Democratic Memes and Populations

Democratic memes spread in the population of members of Parliament in the early nineteenth century. Poaching and illegal game sales were common. Parliament appointed a select committee to investigate the game laws in 1823. The committee reported that, although only elites could legally possess game, members of all classes bought and ate poached animals. Poachers, coachmen, innkeepers, and poultry sellers created an efficient system for transferring poached game from rural estates to markets. The committee thought this trade corrupted "the morals of the lower classes." The middle classes and elites also bought and ate poached game, but they escaped criticism. Legalizing the game trade would, the committee suggested, increase the value of hares and other animals for landowners, which would encourage them to raise and sell game in legal markets. This change would not drive poachers out of business, but competition might reduce their numbers.[1]

The population of members of Parliament evolved when it adopted these new memes and acted in accordance with them. Parliament mulled reform for years before mustering the votes to change the game laws in 1831.[2] Previously, all game had belonged to large land-owners and the aristocracy. They, and only they, could kill game on other people's land without permission. The new law made game the property of the owner of the land where an animal stood, and it legalized the game trade. In eliminating the status-based monopoly over hunting and game ownership, the new law reflected changes in English society. Enclosure of common lands and high crop prices had enabled rural elites to flaunt lavish living at the same time they impoverished rural laborers, which undermined loyalty to the estab-lished order.[3]

Broader reform movements in the early nineteenth century fostered a welcoming environment for new memes about hunting. The same social changes – especially the growth in the size and power of the middle and working classes – that spurred modification of hunting laws led to the Reform Act of 1832, which increased the number of seats in Parliament allocated to cities (which swelled in size thanks to enclosures and indus-trialization) and boosted the representation of the middle classes. Like the change in game laws, the Reform Act challenged the power of landed elites. It reduced the number of seats allocated to "rotten boroughs," where few electors lived and powerful patrons controlled the selection of members of Parliament. The Reform Act affected England and Wales. Scotland and Ireland enacted similar reform in Parliamentary represen-tation in 1832, demonstrating the shifting base of political power throughout the United Kingdom. In 1846, the repeal of the corn laws, which benefited landowners by keeping grain prices high, reflected the growing power of industry and merchants. Even the crown seemed to reflect change in English social structure. Queen Victoria ruled from 1837 to 1901, and her emphasis on personal virtue spoke to values embraced by the middle classes.[4]

Adopting new, written memes about hunting forced Parliament to banish older memes. The 1831 hunting law required three pages to specify the laws it repealed, flagging the degree to which the new law overthrew centuries of tradition. The section dealing with greyhounds was brief. It repealed the "Statute made in the thirteenth year of the reign of King Richard the Second, as relates to such persons as shall not have or keep any Greyhound, Hound or other dog to hunt, and shall not use fyrets [ferrets], heys, nets, hare pipes, cords, or other engines to take or destroy hares, conies or other gentlemen's Game."[5] Because anyone could kill game with a landowner's permission, it no longer made sense to limit the tools for taking game to patricians. A greyhound was one of those tools.

In 1880, the population of Parliament members adopted a new meme that advantaged coursing tenants at the expense of landowners. The Reform Act of 1832 had expanded the power of the middle classes but left the working classes disenfranchised. The Chartist movement responded by pushing for almost universal male suffrage, and the growth of trade unions after 1848 amplified the voice of industrial workers. In 1867, the Second Reform Act expanded the franchise to working-class men, doubling the number of voters in Parliamentary elections.[6] In 1880, a reformed Parliament revised the game laws to make them more democratic. The 1831 game law made game the property of land-owners. Tenants, who watched hares gobble their crops, needed their landowners' permission to kill the pests. In 1880, the Ground Game Act gave tenants permission to kill hares whenever they wished.[7]

The urban, middle, and working classes took advantage of the oppor-tunity to create new populations coevolving with greyhounds. In 1856, John H. Walsh estimated that 4,000 coursers spent about 29,000 pounds for entrance money at more than 600 stakes per year in England, Scotland, and Ireland.[8] Walsh noted that between 1831 and 1859, "the possession of the greyhound has been coveted and obtained by great numbers of country gentlemen and farmers in rural districts, and by professional men as well as tradesmen in our cities and towns, so that the total number in Great Britain and Ireland may be estimated about fifteen or twenty thousand."[9] (See Figure 5.1.) Between 1840 and 1850, Walsh observed, "the public at large began to think themselves entitled to share in the sport" of coursing.[10]

Several memes motivated the middle and working classes to join populations of greyhound owners. One writer suggested that "the increased desire that seems to pervade society of participating in all kinds of field sports," the founding of democratic clubs that sponsored meets, and powerful individuals who promoted the sport helped broaden participation in coursing.[11] By 1879, dog expert Hugh Dalziel reflected, "The alteration of the game laws of modern times, coupled with the great increase of wealth and leisure, have, by giving impetus to the natural desire for field sports, characteristic of Englishmen, led to the present great and increasing popularity of coursing, and consequent diffusion of greyhounds through all classes."[12]

Coursing clubs coevolved in response to democratization of coursing, albeit in a variety of ways. Some patrician clubs tried to evolve as little as

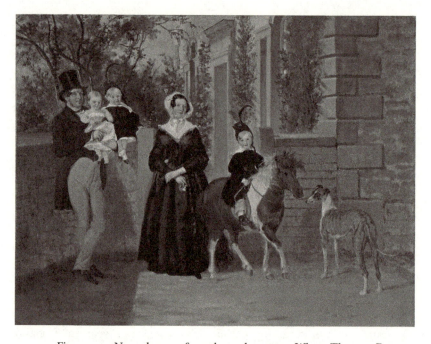

Figure 5.1 New classes of greyhound owners. When Thomas Dawson and his family posed for this portrait in 1842, they included a greyhound named Grace Darling. Twelve years before, keeping Grace Darling might have cost Dawson a fine or three months in jail without bail. Until 1831, a man had to be the heir apparent of a title, have significant property, or work as a keeper to possess a greyhound legally. One of seventeen children of a horse trainer in Scotland, the twenty-one-year-old Dawson probably had none of these when he started a stable in Yorkshire in 1830. The building, clothing, pony, and greyhound symbolized his rising status and wealth in 1842, when Dawson was becoming a leading horse trainer. As ownership and gambling widened, greyhounds lost their elite symbolism. John Frederick Herring, "Thomas Dawson and His Family, 1842," Accession Number 85-492, Virginia Museum of Fine Arts, Richmond, Virginia. Reproduced by permission of Virginia Museum of Fine Arts.

possible. They spurned the middle and working classes. These elite clubs, which limited entries in meets to members and friends, became known as *closed* meetings. Other clubs adopted new memes suited to new realities. Some clubs adopted the meme that anyone, independent of membership status, could participate in contests. These contests became known as *open* meetings. At mid-century, open meetings took place in the south (e.g.,

Amesbury, Ashdown, and Newmarket), the north (e.g., Waterloo and Southport), and in Scotland (e.g., Caledonian and Biggar).[13] One effect of democratization, then, was to increase the variation in memes among coursing clubs. In the transitional era, all clubs relied on the meme that clubs should be exclusive and reinforce inherited privilege. In the democratic era, some clubs retained the exclusive, patrician meme. Other clubs embraced democracy and held open contests.

Variation among clubs increased by the end of the nineteenth century when many embraced both the exclusive meme and the open meme. These clubs became known as *hybrid* clubs. Hybrid meetings included Altcar, Ridgway, North of England, and Yorkshire. Some hybrid clubs offered two types of meets – some closed and others open. Other hybrid clubs let members take all the entry slots they wished in a meet and made the rest available to the public.[14] Open meetings and less restrictive clubs enabled, Walsh noted, "all classes of good sportsmen" to enter meetings in the second half of the nineteenth century.[15]

Although anyone could join populations of coursers, economics deterred many members of the working classes. Coursers had to pay for a dam, stallion fees, taxes, food, and a trainer before a dog entered its first meet.[16] In the mid-nineteenth century, Walsh estimated an owner could raise a brood of greyhounds for twelve pounds per dog. It cost about four pounds to enter a public coursing meet, so the owner of a dog would have invested about sixteen pounds to see a pup into its first match.[17] Additional costs included travel, lodging, meals, and wagers at meets. Kennel buildings could be expensive. In 1856, Walsh recommended a building measuring 25–35 feet on one side and 24–25 feet on the other.[18] (See Figure 5.2.) The kennel of M. G. Hale in Suffolk in 1898 consisted of "a large lofty building divided up into small compartments, and heated by an American stove." Dogs slept on large wooden beds raised a foot from the ground. The kitchen for preparing the dogs' food had a stove large enough to boil two huge copper cauldrons at the same time.[19] Facilities on this scale, which cost a lot to build and staff, lay beyond the reach of working-class budgets.

The working classes helped to create new kinds of greyhound-related populations: spectators and gamblers. These human populations evolved in response to greyhounds even if they did not own greyhounds. Greyhounds created the opportunity for spectators to watch and gamble on matches. Many members of the working classes accepted the opportunity. Their ability to do so expanded as the economic benefits of industrialization, which first flowed to the middle classes, reached workers in

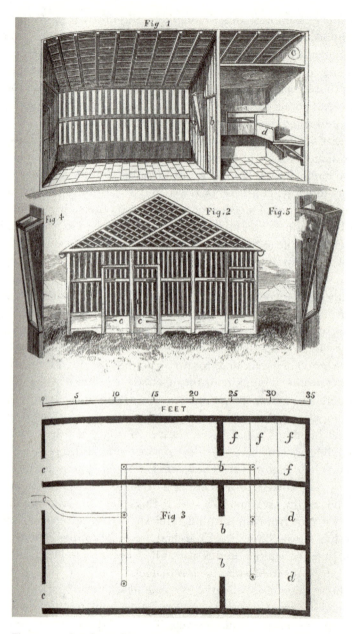

Figure 5.2 Greyhound kennels. Parliament widened access to coursing in 1831, but cost kept most workers out of the sport. John H. Walsh enthused that anyone with five or ten guineas could "compete on favourable terms in any company of coursers, at least as far as his breed of greyhounds is concerned." The last phrase was an important

the second half of the nineteenth century. Real wages doubled between 1800 and 1900, and factory legislation shortened the working day. Workers still worked long hours for low pay, but they gained enough time and money to patronize coursing meets and have a flutter.[20]

In sum, several human populations evolved after 1831 in response to democracy. One evolving population was members of Parliament. For centuries, this population embraced the meme that limited greyhounds and hunting to patricians. In 1831, this population replaced that meme with a new meme allowing all classes to own greyhounds and hunt. In 1880, this population evolved further when it accepted a meme that enabled tenants to kill game. Parliament evolved radically with respect to greyhounds and hunting. Parliament's behavior enabled new populations to form in response to opportunities created by greyhounds. The middle and working classes became greyhound owners, coursers, spectators, and gamblers. These new populations developed memes and behaviors tailored to their new roles, such as attending and betting on coursing contests.

Modern Communication and Transportation

Other aspects of modernity joined democracy in fostering new populations of people enthusiastic about greyhounds and coursing. One aspect was modern *communication*. The introduction of two innovations – universal cheap mail and telegraphy – in the decade after democratization of coursing helped news of coursing reach broader audiences, at a faster speed, than ever before. The penny post reached all of England in 1840, and telegraph lines spread after 1843.[21] Newspapers, magazines, and books exploded in readership.

Newspapers and sporting magazines helped populations of coursers, spectators, and gamblers form by announcing coursing contests in advance. In the early nineteenth century, sporting magazines reported

---

Caption for Figure 5.2 (cont.)

qualification. Walsh's kennel plan, which appeared one page before his comment on stud fees, illustrated one of the investments the middle classes made in their greyhounds beyond stud fees. Few members of the working classes would have access to space for a kennel thirty-five feet long. John H. Walsh, *Manual of British Rural Sports: Comprising Shooting, Hunting, Coursing, Fishing, Hawking, Racing, Boating, Pedestrianism, and the Various Rural Games and Amusements of Great Britain* (London: G. Routledge, 1859), 162. Scan by Pam LeRow, University of Kansas.

the results of meetings after they took place.[22] By the mid-nineteenth century, spectators knew the schedule of meets in time to travel to them. An important new sporting newspaper edited by Walsh, *The Field*, began publishing in 1853 and facilitated this process. In 1864, for example, the January issue of *The Field* published a schedule for the entire year. It showed sixteen meetings in January, twenty-one in February, eleven in March, one in April, none in May through September, one in October, five in November, and one in December.[23]

As the popularity of coursing spread among the middle and working classes, sporting and general newspapers increased coverage of the sport. Early in the nineteenth century, editors of sporting magazines relied on participants in contests to send them news. When the public's interest in coursing rose, magazines and daily newspapers sent reporters to meets. Hugh Dalziel (1887) reflected on the change when he wrote,

> In the early days of free coursing, even *Bell's Life* did not give more than the results of stakes and matches; whilst now no sporting paper of repute exists that does not send its specialist to report on the running at all important public meetings, and even the daily papers of London and the chief provincial towns supply their readers with full information respecting the principal coursing events.[24]

This coverage helped coursing memes spread among the public, including the idea that coursing was of interest to all English people.

Publishers spread coursing memes by explaining coursing to mass audiences and printing specialized books. English elites had been writing hunting manuals for themselves since the Middle Ages, and sporting magazines arose in the transitional decades, but the audience expanded beyond those to the manor born in the democratic era. A national passion for sports led to mammoth encyclopedias in the nineteenth century that explained coursing and its complex memes (along with other sports) to a wide audience.[25] Specialized books on coursing included revisions of titles that appeared during the transitional period, notably Thomas Goodlake's *The Courser's Manual or Stud-Book* (1828 and 1833) and Thomas Thacker's *The Courser's Companion* (1829 and 1834). New titles included Robert Abram Welsh's *Thacker's Courser's Annual Remembrancer and Stud Book* (1849 and after), John Henry Walsh's *The Greyhound* (1853, 1864, and 1875), and Hugh Dalziel's *The Greyhound* (1887).[26] Translations of ancient texts on coursing also appeared.[27]

A third feature of modernity, *industrial infrastructure*, helped populations of coursers, spectators, and gamblers gather. Railroads, which
spread fast after 1830, carried people to coursing meets quickly,
cheaply, and widely. The 1840s alone saw the addition of 6,000 miles of
track.[28] A map illustrated the importance of the press, railroads, and
urbanites (Londoners) for modern coursing. In 1849, *Thacker's Courser's
Annual Remembrancer and Stud Book* included for the first time
"The Courser's Railway Map." It showed the routes of twenty-six railroads and the locations of 109 coursing meetings. A table told readers
how to travel from London to each meeting and where to stay upon
arrival. A Londoner traveling to the meeting in Aldford, Cheshire, for
example, would board the London and North Western train at London
Station, Euston Square, and ride 178 miles to Chester. After traveling
six more miles, the traveler would reach Aldford, where the Grosvenor
Arms offered lodging.[29]

Coursing calendars and railroads made it possible for people from all
classes to compete in coursing meets. In 1869, *The Field* gushed,
"Coursing has now become such a fashionable sport that hundreds of
votaries are added to the ranks of its supporters, season after season, until
it can now fairly hold its own as one of the 'national pastimes'."[30] By one
count, 3,369 greyhounds competed for stakes between October of 1868
and February of 1869.[31] *The Field* credited the rise in spectators, entrants,
and greyhounds to railroads, which made it possible for city dwellers
(especially Londoners) to reach meets.[32]

In sum, mass communication and railroads joined democracy in helping to modernize evolution after 1831. By publishing news of coursing
contests in advance, mass communication enabled populations of coursers, spectators, and gamblers to know when and where to gather.
By transporting people, railroads enabled people from throughout
England to show up at contests. By explaining coursing's complex
memes (rules) to general audiences, books made the sport accessible to
a wider audience. By covering meets, newspapers made coursing
a popular sport with a wide following.

Capitalism

Never eager to be left behind, *capitalism* jumped into the fray to modernize human evolution in the nineteenth century. We have just seen one
effect of capitalism. Profit-seeking individuals and companies produced
newspapers, magazines, and books, which accelerated the spread of

memes about coursing and greyhounds. This section focuses on two other aspects of capitalism: the role of profit-seeking entrepreneurs in organizing coursing clubs and meets, and the addition of bookmakers to the coursing world. Entrepreneurs and bookmakers became important new populations that evolved in response to the opportunities created for them by greyhounds.

Innkeepers led the way in creating a population of profit-seeking entrepreneurs who organized coursing clubs and meets. Their goal was to increase sales of food and drink by gathering crowds of participants and spectators. Innkeepers of Newcastle-on-Tyne founded the large, democratic North of England Club in 1835. Its 215 members included colliers, village tradesmen, and noblemen (Duke of Portland, Marquis of Londonderry, and Earl of Ravensworth). The club's open doors made it, in the words of Harding Cox (1892), "exceedingly popular with all classes of northern coursing-men, and now its hold upon the affections of the districts where it flourishes is so strong that nothing is ever likely to interfere with its well-being."[33] Innkeepers rotated as hosts of the club's meets, and they hired the judge and slipper.[34] The population of inn-keepers evolved by adopting new memes and behaviors: organizing clubs and meets.

Hotelkeeper William Lynn turned out to be the most influential of the new, entrepreneurial meet organizers. In 1836, Lynn organized a coursing meet to generate customers for his business, the Waterloo Hotel in Liverpool. The hotel provided the name for a prize awarded to the winner of the meet, the Waterloo Cup. Eight dogs competed in the first meet. Lynn's hotel served as meet headquarters, but, beyond its proprietor's initiative, had little to recommend it. According to an 1882 history, "The whole place had a dingy appearance; from basement to attic it was smoke begrimmed and dirty, few and far between appeared to be the visits of the painter, and the only redeeming point about it was the fine old fashioned furniture, which, to the credit of the housemaids it must be admitted, was kept well polished." One hundred people bought tickets for the banquet, but only eighty could fit into the hotel dining room, so twenty ticket holders had to eat elsewhere.[35]

From this unpromising start grew the most important coursing contest in England. The entrants doubled to sixteen dogs in the second year, thirty-two the following year, and sixty-four a couple of decades later. The events also multiplied. The first year offered only one event, the Waterloo Cup, while the second year offered the cup and a stakes. In 1857, the events expanded to three (cup, purse, and plate).[36]

In 1870, after the Waterloo Hotel fell to a new railway station, the event upgraded its headquarters to the spacious Adelphi Hotel. The name of the Waterloo Cup survived its eponymous hotel. The new venue offered plenty of rooms for guests, which made it easier to relay information to all participants.[37]

Members of the new, democratic populations of coursers – especially the middle classes – usually won the Waterloo Cup. An innkeeper – Lynn himself – won the first cup using a dog (Melanie) that Lord Molyneux, the Earl of Sefton's son, loaned to him.[38] In 1857, W. Wilson, a waiter at a hotel in Dumfries, Scotland, won with King Lear. The win, according to the National Coursing Club, "enabled him to materially improve his position."[39] Nobles occasionally won, but men without titles dominated the event. Between 1836 and 1886, *Mr.* appeared before the winner's name forty-four times (88 percent of the years). *Lord* appeared five times, but a single dog, Lord Lurgan's Master M'Grath, accounted for three of the five. *Sir* appeared twice, *Captain* once, and *Colonel* once.[40]

Industrial transportation, spectators, and mass communication helped the Waterloo Cup succeed. Coursing expert Hugh Dalziel noted, "The days of railways came in with the Waterloo Cup – the first, and still the chief, of open coursing meetings."[41] Thousands of spectators flocked to the meet – so much so that an 1881 prospectus for a new railroad company listed the Waterloo Cup as one of the reasons the line could expect heavy passenger traffic.[42] Sporting magazines, newspapers, and books carried news of the meeting far and wide.[43] Ordinary newspapers, such as *The Times*, reported on the meeting.[44] The cup benefited from local interest as well. By 1892, Lancashire stood tall as the most prominent county for public coursing thanks to two clubs with grounds twenty miles apart, Altcar and Ridgway. As an author put it, "greyhounds are to the Lancashire man what foxhounds and harriers are to the denizens of more accommodating counties." Plus, at a time when coursers complained of a shortage of hares in most locales, South Lancashire boasted a plethora.[45]

Although modern in many ways, the Waterloo Cup succeeded by allying itself with inherited privilege. The second Earl of Sefton, William Molyneux, made his Altcar estate available to Lynn for the Waterloo Cup. About 12 miles from Liverpool, Altcar stretched along the shores of the River Mersey. An artificial river (the Alt) and ditches divided the land into 30–40 acre meadows used to grow hay for Liverpool. The ditches (6 feet across and 4 feet deep) added complexity for hares and dogs.[46]

The second Earl of Sefton resembled Lord Orford and Lord Rivers, the giants of the transitional coursing era, in offering little proof of the inherited superiority of aristocrats. Although a sportsman, he loved the dining table more than the field. He gained fame for realizing that one need not travel to Dunstable to eat its delectable larks. Instead, he took delivery of tinned Dunstable larks at his house.[47] The earl seemed so ridiculous that he became the butt of popular satire, a powerful tool for mocking pretentious aristocrats in the age of democracy. In the novel *Pelham*, Edward Lytton Bulwer used the earl as the prototype for gluttonous Lord Guloseton, who explained to a companion, "I never dine out: for a bad dinner, Mr. Pelham, a bad dinner is the most serious – I may add, *the* most serious calamity."[48]

Fortunately for the entrepreneur organizing the Waterloo Cup, subsequent earls of Sefton carried on the tradition of hosting the contest at Altcar. The second earl died in 1838, two years after the Waterloo meeting began, but the third earl continued to host the Waterloo Cup on the estate. The third earl loved coursing more than the dining table. He owned some of the best greyhounds in Lancashire, two of which (Senate and Sackcloth) won the Waterloo Cup. When the third earl died in 1855, his son brought similar enthusiasm to coursing. Educated at Eton, the fourth earl served as an officer in the Grenadier Guards before being summoned home to assume his title. He loved to course, shoot, and host guests of the Aintree steeplechase, which became known as the Grand National.[49] (The earls of Sefton were not unique. Nobles provided an important service in the democratic era by making their estates available for meets. Examples included Lord Craven, Lord Londesborough, and Sir Edmund Antrobus.[50] The gentry also contributed. The Letcombe Bowers Coursing Meeting coursed the estate of its founder, Thomas Goodlake, at Wantage, Berkshire.)[51] The Altcar estate hosted the Waterloo meeting until 2005, when hare coursing became illegal in the United Kingdom.[52]

Capitalism spawned a new kind of coursing meet, and attendant behaviors, in 1876. That year, an entrepreneur named Thomas Henry Case organized the first enclosed-coursing meet. *Enclosed* here referred to a ground surrounded by a fence, which made it easier for spectators to watch greyhounds chase hares and for meet organizers to charge admission. (See Figure 5.3.) Case enclosed a ground at Plumpton, East Sussex, and invited coursers to compete for several sweepstakes. Case enlisted the Gloucester Hotel, Brighton, to host the dinner and draw. He corralled a hero of the Crimean War, General Gerald Goodlake, to help organize

Counting the slain

Figure 5.3 Enclosed coursing. Coursing clubs in the eighteenth century metaphorically walled in small groups of rural, male aristocrats and walled out other people. No literal fences kept hares from escaping. In the nineteenth century, entrepreneurs broke down social walls but erected physical ones. Enclosed grounds fenced in entrants, greyhounds, and spectators who paid an admission fee and walled out other people. Enclosed grounds corralled hares, which ratcheted up their death rate compared to coursing over open grounds. "Counting the slain" hares became such a prominent ritual at enclosed meets that humane advocates protested, forcing entrepreneurs to introduce escape routes for hares. Harding Cox and Gerald Lascelles, *Coursing and Falconry* (London: Longmans, Green, and Co., 1892), 10. Courtesy of Special Collections, Kenneth Spencer Research Library, University of Kansas Libraries.

the event. Goodlake arranged for special trains to run from London and Brighton on the morning of the scheduled meet.[53] Enclosed coursing proved popular and grew rapidly. The population of coursers evolved when they competed in the contests. The frequency of competing in enclosed coursing contests increased. Famous coursers participated, including Lord Lurgan, Lord St. Vincent, and Sir John D. Astley.[54] The new model of coursing spread to other cities, including High Gosforth Park in Newcastle-on-Tyne and Kempton Park, near London.[55]

Enclosed coursing spawned a backlash from humane activists. The first enclosed-coursing matches killed hares efficiently. The fences prevented hares from escaping, and the small size of the enclosed areas meant hares ran only a short distance before being caught. As a result, greyhounds caught and killed almost all hares in short order. As an organizer put it, "The advantages this description of coursing possesses over that in an open country is very great; there is no tramping after hares, but, on the contrary, trials can be secured as fast as the judge can decide upon them."[56] Such high mortality led the Society for the Prevention of Cruelty to Animals, some coursers, and newspapers to condemn the meets as cruel and unsporting because the hares had no chance to escape.[57] The matches resembled slaughter more than a fair contest between greyhound and hare.

The population of contest-organizing entrepreneurs evolved in response to criticisms. They adopted the meme that enclosed coursing should appear sporting, which meant hares had some chance of escaping their pursuers. Entrepreneur behavior changed in consequence. One change came in hare procurement. Instead of paying low prices for weak hares, as they previously had, organizers of an 1883 contest at Kempton bought 100 top-quality Norfolk hares at the high price of 13 shillings each. A second behavioral change came in creating an opening in the fence where hares could escape. A third behavioral change came in hare tutelage. Instead of releasing hares in the coursing ground for the first time on match day, they placed hares in the enclosure several weeks before a contest. Fox terriers drove the hares from one end of the enclosure to the other, where hares found the escape route. By the time the meet arrived, the hares knew the ground and where to escape. These measures succeeded. After thirty-five courses during the contest, only ten hares lay dead. This rate resembled those at public coursing meets.[58]

The frequency of enclosed-coursing behaviors in the entrepreneurial population rose and fell in short order, so the population evolved rapidly in this regard. The 1880s marked the heyday of enclosed coursing, after which it declined for reasons described in vague terms in sources.

Gosforth closed in 1889 when its directors decided they did not like the sport.[59] Attendance never reached the desired level at Plumpton, despite the construction of a viewing stand. The last Plumpton coursing meeting took place in 1889, and the Plumpton Coursing Company folded.[60]

Another trait entered and left the population of entrepreneurs at lightning speed in the late nineteenth century. In 1876, entrepreneurs adopted the meme that greyhounds could chase an artificial hare on a track. In a field in Herndon, about an hour from London, entrepreneurs put this meme into practice when they set up a straight track of four hundred yards. They hid a grooved rail in the grass along the track, mounted an "artificial hare" on an "apparatus like a skate on wheels," and pulled the hare along the rail by cranking a windlass. Greyhounds chased the hare and, if they caught it, "tore [it] into shreds with destructive fury." Thus began greyhound racing. The promoters advertised racing, which *The Times* dubbed "coursing by proxy," as exciting and devoid of cruelty.[61] But the sport proved to be stillborn. *The Times* reported only one day of racing, and most people forgot about it. When racing reappeared fifty years later in Manchester, this time relying on an electric hare developed in the United States, *The Times* described it as a "new form of coursing."[62]

Bookmakers comprised another profit-seeking population that emerged in response to greyhounds in the modern era. Recognizing the chance to create a market for betting on coursing, bookmakers streamed to Waterloo and other large contests. There they set up flags and stools to take bets. The amounts wagered were large, so much so that they created an incentive for contestants to cheat. *The Field* rued in 1864 that the large amounts of money wagered "induces nominators [competitors] to resort to all sorts of expedients to hoodwink the bookmakers."[63] Populations of contestants and bookmakers coevolved. Bookmakers displayed a trait (taking large bets). Some contestants responded by adopting a meme (cheating bookmakers) and behaved in accordance with it, which affected the frequency of that behavioral trait in contestants.

At the same time, the population of bookmakers adopted memes and behaviors for cheating. One meme was to bribe contestants to throw matches. A Mr. Warwick reported that a bookmaker offered him five hundred pounds if a certain dog won the cup. The earl of Sefton ordered the man off his property.[64] Another meme was to refuse to pay winners of large bets. An 1882 history of Waterloo noted, "Of late years the objectionable feature of betting, or I should rather say welshing, has developed itself to such an extent as to become a thorough nuisance." The ditches of

Waterloo helped dishonest bookmakers. If someone who bet with a "welsher" tried to claim the winnings, he might find himself in the ditch if he was lucky, and robbed and beaten if he was not. The Earl of Sefton brought things back under control by banning flags, stools, and other paraphernalia of bookmaking. He employed police to enforce the ban.[65]

Mass communication enabled populations of gamblers to emerge off site. One of the most prominent off-site locations was Tattersall's in London, a horse auction house where coursing enthusiasts met. Subscriptions cost two pounds two shillings, and a newcomer had to be introduced by a current subscriber. About 300–400 subscribers belonged in 1850.[66] *The Field* carried news of the odds and amounts wagered at Tattersall's before big meets. Some bets were large. In 1864, two or three people laid 7,000 pounds against some of the favorite dogs at Waterloo.[67] Gamblers sometimes bet on dogs and sometimes on dog owners.[68] Within elite clubs, then, populations evolved when the frequency of betting on Waterloo and other contests at a distance increased.

The press offered a class-biased interpretation of betting at coursing contests and elite clubs. A magazine reported in 1897 that the greyhound had once been a minister to kings and nobles. By the end of the nineteenth century, it had become "the instrument of 'sport' for the gambling multitude," whose "interest in the greyhound centres to-day in the betting on the Waterloo Cup."[69] This version of history overlooked the fact that greyhounds had always been instruments of sport for gamblers. Patricians had gambled on coursing contests for centuries. In the transitional era, elite coursing clubs forced contestants to gamble on every match. The magazine also overlooked the popularity of gambling at elite clubs in the modern era. The same activity was despicable or acceptable depending on the class of the actor. It was reminiscent of the pre-1831 game laws, which made the same activity (killing animals with greyhounds) admirable or despicable depending on the class of the actor.

In sum, capitalism became one of the most important forces driving human evolution in the modern period. Profit-seeking entrepreneurs comprised a new population that evolved in response to opportunities created by greyhounds. This population developed memes and behaviors for organizing coursing contests, selling food and drink, charging admission, and modifying habitats. Some new memes and behaviors, such as organizing the Waterloo Cup, endured in the population. Other memes and behaviors, those associated with enclosed coursing and racing, appeared and disappeared by 1900. The population of entrepreneurs adapted to other populations as well as to greyhounds. In response to criticism from humane activists, entrepreneurs modified memes and behaviors associated with enclosed coursing. They made contests appear more sporting by making it possible for hares to escape. Entrepreneurs enabled populations of coursers to compete in contests, spectators to attend events, and gamblers to place bets on outcomes.

Bookmakers comprised another profit-seeking population that capitalized on opportunities created for them by greyhounds (and entrepreneurs) in the modern period. They flocked to large contests, where they took bets from spectators and contestants. Some bookmakers and contestants adopted illicit memes and behaviors, such as fixing matches and refusing to pay winning bettors. Mass communication enabled populations of gamblers to wager with each other off site.

Standardizing Memes and Niches on a National Scale

Modernization helped to standardize memes and niches on a national scale. Industrial transportation and mass communication played key roles in standardization. In the patrician and transitional eras, when transportation was slow, coursers competed mainly near home. Patrician clubs standardized memes and job descriptions (coursing rules) for members on a local scale, but variation persisted on a national scale. In the modern era, railroads enabled coursers to travel across the land to compete in meets. Coursers from different regions arrived at meets with different understandings of coursing rules. Individuals and clubs set out to standardize rules on a national scale. Broader social forces, including a national passion for organized sports with prescribed rules, created a welcoming environment.

Conflicts over variation in memes (coursing rules) emerged quickly as railroads and open meets threw together coursers from multiple regions. Coursers and judges found they had very different ideas about how to evaluate greyhound performance. As Delabere Blaine noted in his 1840 sporting encyclopedia, "The opinions as to which are the best rules as proper criterions for estimating the relative merits of the contending dogs are very various, not only in the minds of the owners and other amateurs, but also in the minds of the different judges who are appointed to decide the courses at different places."[70] Blaine illustrated variation in rules by including five sets in his encyclopedia – two from the Duke of Norfolk (memes could vary within the same individual), Ashdown rules, Thacker's rules, and the Thatched House Tavern rules.[71]

Conflicting memes caused courser populations to evolve by increasing the frequency of antagonistic behavior. In 1840, Delabere Blaine reported that attending one coursing meeting was sufficient to see that differences in rules and interpretations brought out the worst in people. Coursing crowds still tended to the genteel at that time, but coursing sent them into high dudgeon so often that Blaine thought they resembled the onlookers at events famous for raucous behavior by laborers and workers. Without "judicious rules and laws, clearly defined and implicitly obeyed," Blaine complained, "it would be better that a bear-garden should be the arena, and that a badger bait, bull bait, or a dog fight, in the kens of the fancy in Tothill-fields, should be visited."[72] Blaine's argument was class-based. The middle classes condemned badger baiting, bull baiting, and dog fighting as "lower" class because they attracted workers and seemed inhumane. (Patricians also favored blood sports, but the moralizers turned a blind eye to their participation.) Clear, standardized memes (rules), it seemed, would help courser populations evolve toward greater gentility by reducing the frequency of antagonistic behavior.

Some experts tried to simplify coursing rules by adopting a common feature of modernity: quantification. Rules from earlier centuries told judges how to convert the value of one behavior into an equivalent value for another behavior. In Gascoigne's rules, two wrenches equaled a turn, and two turns equaled a cote. It was quantification, but of almost impossible complexity. Complexity advanced the patrician goal of creating an elite within the elite by raising high barriers to entry. In the democratic era, individuals without titles advocated simpler arithmetic understandable to a wider audience. A Mr. Welsh realized that assigning point values to each valued greyhound behavior would simplify calculations. He allocated two points to a go-by and half a point to a jerk or trip. Many meets adopted his system.[73]

Although a step toward simplification, Welsh's rules failed to standardize memes among coursers. The rules invited dispute by forcing judges to, among other things, assess a greyhound's intention, effort, and caliber of thought. A kill was worth zero points if done "by accident," one point if done "with fair merit," and two points if done with "a great effort and cleverness." The criteria for distinguishing "fair merit" from "great effort" went unstated. Similarly, the difference of one degree led one turn to earn twice as many points as another. A dog earned half a point for turning a hare fifteen to forty-five degrees, and one point for turning it more than forty-five degrees. Judges must have been hard pressed to distinguish turns of forty-five and forty-six degrees while dogs and hares raced at top speed. Judges also had to assess the motives of hares. A turn earned zero points if the hare turned "for her own convenience."[74] Although covered with a veneer of objective quantification, Welsh's rules were subjective.

Another individual who tried to standardize memes on a national scale was Thomas Thacker, who published books on coursing. He began his efforts near the end of the transitional decades. In 1829, he published an analysis of existing rules, including their defects, and proposed a new code.[75] Like Welsh, Thacker recommended the use of points to evaluate performance. At the beginning of the modern era, Thacker took his analysis to a new scale. In 1834, he published a coursing guide with 156 pages devoted to his rules and their interpretation.[76] Fifty pages reviewed existing rules, including those of the Duke of Norfolk and the Ashdown Park meeting. Thacker's new rules covered seven pages, which seemed clear and concise, but Thacker devoted ninety-nine pages to explaining them.[77] Complexity in rules and their interpretation continued.

Decades after Thacker tried to standardize rules, variation in memes continued to spark antagonistic behaviors in populations of coursers. In 1869, *The Field* rued the absence of a "general code of laws by which either the management of public meetings or the decisions of judges could be regulated. Several codes had been previously drawn up, some of which were in force in certain districts, but were ignored in others, causing endless confusion, and leading to constant disputes."[78] In an age of national competition, regional variation in memes made conflict a feature of coursing contests.

The difficulty of agreeing on rules contrasted with the ease of adopting a technological solution to a different problem. A fair contest required a man (the slipper) to release two greyhounds simultaneously. Because small differences in release time could determine which greyhound reached a hare first, which in turn could decide the match, coursers cared a great deal about even slipping. It was easy to charge a slipper with favoring one dog or the other, being susceptible to bribery, and more. A simple device solved the problem. It featured two collars attached to each other. When the slipper pulled a cord, both collars opened and released dogs at the same time.[79] (See Figure 5.4.) The device had the virtue of being transparent. In contrast to coursing rules, the slipping device operated the same in anyone's hands and struck everyone as fair. The meme that slippers should use a slipping device became standard among coursers.

National *standardization* of coursing rules (memes) came with the rise of a national *bureaucracy*. In the transitional era and the first decades of

AN EVEN SLIP

Figure 5.4 Slipping greyhounds at a coursing meet. After giving a hare (the small, dark shape on the right edge of the image) a head start, the slipper on the left has released two greyhounds. A judge observes from horseback. The leash has two open collars on the end. They are yards from the horse but appear to be tangling its forelegs. Pulling the wooden peg (below the slipper's right hand) on the leash opened both collars simultaneously. Before the invention of these devices (called slips), dogs wore individual collars around their necks. Slippers held one collar in each hand. They were supposed to release dogs at the same time, but gamblers accused them of uneven slipping. A coursing book titled this image "An Even Slip," which highlighted the value of technology for reducing disputes among gamblers. Harding Cox and Gerald Lascelles, *Coursing and Falconry* (London: Longmans, Green, and Co., 1892), after 140. Courtesy of Special Collections, Kenneth Spencer Research Library, University of Kansas Libraries.

the modern era, local bureaucracies created local uniformity in coursing memes. National contests highlighted regional variation and sparked conflict. The most important national contest, the Waterloo Cup, became the vehicle for organizing a national bureaucracy. In 1858, a prominent courser named C. Jardine (publications used only his initial) organized a National Coursing Club to standardize rules and adjudicate disputes. The early club consisted of thirty to thirty-five members (the number fluctuated) with Jardine as president.[80] It met twice a year: once in London, and once in Liverpool in conjunction with the Waterloo Cup.[81]

The National Coursing Club standardized memes for management of meetings (election of judges, method of slipping, etc.) and scoring of matches. Based on Thacker's rules, the National Coursing Club's rules relied on a point system.[82] Mass communication helped spread these memes across the nation. Leading experts encouraged the coursing population to accede to the authority of the national club to standardize rules and settle disputes. The importance of dispute resolution can be seen in the first sentence discussing the club in Walsh's 1859 edition of *Manual of British Rural Sports*, which came out a year after the club formed. The sentence read, "The National Coursing Club has now been established, and all complaints, of whatever description, connected with coursing, or any matters in dispute, can be referred to it for arbitration and adjustment."[83] Problems brought to the club included entering dogs without paying the entry fee, secretly altering names of dogs, running someone else's dog as one's own, interfering with the slipping of the dogs, riding horses over other people's dogs, impugning the judges, serving as judge despite having a stake in the outcome, and defaulting on bets.[84]

The National Coursing Club succeeded in reducing variation in rules on a national scale. Before the 1859 Waterloo Cup, Jardine announced that the meet would follow the rules of the National Coursing Club.[85] Getting Waterloo to adopt the rules was probably easy. Jardine served as president of the National Coursing Club and as chairman of the Waterloo meeting at the same time.[86] Waterloo's adoption created a powerful precedent for others to follow, and they did. In 1887, Hugh Dalziel described the National Coursing Club as "the supreme authority on all coursing matters – framing and administering laws, arbitrating on disputes, settling betting questions, and with power to disqualify from participation in the sport at all meetings held under its rules those who infringe or set at nought its rulings."[87]

The population of members of the National Coursing Club included patricians but was dominated by men without titles (no women belonged). The 1859 members included six earls and lords, four men with military ranks, and twenty-two men without titles (listed by the club in that order). The club seemed unable to let go of patrician aspirations for coursers, whatever their background. Coursers had traditionally identified untitled men as "Mr." in publications, but the list of National Coursing Club members dropped "Mr." and added "Esq." to the names (e.g., C. Jardine, Esq.) of men without noble or military honorifics. This practice probably reflected a desire to retain the status coursing had enjoyed before the democratic era. Before 1831, the lowest rank qualifying a man to own a greyhound was son of an esquire.[88]

The National Coursing Club grew less democratic and more republican over time. In the early years, coursers at the Waterloo meeting chose the members of the National Coursing Club. Waterloo was an open meeting, so the participants probably included men who belonged to no coursing club.[89] Under National Coursing Club laws published in 1861, however, electors consisted of Waterloo participants who were "members of any recognised coursing club."[90] By 1869, coursing clubs elected the members of the National Coursing Club. Clubs could elect members if they were located in the United Kingdom, had been existence at least a year, had at least twenty-four members, and paid dues to the national club.[91] In 1870, twenty-six coursing clubs elected members of the National Coursing Club.[92] The members of the National Coursing Club in 1882 came mainly from outside the nobility. Of the fifty-one honorifics (the size of the club had grown), thirty-nine (76 percent) were "Mr.," one was "Dr.," two were military ranks (Colonel and Captain), and nine (18 percent) were noble or chivalrous titles (two sirs, five earls, one marquis, and one lord).[93]

By standardizing memes, the National Coursing Club narrowed variation in human niches. The rules governing coursing matches were job descriptions for coursers and officials. National rules meant standardization of the job half of niches. Coursers competing in the Waterloo Cup saw national standardization in the habitat half of niches, too. The cup always took place on the same estate, Altcar. For Waterloo competitors, the standardization of job and habitat created a narrow niche. Many coursers, however, continued to compete in contests held in other locations. Even if the job side of their niche was uniform, the habitat side varied. The trend in niches in the modern era, then, was toward uniformity in job description, standardization in habitat for some coursers, and variation in habitat for other coursers.

In sum, populations of coursers in the modern era evolved when variation in memes, behaviors, and niches narrowed. Narrowing of memes and behaviors took decades. Local variation in memes (coursing rules) persisted, which led to frequent conflicts as railroads brought coursers from multiple locations to the same contests. Efforts to

standardize memes on a national scale failed until a national bureaucracy, the National Coursing Club, emerged in 1858. The club issued
standard rules and got them adopted by the most important contest
(Waterloo). Many local clubs followed suit. The representative nature
of the National Coursing Club helped create legitimacy and influence.
All coursing clubs had representation in the national club. National
standardization in coursing memes standardized job descriptions, and
thus the job side of human niches, on a national scale. The habitat side of
niches was standardized for contestants in the Waterloo Cup but continued to vary nationally.

Patrician Evolution

Patrician populations evolved in response to democratization of coursing. The overall pattern was a reduction in the frequency of coursing
behaviors. As Walsh noted in 1856, nobles and large landowners who
coursed "are the exceptions to the rule, and the great bulk of its [cour-
sing's] supporters are those gentlemen in middle life who are neither
noblemen nor even men of large landed property."[94] This trend hid
variation in memes and behaviors. As noted earlier, some patricians
adopted the meme that coursing remained worthwhile. They joined
democratic clubs, competed in open and hybrid meets, hosted meets
on their estates, and helped lead the republican National Coursing Club.
And we saw that other patricians adopted a meme that rejected democracy. They competed in closed meets to keep the hoi polloi at bay.

Patricians adopted additional memes that denigrated democratic
coursing. One derogatory meme, which seems to have originated in the
democratic era, was the idea of *pot-hunting*. It meant that killing game for
food was objectionable. The first use may have been in 1840, when it
appeared in Blaine's sporting encyclopedia. Blaine warned readers that
pot-hunting had the "savour of poaching."[95] A subsequent appearance
was in an 1842 short story. When soldiers proposed killing hares,
a gamekeeper exclaimed, "The whole barony would rise against you for
shooting a hare in a hunting country. The like was never heard of –
'twould be regular pot-hunting."[96] Use of *pot-hunting* soared over the
nineteenth century.[97] (See Figure 5.5.)

The *pot-hunting* meme reversed the symbolism of hare hunting. For
centuries, patricians had argued that hunting hares was one of the highest pursuits of men. Hunters developed elaborate rituals for butchering,
cooking, and eating hares. Suddenly, once anyone could legally hunt,

COURSING. *Going Home.*
London, Published by Thos. Mc Lean, 26 Haymarket, 1823.

Figure 5.5 Reversal of values. Before 1831, patricians regarded hare hunting as one of the highest, most aristocratic of sports. It often occurred in private, and hunters loved to eat the hares they killed. This image from 1825, which Henry Alken published in a book lauding British sports, reflected that tradition. It showed a patrician, a servant, and greyhounds heading home with two dead hares after coursing with no one else around. It would have been illegal for anyone other than patricians and their servants to hold a hare or keep greyhounds. After 1831, when Parliament democratized greyhound ownership, sportsmen reversed course. They introduced a new term, *pot-hunting*, in 1840 to redefine hare hunting as a low-class activity akin to poaching. Sportsmen claimed chasing (and sometimes killing) hares for fun was morally superior to killing hares to feed one's family or earn a living. Another new term in 1840, *private coursing*, voiced a novel distrust of the character of coursers once anyone could legally own a greyhound. Without the discipline imposed by a public gaze, sportsmen feared, men coursing in private degenerated into pot-hunters. If published in the 1840s, then, Alken's image might have been used to illustrate the evils of pot-hunting and private coursing rather than admirable, aristocratic behavior worthy of emulation. Henry Alken, *The National Sports of Great Britain* ([1825] New York: D. Appleton, 1903), Going Home, NE960 .A4 1825. Special Collections, University of Virginia, Charlottesville, VA.

criticism of hare hunting burst out. The association with poaching was telling. Poaching was illegal killing of animals. Although all classes poached before 1831, patricians chose to assign blame to the poorest classes.

Saying that hare hunting was like poaching, then, converted an activity (hare hunting) from one of the most admirable activities of elites to a despicable activity of poorer classes (even when legal).

Absent a legal monopoly on hunting, patricians turned to the distinction between need and sport to distinguish elites from everyone else. Patricians narrowed admirable killing of hares to match coursing alone. Match coursing, patricians argued, was not about killing hares. Its purpose was to test greyhounds. It was sport. A person who needed to hunt for food (that is, pot-hunt) was poor and objectionable. One who chased hares for sport (match coursing) was admirable.

Another meme, *private coursing*, made it easier to question the character of the new classes of coursers. The term *private coursing* may have appeared in print only once before 1831. In 1828, Goodlake used it to refer to informal coursing contests among patricians. These informal contests led, in some places, to the formation of patrician coursing clubs.[98] After 1831, *private coursing* became common. It stood in contrast to *public coursing*, which referred to organized, formal contests with spectators. The only printed use of *public coursing* before 1831 may have been in 1807, when a source described a coursing contest at Flixton.[99] In 1835, a sporting magazine referred to "our great public Coursing Meetings."[100] *Public coursing* appeared frequently after that. After 1831, then, it seemed important to distinguish coursing behavior monitored by others from behavior monitored by oneself.

The pot-hunting and private coursing memes worked in tandem to throw doubt on the morals of democratic coursers. Having narrowed acceptable killing of hares to sport (match coursing), patricians worried that coursers would hunt hares (pot-hunt) outside the disciplining gaze of others. This worry led Blaine, in 1840, to warn coursers they should show the same sporting spirit in "private" as in "public or match coursing."[101] In 1856, John Walsh elaborated on the distinction between shameful, unsporting pot-hunting in private and admirable, sporting coursing in public. He complained, "most men in *private* go out for the sake of *killing hares*, and *not* for the purpose of *competing* with their neighbors and friends." Walsh disdained hare hunting, saying,

> I should despise myself for partaking in such a *bastard kind of hunting*, for it certainly *cannot be called coursing*. In any case, *private coursing* is too often converted into a *"pot-hunting"* kind of business, in which the hare is the great object of the pursuit. On the other hand, in *public coursing*, the hare is only a means of trying the powers of the dogs, which are pitted against one

another, and her capture or escape is not immediately connected with the success of failure of the *sport*.[102]

Another meme that spread among patricians was that working-class
audiences debased coursing contests. In 1840, Delabere Blaine reported
that the coursing was delightful at the Epsom Coursing Club meeting
"when the cockney crowd is not abroad."[103] But, because coursing took
place in large, open areas linked to cities by trains, it was hard to exclude
spectators looking for outings. In 1874, a writer rued, "It is impossible,
perhaps, to eliminate the cockney element entirely from any kind of sport
held within convenient distance of the metropolis."[104] Elite coursers
believed gamblers, bookmakers, poachers, and thieves were common
among working-class spectators. In 1883, *The Kennel Gazette* reported,
estate owners were tired of seeing "the betting element" attract "the
lowest characters as hangers-on to every meeting." Opening estates to
coursing meetings offered "poachers and ruffians of the big towns"
a chance to scout game preserves.[105]

Allied with the "anti-cockney" meme was an anti-urban meme focused
on enclosed coursing. Advocates of rural sports mocked fashion-
conscious urban spectators – or what they assumed were fashion-
conscious urban spectators – at enclosed-coursing meets. Hugh Dalziel,
who had never attended an enclosed-coursing meet, was certain the
events attracted "multitudes of onlookers, the majority of whom probably
know nothing of natural coursing, and a large section of whom consist of
the 'sharps' and 'flats' who hang on to the skirts of modern sport, and to
whom life without betting would be insipid." This "modern innovation
debased the sport to suit men who would be coursers in patent leather
boots, and the parasites of sport whose only idea of it is that of a medium
for enabling them to become possessed of 'unearned increment.'"[106]
Enclosed coursing was "the effeminate Cockney coursing so popular today."[107] Some patricians believed that enclosed coursing hurt club meets
in the countryside.[108]

Some patricians adopted the meme that capitalism ruined the nobility
of coursing. Enclosed coursing raised hackles the highest. One reason
was its frankly commercial nature, which seemed contrary to the spirit of
sport. One could almost hear Hugh Dalziel spit as he called enclosed
coursing "a mere caricature of the ancient and noble sport, thus traves-
tied for purposes of gate money and gambling."[109] The founding of
companies that specialized in enclosed coursing put an exclamation
point on the sport's commercial nature. In 1882, the Plumpton

Coursing Company, Ltd., formed to manage the enclosed Plumpton meeting.[110] *The Kennel Gazette* complained in 1883 that a "total change" had overtaken coursing, "and whether old sportsmen like it or no, the power of the pastime is in the hands of those who look to it for commercial returns."[111]

In sum, patrician populations evolved in the democratic era by increasing the frequency of memes that denigrated democratic coursing and reducing the frequency with which they coursed. Once coursing lost its elite symbolism, its appeal to elites declined. Some patricians continued to course, but they became rare. After centuries of coevolution between patricians and greyhounds, the middle classes displaced patricians as the primary partner population of greyhounds.

Conclusion

In 1887, Hugh Dalziel concluded that coursing had changed over the nineteenth century because "The giant Democracy, having given many uneasy turns in his long sleep, was now rubbing his eyes and stirring in earnest."[112] He pointed to the press, railroads, and open competitions as democratic forces. To that list, we must add democratic greyhound ownership, a national bureaucracy, standardization, and capitalism. Patricians founded coursing clubs in the eighteenth century to protect inherited privilege, so it came as a shock in the nineteenth century to see coursing become a Trojan horse for the people they had excluded. Coursing meets provided a way for the people they saw as barbarians at the gate – toughs, bookmakers, poachers, and city dwellers – to flood onto the estates of aristocrats. Some patricians accepted democratic coursing, and they enjoyed good relations with their neighbors, but others clung to exclusive clubs. To their chagrin, the dogs that had symbolized patrician and royal privilege had come to symbolize democracy and commerce.

The democratic, or modern, era sparked rapid cultural evolution in human populations. It created new populations that coevolved with greyhounds, including entrepreneurs, the middle classes, the working classes, and bookmakers. These populations evolved the memes and behaviors suited to their roles with greyhounds, such as organizing contests, competing in meets, watching and wagering on meets, and bookmaking. Greyhounds did not cause these populations to evolve these traits. The catalyst to a new era was evolution in the population of Parliament members. They adopted a new meme that allowed anyone to own a greyhound and course. Many of the traits seen in these new populations reflected broad social trends – capitalism, democracy, mass communication, industrial transportation, and standardization – more than the direct impact of greyhounds. But greyhounds were essential to the evolution of these populations. Without the dogs that made coursing memes and behaviors realistic, this human evolution would not have occurred.

Notes

1. House of Commons, "Report from the Select Committee on the Laws Related to Game 1823 (260)," *Parliamentary Papers* IV (1823): 109–11.
2. House of Commons, "A Bill (as Amended by the Committee) to Amend the Laws in England Relative to Game," *Parliamentary Papers* 11 (1831): 29–50; House of Lords, "Game Laws," *Parliamentary Debates* XVI (1827): 680–92; House of Commons, "Game Laws. An Account of the Number of Convictions under the Game Laws from 1820 to 1826 ...," *Parliamentary Papers* 20 (1827 1826): 517–26. These citations are examples rather than an exhaustive list.
3. P. B. Munsche, *Gentlemen and Poachers: The English Game Laws, 1671–1831* (Cambridge: Cambridge University Press, 1981), 132–58.
4. Frederick C. Dietz, *A Political and Social History of England* (New York: Macmillan, 1932), 520–42.
5. House of Commons, "A Bill (as Amended by the Committee) to Amend the Laws in England Relative to Game," 29–50, see 29.
6. Dietz, *A Political and Social History of England*, 568–70.
7. J. H. Porter, "Tenant Right: Devonshire and the 1880 Ground Game Act," *The Agricultural History Review* 34, no. 2 (January 1, 1986): 188–97, doi:10.2307/40274469.
8. John Henry Walsh, *The Greyhound: Being a Treatise on the Art of Breeding, Rearing, and Training Greyhounds for Public Running* (London: Longman, Brown, Green & Longmans, 1853), 151.
9. John Henry Walsh, *The Dog, in Health and Disease* (London: Longman, Green, Longman, and Roberts, 1859), 26.
10. John Henry Walsh, *The Dog in Health and Disease. Comprising the Various Modes of Breaking and Using Him for Hunting, Coursing, Shooting, Etc., and Including the Points or Characteristics of All Dogs, Which Are Entirely Rewritten*, 3rd edn. (London: Longmans, Green, 1879), 20.
11. Robin Hood, "The Coursing Season," *Field*, December 25, 1869, 533.
12. Hugh Dalziel, *British Dogs: Their Varieties, History, Characteristics, Breeding, Management, and Exhibition* (London: The Bazaar Office, 1879), 15.
13. J. H. Walsh, *Manual of British Rural Sports: Comprising Shooting, Hunting, Coursing, Fishing, Hawking, Racing, Boating, Pedestrianism, and the Various Rural Games and Amusements of Great Britain* (London: G. Routledge, 1856), 202–3.
14. Harding Cox and Gerald Lascelles, *Coursing and Falconry* (London: Longmans, Green, and Company, 1892), 163.

15. Walsh, *Dog in Health and Disease [1879]*, 21.

16. Walsh, *Greyhound [1853]*, 288.

17. Walsh, *Greyhound [1853]*, 151.

18. Walsh, *Manual of British Rural Sports [1856]*, 162.

19. Wellesley Pain, "How Greyhounds Are Trained," *Ludgate* 5, February (1898): 435–36.

20. Dietz, *A Political and Social History of England*, 565–67.

21. Dietz, *A Political and Social History of England*, 533.

22. Anonymous, "Coursing Calendar 1834," *New Sporting Magazine* 8, April (1835): 1.

23. Anonymous, "Coursing Meetings to Come," *Field*, January 16, 1864.

24. Hugh Dalziel, *The Greyhound; Its History, Points, Breeding, Rearing, Training, and Running* (London: L. Upcott Gill, 1887), 42.

25. Delabere Pritchett Blaine, *An Encyclopaedia of Rural Sports: Or a Complete Account, Historical, Practical, and Descriptive, of Hunting, Shooting, Fishing, Racing, and Other Field Sports and Athletic Amusements of the Present Day* (London: Longman, Orme, Brown, Green and Longmans, 1840); John Scott, *The Sportsman's Repository: Comprising a Series of Highly Finished Engravings, Representing the Horse and the Dog, in All Their Varieties* (London: Henry G. Bohn, 1845); Walsh, *Manual of British Rural Sports [1856]*.

26. Anonymous, *A Treatise on Greyhounds, with Observations on the Treatment and Disorders of Them* (London: [n.p.], 1816); Thomas Goodlake, *The Courser's Manual or Stud-Book* (Liverpool: Geo. B. Whittaker and Jos. Booker, 1828); Thomas Goodlake, *Continuation of the Courser's Manual, or Stud Book. Containing the Pedigrees and Performances of Winning Dogs* (London: Simpkin and Marshall, 1833); Thomas Thacker, *The Courser's Companion; Or, a Practical Treatise on the Laws of the Leash; with the Defects of the Old Laws Considered; and a New Code, with Notes of Explanation, by an Experienced Courser* (Derby: Thomas Richardson, 1829); Thomas Thacker, *The Courser's Companion, Revised and Enlarged, to Which Is Added the Breeder's Guide, or Breeding in All Its Branches*, 2nd edn., vol. 1 (London: S. T. Probett, 1834); Robert Abram Welsh, *Thacker's Courser's Annual Remembrancer and Stud Book; Being an Alphabetical Return of the Running at All the Public Coursing Clubs in England, Ireland, and Scotland, for the Season 1848–1849; with the Pedigrees (as Far as Received) of the Dogs That Won, and the Dogs That Ran Up Second for Each Prize; Also, a Return of All Single Matches Run at Those Meetings, and of All Mains of Greyhounds, during the Season, That Have Been Made Publicly Known*, vol. 9 (London: Lonngman, 1849); Walsh, *Greyhound [1853]*; John Henry Walsh, *The Greyhound in 1864* (London: Longman, Green, Longman, Roberts, and Green, 1864); John H. Walsh, *The Greyhound, a Treatise on the Art of Breeding, Rearing, and Training Greyhounds for Public Running, Their Diseases and Treatment, Containing Also the National Rules for the Management of Coursing Meetings and for the Decision of Courses, Also, in an Appendix, an Extended List of Pedigrees* (London: Longmans, Green, 1875); Dalziel, *Greyhound*.

27. Arrian, *Arrian on Coursing: The Cynegeticus of the Younger Xenophon, Translated from the Greek, with Classical and Practical Annotations, and a Brief Sketch of the Life and Writings of the Author. To Which Is Added an Appendix, Containing Some*

Account of the Canes Venatici of Classical Antiquity, trans. William Dansey (London: J. Bohn, 1831); Xenophon, "On Hunting: A Sportsman's Manual Commonly Called Cynegeticus," text, trans. H. G. Dakyns (1897), http://ebooks.adelaide.edu.au/x/xenophon/x5hu/.

28. Dietz, *A Political and Social History of England,* 533.

29. Welsh, *Annual Remembrancer [1849],* 9:1–5 plus unpaginated map.

30. Hood, "The Coursing Season," 533.

31. J. H., "Ashdown Coursing Meeting," *Field,* February 6, 1869, 119.

32. Hood, "The Coursing Season," 533.

33. Cox and Lascelles, *Coursing and Falconry,* 195–96.

34. Cox and Lascelles, *Coursing and Falconry,* 195.

35. David Brown, *The Greyhound Stud Book, Established by the Authority of the National Coursing Club 1882,* vol. 1 (Dalry: David Brown, 1882), 33, 35, 62.

36. Brown, *Greyhound Stud Book,* 1:62–63.

37. Brown, *Greyhound Stud Book,* 1:43.

38. Brown, *Greyhound Stud Book,* 1:62.

39. Brown, *Greyhound Stud Book,* 1:34.

40. The number of winners exceeded the number of years because two winners occasionally shared the cup. Dalziel, *Greyhound,* 82–84.

41. Dalziel, *Greyhound,* 41.

42. Anonymous, "Southport and Cheshire Lines Extension Railway Company," *Times [London],* July 21, 1882, 13.

43. By 1863, "Waterloo Cup" had appeared in 36 books and magazines in the Google Books collection. Most of the sporting magazines, which offered the most intensive coverage of the event, are not in Google Books. Google Books, searched February 26, 2014.

44. Anonymous, "Coursing. The Waterloo Cup Meeting," *Times [London],* February 23, 1878.

45. Cox and Lascelles, *Coursing and Falconry,* 164–65.

46. Brown, *Greyhound Stud Book,* 1:33–34.

47. Anonymous, "The Earl of Sefton," *Baily's Monthly Magazine of Sports and Pastimes* 6, no. 36 (1863): 1–4.

48. Edward Bulwer Lytton, *Pelham; Or, Adventures of a Gentleman* (London: G. Routledge, 1875), 232; Anonymous, "The Earl of Sefton."

49. Anonymous, "The Earl of Sefton."

50. Walsh, *Manual of British Rural Sports [1856],* 152.

51. Blaine, *An Encyclopaedia of Rural Sports [1840],* 586–88.

52. Altcar Estate, www.altcarestate.com/Altcar_Experience/Heritage.htm, viewed July 25, 2014.

53. Cox and Lascelles, *Coursing and Falconry,* 93; Michael Springman, *Sharpshooter in the Crimea: The Letters of the Captain Gerald Goodlake VC 1854-56* (Barnsley: Pen and Sword, 2005).

54. Cox and Lascelles, *Coursing and Falconry,* 93–95.

55. Cox and Lascelles, *Coursing and Falconry,* 95–97; Anonymous, "Modern Coursing," *Kennel Gazette,* February 1883; Dalziel, *Greyhound,* 46.

56. Dalziel, *Greyhound,* 47.

57. Cox and Lascelles, *Coursing and Falconry,* 94.

58. Anonymous, "Modern Coursing."

59. Cox and Lascelles, *Coursing and Falconry*, 96.

60. Cox and Lascelles, *Coursing and Falconry*, 93–95.

61. Anonymous, "Coursing by Proxy," *Times [London]*, September 11, 1876.

62. Anonymous, "New Form of Coursing. Greyhound Racing with an Electric Hare," *Times [London]*, October 9, 1926.

63. Anonymous, "Great Waterloo Meeting," *Field*, February 20, 1864.

64. Anonymous, "Great Waterloo Meeting."

65. Brown, *Greyhound Stud Book*, 1:34.

66. Peter Cunningham, *Handbook of London: Past and Present* (London: John Murray, 1850), 75.

67. Anonymous, "Coursing," *Field*, February 20, 1864, 132.

68. Robin Hood, "Coursing," *Field*, January 29, 1870, 97.

69. St. Bernard, "Notable Dogs of the Chase: The Greyhound," *Good Words* 38 (1897): 848.

70. Blaine, *An Encyclopaedia of Rural Sports [1840]*, 589.

71. Blaine, *An Encyclopaedia of Rural Sports [1840]*, 589–600.

72. Blaine, *An Encyclopaedia of Rural Sports [1840]*, 598.

73. Walsh, *Manual of British Rural Sports [1856]*, 210.

74. Walsh, *Manual of British Rural Sports [1856]*, 212.

75. Thacker, *Courser's Companion [1829]*.

76. Thomas Thacker, *The Courser's Companion, Revised and Enlarged, to Which Is Added the Breeder's Guide, or Breeding in All Its Branches*, 2nd ed., vol. 2 (London: S. T. Probett, 1834).

77. Thacker, *Courser's Companion [1834]*, 1:99–256.

78. Anonymous, "Revision of the Laws of Coursing and Croquet," *Field*, October 23, 1869.

79. Blaine, *An Encyclopaedia of Rural Sports [1840]*, 597.

80. Walsh, *Dog in Health and Disease [1859]*, 297–98; John Henry Walsh (Stonehenge), *Manual of British Rural Sports: Comprising Shooting, Hunting, Coursing, Fishing, Hawking, Racing, Boating, Pedestrianism, and the Various Rural Games and Amusements of Great Britain*, 5th edn. (London: Routledge, Warne, and Routledge, 1861), 204–5.

81. Dalziel, *Greyhound*, 42–43.

82. John Henry Walsh, *Manual of British Rural Sports*, 4th edn. (London: Routledge, Warnes, and Routledge, 1859), 204–11.

83. Walsh, *Manual of British Rural Sports [1859]*, 204–11.

84. Rule Revision Committee of National Coursing Club, "Draft of Rules," *Field*, November 27, 1869; the revised rules were adopted in December 1869. Anonymous, "The Revision of the Laws of Coursing," *Field*, January 29, 1870.

85. John H. Walsh, *The Coursing Calendar and Report of the Spring Season 1859* (London: John Crockford, 1859), 80.

86. The club allowed some local variation in rules, saying it could see "clubs merely adding such special or local regulations as may be required to adapt the National code to their own peculiar use." Walsh, *Manual of British Rural Sports [1859]*, 204.

87. Dalziel, *Greyhound*, 42.

88. Originally, the club decided to limit the membership to thirty-five individuals. Five members rotated out each year, and the coursers at the Waterloo meeting either re-elected them or elected their replacements. Walsh, *Manual of British Rural Sports [1859]*, 204; Walsh (Stonehenge), *Manual of British Rural Sports [1861]*, 205–6.

89. Walsh, *Manual of British Rural Sports [1859]*, 204; Walsh, *Dog in Health and Disease [1859]*, 297; Walsh, *Coursing Calendar [1859]*, 80.

90. Walsh (Stonehenge), *Manual of British Rural Sports [1861]*, 205.

91. Rule Revision Committee of National Coursing Club, "Draft of Rules."

92. Anonymous, "Members of the National Coursing Club for 1870," *Field*, January 22, 1870.

93. Brown, *Greyhound Stud Book*, 1:xi–xii.

94. Walsh, *Manual of British Rural Sports [1856]*, 152.

95. Blaine, *An Encyclopaedia of Rural Sports [1840]*, 294. This source did not appear in a search of Google Ngram on October 9, 2014, which cited an 1842 publication (see next note) as the first use. The earliest use in the *Oxford English Dictionary* dates from 1843.

96. Phelim O'Toole, "Minor Bodkin's Cure for Conceit," *Bentley's Miscellany* 10 (1842): 285–97, see 290. This is the earliest use of the term found in a search of Google Ngram on October 9, 2014.

97. Google Ngram searched October 9, 2014.

98. Goodlake, *Courser's Manual [1828]*, xliii, li, lxiii. Google books, searched February 23, 2017.

99. Pierce Egan, *Sporting Anecdotes: Original and Select; Including Characteristic Sketches of Eminent Persons Who Have Appeared on the Turf: With an Interesting Selection of the Most Extraordinary Events Which Have Transpired in the Sporting World; a Correct Description of the Animals of Chase; and of Every Other Subject Connected with the Various Diversions of the Field* (London: J. Cundee and J. Harris, 1807), 94.

100. Anonymous, "Coursing. Engraving by Greig from a Painting by Lambert Marshall," *Sporting Magazine* 11 (1835): 228–229, see 228. Date of appearance determined by search of Google Ngram for *public coursing* on October 7, 2014.

101. Blaine, *An Encyclopaedia of Rural Sports [1840]*, 294.

102. Walsh, *Manual of British Rural Sports [1856]*, 152 (emphasis added).

103. Blaine, *An Encyclopaedia of Rural Sports [1840]*, 588.

104. Sirius, "Her Majesty's Staghounds," *Gentleman's Magazine* 12, January–June (1874): 88.

105. Anonymous, "Modern Coursing," 282.

106. Dalziel, *Greyhound*, 47–48.

107. Dalziel, *Greyhound*, 48–49.

108. Cox and Lascelles, *Coursing and Falconry*, 178.

109. Dalziel, *Greyhound*, 47.

110. Plumpton Racecourse, http://plumptonracecourse.co.uk/general-information/history/, viewed July 25, 2014.

111. Anonymous, "Modern Coursing," 281–82, see 281.

112. Dalziel, *Greyhound*, 41.

6

MODERN COEVOLUTION FOR
COURSING (1831–1900)

Greyhounds evolved rapidly after 1831. One reason was that the modern forces that standardized human niches also standardized greyhound niches. The most important forces were democracy, capitalism, bureaucracy, mass communication, and industrial transportation. These forces standardized greyhound niches at the same time, and for the same reasons, that they standardized human niches (see previous chapter). The two most important, standardized niches were the Waterloo Cup and enclosed coursing. Greyhound populations evolved when narrowed variation in niches led to narrowed variation in traits. A second reason greyhounds evolved rapidly was that modern forces facilitated narrowing of greyhound traits as well as narrowing of niches. Bureaucracy, capitalism, mass communication, and industrial transport facilitated public studs and a national breeding pool, which helped to homogenize greyhound traits across England.

Although greyhounds in general evolved toward less variation in traits, variation persisted. Some of the clearest contrasts came among three subpopulations: greyhounds in public coursing, greyhounds in private coursing, and greyhounds in hare hunting. Greyhounds in public coursing saw the greatest standardization of niches and the greatest narrowing of traits. Homogenization of agricultural practices narrowed variation in habitat dimensions of niches for greyhounds in private coursing and hare hunting. Narrowed niches encouraged narrowed variation in these populations. Because job dimensions of niches for public greyhounds, private greyhounds, and hare hunters differed, however, populations of greyhounds in the three occupations differed from each other.

Human populations coevolved rapidly with greyhounds after 1831. In response to the success of a rough greyhound in public coursing, a meme spread that rough greyhounds were superior to smooth greyhounds. The overall trend toward smoother greyhounds, however, encouraged the spread of the smooth-superiority meme seen in the transitional era.

A related meme held that the greyhound breed progressed when rough, inferior dogs evolved into smooth, superior dogs. Human populations evolved in response to wider social trends as well as in response to greyhounds. The nationalistic fervor that swept through Europe in the nineteenth century encouraged memes that classified greyhounds by nationalistic and imperial categories.

Human populations also evolved with respect to memes about breeding. One of the most curious changes came with the rejection of crossbreeding. The favored method of improving greyhounds in the transitional decades, crossbreeding came under attack after 1831. Opponents argued that purity, rather than crossbreeding, was the route to superiority. Because evidence from greyhounds contradicted this claim, it seems unlikely that the purity meme spread in response to greyhounds. It appears more likely to be a backlash against democratization of greyhound ownership. A desire to reify a hierarchical class system, coupled with Christianity and a grab bag of other ideas, appears to have driven support for the purity meme for greyhounds.

The purity meme did spark coevolution in greyhounds. The spread of the purity meme, coupled with a bureaucratic turf battle, apparently drove the National Coursing Club to "close" the breeding pool of greyhounds used in public coursing in 1882. A breed that had evolved for centuries with porous boundaries suddenly became an isolated population. This event created an evolutionary bottleneck, also known as a "sampling effect" among evolutionary biologists, in which the traits available to future generations of greyhounds were limited to traits already in the greyhound population.

Standard National Niches

Modern social forces standardized job descriptions for greyhounds at the same time, for the same reasons, and in the same ways that they standardized job descriptions for human coursers. In the first decades of the modern era, variation was the rule. As in the transitional decades, clubs and contests used the coursing rules they wished. These practices created local uniformity, and national variation, in greyhound job descriptions. When the National Coursing Club standardized memes (coursing rules) on a national scale after 1859, it standardized job descriptions for greyhounds on a national scale.

The habitat dimensions of greyhound niches standardized in lock step with standardization of habitats for human coursers. The Altcar estate became the standard, national habitat for many greyhounds. Altcar achieved this status because the Waterloo Cup served as the de facto British coursing championship. When Hugh Dalziel published *The Greyhound* in 1887, he included a list of winners of only one coursing contest, the Waterloo Cup.[1]

Enclosed coursing differed from the Waterloo Cup in that it took place in multiple locations, but it offered standardized habitats. As *The Kennel Gazette* reported in 1883, "the ground for all [enclosed coursing] is the same, a beautiful piece of turf, nearly as level as a bowling green, free from fence or obstacle."[2] (In this passage, "fence" meant something the dogs needed to jump to follow hares. Another kind of fence, high barriers that greyhounds could not jump, surrounded enclosed coursing grounds.) The enclosures were small by coursing standards, with the ground at Newcastle-on-Tyne advertised at 700 yards by 100 yards, which limited the distance greyhounds ran.[3]

Outside Altcar and enclosed-coursing grounds, variation in habitats narrowed in the modern period as farmers adopted similar practices across the country. Two key features of habitats – degree of openness and traits of hares – did not become uniform, but they did homogenize. Farmers in rough areas opened up landscapes by combining small fields, tearing out hedges, and dropping the ridge and furrow system. Fans of fast, stout hares introduced them to regions with slow hares.[4]

In sum, modernization narrowed variation in greyhound niches by standardizing job descriptions and habitats. The National Coursing Club standardized job descriptions by standardizing coursing rules. Altcar and enclosed coursing created two, standard, national greyhound habitats. Other habitats homogenized (but did not become uniform) when farmers removed hedges and coursers transplanted hares among regions.

Adapting National Populations to National Niches

Greyhound populations adapted to standard, national niches by narrowing variation in traits. At the beginning of the modern era, as in the transitional era, local uniformity and national variation were the rule in greyhound traits. The six regional populations Walsh identified (see Chapter 4) persisted at the beginning of the modern era. They continued because regional variation in both niche dimensions – job descriptions and habitats – remained.

Greyhound populations evolved on a national scale in the mid-nineteenth century when variation in traits narrowed in response to identical job descriptions. After 1859, almost all match greyhounds in the nation adapted to the same job dimensions of their niches: the National Coursing Club's rules. Breeders fine-tuned greyhound traits (especially behavioral traits) to the rules. When the National Coursing Club considered modifying its rules in 1869, *The Field* editorialized against the move. "The club should recollect that breeders have selected their strains with a view to carry out the principles hitherto laid down," the newspaper cautioned, "and that any deviation is by so much a breach of faith with them."[5] National uniformity in job descriptions rewarded national uniformity in behavioral traits. Once the job dimension of niches standardized, the main reason for variation in greyhounds was variation in the other niche dimension: habitats.

A national population of greyhounds with narrow traits evolved in response to one standard national niche (that is, a niche identical in habitat and job description for greyhounds that lived anywhere in England). The population was greyhounds bred for the Waterloo Cup. The standard, national habitat was the Altcar estate. Breeders who wanted to win the Waterloo Cup adapted their greyhounds to Altcar, not to the habitats where they lived. Almost always, Altcar differed from a greyhound's home habitat. Narrow ditches crisscrossed Altcar. Other coursing grounds lacked ditches or had wider ditches. Narrow ditches made Altcar unusual, and perhaps unique, as habitat.

The importance of fine-tuning greyhound traits to Altcar became visible when dogs good in other ditched habitats failed at Waterloo. Coursers in the south who wanted to see how their dogs would fare at Waterloo entered meetings organized by a club in Kent with the wonderful name of the Cliffe and Hundred of Hoo Association for the Preservation of Hares and Wildfowl. The Cliffe's grounds, like Altcar, had ditches, so southern coursers thought greyhounds good at Cliffe would succeed at Altcar. They usually were disappointed.[6]

The reason was a difference in habitat invisible to many coursers but decisive during matches. Cliffe's ditches were wider than Altcar's. Hares and greyhounds had to swim or use bridges to cross ditches at Cliffe. Swimming and bridge-crossing were irrelevant at Altcar, where narrow ditches permitted jumping. (See Figure 6.1.) Greyhounds that excelled at Cliffe failed at Waterloo. Harding Cox reported in 1892, "I have frequently met disappointed individuals who have taken dogs into [the Cliffe grounds] at Kent with a view to a Waterloo trial, and who, when considering the matter afterwards, have recollected that no drain [ditch] jumping was brought into play."[7] The lesson was that Waterloo aspirants,

Figure 6.1 Making one environment stand for all. Coursers considered Waterloo Cup winners to be the best greyhounds in the land. The Altcar estate outside Liverpool hosted the cup, which made its landscape and hares the national tests of quality. Hares leapt across the narrow ditches that crisscrossed Altcar, so Waterloo winners had to be skilled ditch-jumpers. Coursing grounds elsewhere had no ditches, or they had wide ditches that hares and greyhounds crossed by swimming or using bridges, so skilled coursers in other environments often failed at Altcar. Winning the Waterloo Cup meant a greyhound excelled in one environment, not all environments. An act of imagination converted local excellence into universal superiority. Harding Cox and Gerald Lascelles, *Coursing and Falconry* (London: Longmans, Green, and Co., 1892), frontispiece. Courtesy of Special Collections, Kenneth Spencer Research Library, University of Kansas Libraries.

no matter how far away their habitation, needed to adapt their dogs to Altcar. Breeders across the land adapted greyhounds to one standard, national niche created by the Waterloo Cup.

A second national population of greyhounds with narrow traits evolved in response to a second standard, national niche. This population comprised greyhounds bred for enclosed-coursing grounds. The traits of the enclosed-coursing population differed from the traits of the Waterloo population because the habitats of the contests differed. The Waterloo population was fast but sacrificed some speed for endurance. Altcar was unenclosed. Hares could run far, and greyhounds needed endurance to catch them. The enclosed-coursing population of greyhounds was fast and had little endurance. Enclosed-coursing grounds were small. Hares could run only short distances, and greyhound speed was more important than endurance. Breeders tailored greyhounds to this goal. As *The Kennel Gazette* put it, "an animal specially to run seven furlongs is the requirement of the day."[8] Seven furlongs was roughly the distance from one end of an enclosure to the other and back again. Because short distances led breeders to select against endurance, Hugh Dalziel thought enclosed coursing eliminated one of the defining characteristics of greyhounds. "I contend that to breed Greyhounds for coursing in enclosures of half-a-mile in length," he complained, "is to take the most certain means of destroying one of the most valuable qualities of the breed."[9]

Greyhounds outside the Waterloo and enclosed-coursing populations also evolved narrower traits in response to narrowed niches – so much so that experts declared the development of a new kind of dog, the modern British greyhound. The National Coursing Club rules standardized the job dimension of niches on a national scale. Homogenized agricultural practices and transplantation of hares reduced variation in the other dimension of niches: habitats. Breeders adapted greyhounds to standard jobs and homogenized habitats, which mixed hares from multiple regions, by mixing regional populations of greyhounds. In 1859, Walsh announced that the half-dozen varieties he described earlier in the century had merged into one national population. The old varieties "are now so completely amalgamated that it is useless to attempt a description of them."[10] Dalziel agreed. In 1879, he said a new, uniform dog, "the modern British greyhound," had replaced distinct greyhound varieties.[11]

The development of "the modern British greyhound" marked a new stage in evolution. Hitherto, greyhounds showed national variation in traits. In the transitional era, clubs created local islands of uniformity amidst a sea of variation. Now experts saw national uniformity. Both adjectives Dalziel attached to *greyhound* – *modern* and *British* – were important. British greyhounds were modern in the sense of *recent and up-to-date*. They were also modern in that modern social forces shaped their evolution. Democracy, capitalism, bureaucratization, mass communication, industrial transportation, and a belief in progress powered their development. Dalziel exaggerated in implying that the British greyhound was one uniform thing. Some variation persisted among greyhounds, so *similarity* would be a more accurate term than *uniformity*. But Dalziel was right that variation declined across Britain, and regional varieties mixed, making *British* an appropriate adjective.

The spread of a capitalist meme facilitated the creation of similar, national populations of greyhounds for Waterloo, enclosed coursing, and other contests. In the patrician and transitional eras, an anti-capitalism meme discouraged public studs. Some coursers believed that offering studs for fees would convert owners from sportsmen to business people, an association they wished to avoid. This meme continued into the first decades of the modern era. Mr. W. G. Borron had one of the best kennels in Britain in the mid-nineteenth century, but he refused to allow others access for breeding. As one observer noted, Borron looked "upon those who made public property of their dogs as sacrificing to pelf the purity of the Greyhound strain."[12] A key capitalist meme – that profit-seeking was legitimate and even admirable – spread among coursers in the modern era. Borron shocked the coursing world in 1857 when he decided to auction off all his twenty-five dogs. The new owners offered the dogs at stud.[13]

Two other modern forces – mass communication and railroads – facilitated public studs, mixing of regional populations, and adaptation of greyhounds to specific contests. Studbooks advertised studs, stated their prices, supplied pedigrees, and listed prizes won by studs (which helped customers surmise the likely traits of offspring). Thomas Goodlake published a greyhound studbook in 1828, but the popularity of the genre surged in the democratic era. In 1833, Goodlake published an update. It listed honors (prizes and dates), owner, color, sex, sire, sire's owner, dam, and dam's owner for each greyhound (when known).[14] Thomas Thacker began publishing data-packed, annual studbooks in 1841.[15] He supplied a list of stallion greyhounds with fees and contact information of owners. The prices varied according to the record of the dog.[16] Trains enabled greyhounds from anywhere in the country to mate with public studs. Sporting periodicals complemented studbooks, which appeared annually, by updating coursers on their competitors' breeding strategies during the year.[17]

Public studs prompted evolution in greyhound populations by spreading match-winning traits beyond the kennels of patricians. Early giants of public coursing, such as Lord Orford and Lord Rivers, kept competitors at a disadvantage by refusing to make their best dogs available for breeding. At most, a competitor might hope for access to an inferior dog, a privilege restricted to a favored few.[18] Public studs made match-winning greyhound traits available to all. "Any person who can procure a bitch, and has the command of five or ten guineas, is enabled to obtain as good blood as the highest nobleman in the land, and can compete on favourable terms in any company of coursers, at least as far as his breed of greyhounds is concerned," Walsh observed in 1856.[19] Borron's dogs illustrated Walsh's point. Once offered as studs, the dogs sired several Waterloo winners.[20]

Evolution of greyhound populations prompted human populations to coevolve in response. One example is the response to the spread of match-winning traits in greyhound populations. Access to public studs enabled middle- and working-class coursers to defeat patricians in coursing contests. As Walsh noted in 1856, public studs meant a "tenant-farmer or the professional man has as good a chance [of winning], or even a better one, than the most wealthy and large-acred noblemen."[21] Victories encouraged middle- and working-class coursers to stay in coursing. Losses motivated patricians to leave. Populations of human coursers coevolved when the frequency of middle- and working-class members increased, and the frequency of patrician members decreased, in response to the diffusion of match-winning traits in greyhounds.

In sum, greyhound populations evolved toward greater similarity in the modern era for several reasons. The national standardization of the job half of niches encouraged national standardization of greyhound behavioral traits. The national standardization of the habitat half of two niches – Waterloo and enclosed coursing – pushed breeders across England to tailor their dogs to those two habitats. The homogenization of other niches, thanks to agricultural practices and hare transplantation, encouraged homogenization of greyhound traits. Breeders responded by mixing regional varieties to create national greyhound populations with similar traits. Public studs, railroads, studbooks, and public pedigrees helped breeders mix regional greyhound populations and tailor their dogs to narrowed, national niches. The spread of match-winning traits prompted human populations to coevolve in response. The frequency of participation in coursing by the middle and working classes rose, and the frequency of patrician participation declined.

Greyhound populations evolved toward greater smoothness because of change in niches, not because rough greyhounds were inferior. Coat length did not determine victory or defeat. Behavioral traits – speed, frequent turning of hares, and endurance – determined outcomes. Over the nineteenth century, however, job and habitat dimensions of niches increasingly favored smooth greyhounds. Waterloo and enclosed coursing took place in open habitats hospitable to smooth greyhounds.

Breeders around the nation tailored greyhounds to the Waterloo and enclosed-coursing habitats. Other breeders adapted greyhounds to local habitats, but the trend in farming practices over the nineteenth century was to rip out hedges and create open fields. The spread of open, local habitats helped smooth greyhounds succeed. Uniformity in habitats narrowed variation in human behavior, too. It also made it easier for coursing to become a spectator sport.

Three Niches, Three Populations

Public greyhounds (those that competed in public meetings) seized the headlines in the nineteenth century, so it was easy to think all greyhounds were public. In fact, public greyhounds were a minority. In 1859, John H. Walsh estimated that about a fourth to a third of British greyhounds worked in public match coursing. Most greyhounds worked in private match coursing and hare hunting (which became known as pot-hunting).[22] Job descriptions for public coursing standardized thanks to the National Coursing Club's rules, but greyhounds outside public coursing worked under other job descriptions.

Three jobs – public match coursing, private match coursing, and hare hunting – led to three niches with overlapping but different job descriptions, which produced greyhound populations with overlapping but different traits. (A fourth job, working in dog shows, led to a fourth niche and a population with distinctive traits. This is the subject of the next chapter.) The traits of the three populations differed in inconsistent ways. For some traits, public and private match greyhounds differed from each other. For other traits, match greyhounds (public and private) resembled each other and differed from hunters. (See Figure 6.2.)

Jobs in public coursing and private coursing required greyhounds to turn hares to win matches, which led to similarities in that behavior, but differences in other duties led to divergence in traits. Public coursers wanted greyhounds to win specific contests, so they preferred greyhounds that sacrificed endurance to speed (to reach hares before other dogs), had mixed greyhound–bulldog ancestry (because bulldogs added courage and intelligence), and were born early in the year (because greyhounds competed in age-restricted categories, and all those born in a calendar year were treated as the same age). Private match coursers sacrificed speed for endurance (because they wanted years of service, not one win), avoided bulldog crosses (because intelligent greyhounds lost interest in turning hares after a couple years), and wanted pups born later in the year (because those born

Job	Speed v. endurance	Behavior toward hares	Lagging	Bulldog cross	Birth	Landscapes
Public coursing (matches)	speed	turn often	bad	good	Feb.–March	1x4
Private coursing-- matches	endurance	turn often	bad	bad	March–May	1
Private coursing-- hunting	endurance	kill soon	good	bad	March–May	<1

Figure 6.2 Three jobs, three populations. Breeders selected greyhounds for job-specific traits, which led to divergent, if porous, populations. Greyhounds that looked similar differed in the traits that breeders valued most, such as speed, endurance, behavior, birth month, and suitability to landscapes. Even similar jobs spawned divergent populations. Public match coursers valued speed over endurance and wanted pups born in February. Private match coursers valued endurance over speed and wanted pups born in March–May. Public match coursers wanted four greyhounds, each tailored to a different landscape. Private match coursers sought individual greyhounds that could do all tasks in a local landscape well. Hunters wanted individuals that specialized in tasks within a local landscape; they paired complementary individuals to create teams with the full suite of desired traits. Table by author.

in warmer weather were healthier).[23] Contrasts in jobs led public and private greyhound populations to evolve different traits, especially behavioral traits. In 1859, Walsh noted, "externally there is no difference whatever [between public and private greyhounds], yet in the more delicate organization of his brain and nerves there is some obscure variation, by which he is rendered more swift and clever in the one case [public greyhounds], and more stout and honest in the other [private greyhounds]."[24]

Contrasts between match coursing and hunting led to trait divergence in greyhound populations. Match coursers wanted greyhounds to turn hares frequently while postponing killing in order to rack up points. They sought dogs that excelled as individuals (because matches were one-on-one contests) in one of four environments (hilly, level, open, and closed). Hunters wanted greyhounds that killed quickly because they wanted hares in the pot. They sought greyhounds with more specialized skills than match greyhounds because their dogs worked in teams. Rather than having one dog that was decent at running uphill and downhill, as match coursers did, hunters wanted one dog that excelled at running uphill and another that excelled at running downhill. Hunters adapted greyhounds to one landscape (the owner's estate).[25]

In sum, differences among these three groups of dogs were important because they falsified the idea of a uniform British greyhound and highlighted the importance of variation in behaviors. The British greyhound was an abstraction made possible by the uniformity of dogs bred to win at Waterloo and similar contests. Greyhounds bred for private coursing differed from greyhounds tailored to public coursing because their owners had different goals, and coursing greyhounds of either sort differed from hunting greyhounds because the latter's owners had yet other goals. Variation in job–environment combinations continued to reward variation in greyhound traits. Because the key differences were behavioral more than physical, they remained invisible to many people in England in the nineteenth century and after. Two greyhounds might look identical in pictures but behave in very different ways. (See Figure 6.3.)

Human Coevolution: Memes about Symbolism and Classification

Human populations evolved in several ways in response to changes in greyhound traits. In the transitional decades, some patricians promoted the meme that rough greyhounds were lurchers (poachers' dogs) and inferior, which implied that the working classes, the Irish, and Scots were inferior. The smooth-superiority meme led some clubs to ban rough greyhounds. In the modern era, some human populations promoted a meme that turned the rough-inferiority meme on its head. Rough greyhounds, the new meme held, were superior to smooth dogs. By implication, the working classes, northerners, Irish, and Scots were superior to southern English patricians.

In the 1830s, a rough dog named Gilbertfield carried the rough-superiority meme on his back. Some coursing clubs banned Gilbertfield (and other rough dogs) from competition. Critics called Gilbertfield a "third-rate" dog and a lurcher (poacher's dog).[26] The lurcher association made clear the class-based denigration of Gilbertfield. All classes of people poached, but patricians blamed the working classes for the practice. To say Gilbertfield was a lurcher was to imply that the owner was a poacher and a member of the working classes. But the anti-rough meme was not universal in coursing clubs. Four clubs allowed Gilbertfield to compete. He excelled during a four-year career in the 1830s. One of his triumphs came in the 1835 Glasgow Gold Cup, when he defeated a field of ninety competitors.[27] By 1836, he was one of the most famous coursing dogs in the United Kingdom. When given the chance to compete on an

Figure 6.3 Defining breeds by behavior. John Henry Walsh, the foremost expert on dogs in the nineteenth century, published this image in 1859 to illustrate "The rough Scotch greyhound and deerhound," which he described as one breed in appearance and two breeds in behavior. Walsh republished the image in an 1879 edition of the same book, but the intervening rise of dog shows led him to revise his text. Shows defined breeds by appearance, considered the deerhound an independent breed, and punished long coats in greyhounds. In the 1879 revision, Walsh focused on the physical traits of the deerhound and ignored the rough greyhound. John Henry Walsh, *The Dog in Health and Disease* (London: Longman, Green, Longman, and Roberts, 1859), 20, and John Henry Walsh, *The Dog in Health and Disease*, 3rd edn. (London: Longmans, Green, 1879), 33, courtesy of Hathi Trust. https://catalog.hathitrust .org/Record/008902739.

even footing (that is, when coursing was democratic for dogs as well as people), this rough greyhound falsified the rough-inferiority meme.

Publicists seized on Gilbertfield's success as evidence of rough superiority. As the *Kilmarnock [Scotland] Journal* put it in 1836, Gilbertfield's victories should lead to "an absolute change in language, so that henceforth, the word lurcher is to designate superiority, instead of, as heretofore, inferiority of blood; and the word third-rate, to apply to the ascending scale in degrees of comparison, or in other words, to denote the superlative degree of excellence."[28] Gilbertfield succeeded because he showed the traits that lurchers and rough greyhounds supposedly lacked – speed, endurance, and honesty. By *honesty*, coursers meant that a dog performed well under the rules of coursing (running in the lead and turning hares often) rather than lurching (hanging back and killing a hare after a lead dog turned it). Among the dogs he faced, only one – a famous champion named Major – seemed faster. Gilbertfield showed remarkable endurance over long meetings.[29]

Some sporting magazines generalized the rough-superiority meme. In 1833, a magazine suggested that greyhounds in "early days" were large, rough animals. In converting rough dogs into "the modern greyhound," breeders enhanced "speed and beauty ... at the expense of strength, of courage, and of sagacity ... The modern high-bred greyhound, on the score of sagacity, is inferior to every other variety of the dog tribe."[30] The same year, another magazine argued that greyhounds in earlier centuries were larger, stronger, and hardier than "the modern greyhound."[31]

A trend toward evolutionary thinking helped both rough-superiority and smooth-superiority memes spread. Although these memes offered opposite claims about greyhound quality, they both capitalized on the idea that greyhounds evolved from rough to smooth dogs. The conflict came in the evaluation of that change. Southern English breeders embraced one of the key ideas of modernity, progress through science, to claim that evolution in their hands created progress. Northerners, the Irish, Scots, and the working classes at times promoted that curious feature of modernity: anti-modernity. They argued that change sometimes brought regress instead of progress. Greyhounds offered examples for both sets of beliefs.

One of the strongest promoters of memes that equated modern change in greyhounds with progress was Delabere Blaine. In his influential 1840 sporting encyclopedia, Blaine suggested that greyhounds probably originated in ancient Greece. The breed spread to Gaul, where it was known as *Canis Gallicus* or *Canis Leporarius*. The Gauls brought dogs called *vertagus* or *vertraha* to Britain and developed them into Irish and Scotch greyhounds. *Canis Gallicus*, *Canis Leporarius*, *vertagus*, and *vertraha* were the same dogs. The English refined coarse Irish and Scotch greyhounds into the English greyhound "as his master increased in civilization and became more reclaimed." This evolution culminated in "the elegant courser or long dog, seen in its highest form at our great coursing meetings."[32] This was a theory of progressive evolution, then, of master and dog in tandem.

Blaine argued that change in greyhound jobs led to evolution in greyhound traits. The extinction of fierce prey, Blaine believed, enabled the
English to develop their fine greyhounds out of coarse Scotch and Irish
varieties. Ireland and Scotland had boars, wolves, and bears that called for
powerful dogs. England exterminated these dangerous beasts before the
Gaelic regions did, "and consequently the same type of dog was not kept
up here, but, on the contrary, by culture was made finer in coat, and of
greater tenuity of form." As prey shifted to stags, greyhounds remained
large and powerful but gained speed. When stags declined, the focus
switched to foxes, which were pursued with "strong wire-haired
greyhounds ... descended from the stock of Scotia." The demand for
speed to chase foxes led to a "more attenuated appearance."[33]

The result was "the cultivated English greyhound." Blaine thought its
elegance and symmetry unrivalled by any animals but racehorses.
Greyhounds provided evidence of "the great alterations which can be
effected in the animal frame by culture; for no naturalist could by possibility be made to believe that the greyhound form, coupled with the
peculiarities which attach thereto, could have originated in nature."[34]

Blaine credited evolution in greyhounds to selection. Hounds (dogs
that used scent and sight) "existed without doubt from the beginning of
animal creation." Selection for speed and reliance on sight shaped
hounds into greyhounds. As Blaine put it,

> Selections would be made from those dogs which exhibited
> sufficient lightness of frame to enable them to compete with
> the smaller deer, the wild goat, the fox, jackal, hare, &c. &c. by
> coursing in sight, instead of employing numbers [of dogs] in
> a more lengthened pursuit by scent. Such an origin we may
> very naturally attribute to the first greyhound types ... This
> change was not effected at once, its gradations were therefore
> not marked; nor has history recorded the physical phenomena
> connected with it in the order of their occurrence ... [The]
> *greyhound form is the effect of cultivation.*

In addition to human selection, Blaine attributed traits to climate. Smooth
coats suited warm climates, and curly coats suited cold Scotland.[35] Because
he regarded smooth greyhounds as superior to rough dogs, Blaine disdained crossing the two. He warned that occasionally "a wire-haired taint
gets among reputed breeds" of greyhounds.[36]

If Blaine's idea of evolution by selection sounds like Charles Darwin's
theory of evolution by selection, it should. Darwin used Blaine's book,
along with works by animal improvers, to develop his theory.[37] Darwin

realized that nature did something like animal breeders. Nature selected animals with certain traits to survive while killing others with traits less suited to their environments. This selection slowly changed the traits of organisms, which eventually led to new species. Darwin used the term "selection" to highlight similarities between the actions of breeders and of nature. Darwin identified four kinds of selection that caused evolution. He added *natural* in front of *selection* to create *natural selection*, which meant differential survival because of differences in traits. He identified *sexual selection* as differential reproduction due to mate choice. He used *methodical selection* to refer to deliberate efforts by breeders to change traits. He used *unconscious selection* to refer to accidental impacts of animal owners on traits.[38]

Blaine's meme projected the patrician-era meme about southern improvement of greyhounds onto the deep past. In the patrician era, southerners argued that they had improved greyhounds using the breeding techniques of the eighteenth and early nineteenth centuries. Selection, they suggested, made southern greyhounds superior to northern dogs. Blaine argued that the English had been improving greyhounds for centuries. He credited English civilization, more than new breeding techniques, for the improvement. The English had always been selecting greyhounds for desired traits, he suggested. This argument shifted the basis of superiority from an elite class of people within England to English civilization as a whole. The smooth English greyhound now symbolized not southern patricians, but the English as a people and a nation.

Memes using greyhounds as national symbols found a welcoming environment in the nineteenth century. Many nation-states took form in Europe in the nineteenth century, so historians have referred to the period as an age of nationalism. Nationalism was not new, but it did spread, including in Britain. The spirit of nationalism extended beyond citizenship. It enlisted culture, including sports, to argue that groups of people shared essential traits that made a nation-state natural, even inevitable. In Britain, nationalism pulled in conflicting directions because it highlighted differences between English, Scottish, Irish, Welsh, and Cornish people. At the same time, many English people pushed to minimize national differences in favor of a unified British identity.

These conflicting strains in political culture helped multiple memes about greyhound classification spread in human populations. Four memes emerged. We have just discussed one, the evolutionary meme, which suggested that smooth greyhounds evolved from rough Irish and Scotch greyhounds. After Blaine, other evolutionists argued that regional breeds of greyhounds merged into one national population. A second meme, lumping, argued that greyhounds and other so-called breeds were one breed, even before merging of populations. A third meme, nationalism, argued that greyhounds came in nationalities throughout the nineteenth century. A fourth meme, arbitrariness, argued that all breed distinctions were social conventions rather than biological realities. Books on dogs in general, and greyhounds in particular, spread these memes widely.[39]

The first meme, evolutionism, developed after the publication of Blaine's encyclopedia in 1840. Later in the century, this meme held that regional varieties merged to create a national population with relatively uniform traits. In the 1830s, greyhound expert John H. Walsh noted, coursers considered half a dozen regional varieties of greyhounds to be "distinct breeds." In mid-century, regional breeds merged to form a unified British population. In 1859, Walsh observed, "it would be wholly impossible in the present day to find a single specimen of either [Newmarket or Wiltshire greyhounds] uncrossed with the blood of some other variety . . . Locality has now little to do with it, and throughout Great Britain and Ireland the public greyhound is the same animal." Lancashire and Yorkshire were exceptions in that they had retained some unique strains, but 90 percent of the greyhounds in those counties descended from mixes with greyhounds from elsewhere. Greyhounds from southern and midland counties had a big impact on the British population, but dogs from other regions (such as Lancashire and Scotland) also contributed.[40]

The second meme, lumping, held that greyhounds and other so-called breeds had been one breed all along. The lumpers thought greyhounds and other dogs varied in appearance, behavior, and name, but they belonged to one breed. In 1836, *The British Cyclopedia* said that the Scotch greyhound was "in all probability the *gazehound* of England."[41] In 1838, William Scrope complained that, in the past, different regions called the same dogs by different names.

> One great obstacle in the way of investigating the history of this dog [the Highland deerhound] has arisen from the different appellations given to it, according to the fancy of the natives in different parts of the country, of Irish wolfdog, Irish greyhound, Highland deerhound, and Scotch greyhound. But for these apparently distinctive designations, sufficient information would probably have been recorded regarding a breed of dogs really the same, and in such general use throughout the different parts of the kingdom.[42]

To Scrope and his allies, national names were misleading because they implied biological differences that did not exist.

The third meme, nationalism, held that greyhounds were not one breed; they were a family of national breeds or varieties. In his 1840 *Natural History of Dogs*, Charles Hamilton Smith identified five members of the greyhound group in Britain, four of them with national or imperial names. The five were the Scottish greyhound, Irish greyhound, Italian greyhound, British greyhound, and lurcher.[43] (Smith's replacement of *English* with *British* was an early example of a practice that grew more common later in the century.) In 1845, William Youatt, a veterinary surgeon who played an important role in animal breeding and the dog world, identified seven greyhounds in Britain. Five had national names, and a sixth (Highland greyhound) was easy to assign to a nation (Scotland). Youatt's seven were English greyhound, Irish greyhound, Scotch greyhound, Highland greyhound or deerhound, gazehound, Irish wolfhound, and Italian greyhound.[44]

For the nationalists, the Waterloo Cup offered the ideal metaphor for international conflict. The cup drew coursers and greyhounds from throughout the United Kingdom. In 1843, *The Sporting Review* described the Waterloo Cup as "a splendid competition between the Scotch, English, and Irish greyhounds." That year marked the first time "the Waterloo Cup has been borne away from England" because a dog from Scotland, Major, won.[45] (Major was the one dog that ran faster than Gilbertfield.) It was unclear, in passages such as this, whether authors thought greyhounds differed in more ways than in residence. But, as with classification of people by nationality, differences in greyhounds were not essential for the nationalism meme to thrive.

Hugh Dalziel synthesized the evolutionary and nationalist memes. He argued that mixing of greyhound varieties created a new kind of greyhound, the *British* greyhound. The term *British greyhound* appeared in 1675 but may not have appeared in print again until 1839, after which its use increased.[46] The *British* greyhound, Dalziel declared in 1879, consigned English, Scotch, and Irish greyhounds to the past.[47] The British greyhound was uniform and superior in all terrains. Dalziel called it "the acme of perfection in beauty of outline and fitness; and whether we see him trying conclusions on the meadows of Lurgan, the rough hillsides of Crawford John, or for the blue ribbon of the leash on the flats of Altcar, he is still the same."[48] Dalziel located this dog in time as well as space. Modern British rules of coursing had molded "the greyhound of the day."[49]

Dalziel's British-superior meme appears to be a political argument in disguise. Blaine argued in 1840 that the *English* greyhound was superior to other greyhounds. Almost forty years later, Dalziel argued that the *British* greyhound rendered the English greyhound, as well as Irish and Scottish greyhounds, obsolete. The three locations he mentioned – Lurgan, Crawford John, and Altcar – were in Ireland, Scotland, and England. In 1879 (the year Dalziel's book appeared), the Irish potato crop tumbled to one-third of the average. Landlords evicted tenants who could not pay their rent. Violence erupted, and Irish leaders renewed calls for independence.[50] In this context, "the modern British greyhound" sounds like a metaphor for the United Kingdom. The English, Irish, and Scots should forget their differences, Dalziel seemed to imply, in favor of a common British identity that would improve life for all.

The fourth meme, arbitrariness, held that all breed classifications were social constructs rather than biological realities. In 1859, John H. Walsh described one group of dogs as both one breed and two breeds. The section on "the rough Scotch greyhound and deerhound" in one of his books opened, "This *breed* of dogs is, I believe, one of the oldest and purest in existence." A subsequent sentence stated, "In spite of the external form being the same in the rough Scotch greyhound used for coursing hares, and the deerhound, there can be no doubt that the *two breeds*, from having been kept to their own game exclusively, are specially adapted to its pursuit by internal organization, and the one cannot be substituted for the other with advantage."[51] Using *breed* two ways reflected Walsh's view that breed divisions were arbitrary social conventions. Classified by appearance, the rough Scotch greyhound and the deerhound were one breed. Classified by behavior, they were two breeds.

Walsh elaborated on the arbitrariness of breed classifications when discussing so-called mongrels, including greyhound–bulldog crosses. He argued that writers misrepresented the complexity of the dog world by ignoring crossbreeds in their canine taxonomies. Breeds originated as crossbreeds, so crossbreeds had as much claim to being breeds as other dogs. If writers recognized this fact, Walsh suggested, "there is scarcely any limit to the numbers [of breeds] which may be described." It was only favoritism for existing breeds that led fanciers to despise mongrels. He observed, "as a certain number of breeds are described by writers on the dog, or defined by 'dog-fanciers,' these 'mongrels,' as they are called from not belonging to them, are generally despised, and, however useful they may be, the breed is not continued." Walsh thought this bias hypocritical because crossbreeding improved many breeds, including greyhounds (via crossing with bulldogs). It was only a sleight of hand that classified certain crossbreeds as single breeds. Crossbred greyhounds and others "are now recognized and admitted into the list of valuable breeds," Walsh noted, "and not only are not considered mongrels, but on the contrary, are prized above the original strains from which they are descended."[52]

In sum, human populations evolved in the modern era when the frequency of memes about greyhound symbolism and classification changed. After 1831, a meme emerged that flipped the smooth-superiority meme on its head. Capitalizing on the success of Gilbertfield, this meme held that rough greyhounds were superior to smooth dogs (and, implicitly, that workers, northerners, Scots, and Irish people were superior to elite, southern English people). A meme that smooth greyhounds evolved from rough dogs supported this meme. This meme expanded over the nineteenth century to include the idea that regional varieties merged to create a uniform national population. A meme held that greyhounds (under multiple names) had been one breed all along. Another meme suggested that greyhounds came in nationalities. Yet another meme argued that all breed classifications were social conventions rather than descriptions of biological reality. These memes coexisted. They created variation in traits of human populations.

Human Coevolution: Memes about Breeding

Memes about breeding coevolved at the same time as memes about classification and symbolism. Most of the memes that guided breeders in the democratic era developed in the transitional decades of the patrician era. Breeders after 1831 accepted the idea that *breeding* meant mating males and females with desired traits, and they culled the offspring for physical and behavioral traits. As we saw earlier, they intensified practices from the transitional era, such as using pedigrees and contest results to assess the quality of sires. They relied on public studs. This section focuses on two related memes that had a low profile before 1831 and became more popular after that watershed: purity and inbreeding.

Purity meant the absence of cross breeding. The key idea of the purity meme was that pure breeding produced superior greyhounds. Populations of human coursers were unlikely candidates for the spread of a purity meme. Although the term was popular among livestock breeders, coursers showed little interest in it before 1831. Breeders in the patrician era considered crossbreeding one of their standard tools. In the transitional era, coursers credited Lord Orford with improving greyhounds by crossing them with bulldogs (and other breeds). The most famous champions of that era (Snowball, Czarina, Major, and Sylvia) descended from Orford's crossbreeding.[53] Crossbreeding was not just acceptable in the transitional decades. It was praised as the route to greyhound excellence. In the modern era, public coursers continued to rely on bulldog crosses to cultivate the traits needed to win championships.

In the early years of the modern era, the strongest advocate for the purity meme for greyhounds was Thomas Thacker. The author of a coursing calendar, breeding guide, and studbook, Thacker had a practical incentive to promote purity. The way to determine whether a dog was pure was to buy Thacker's studbook and study its pedigree for many generations. As Thacker claimed in his 1834 breeding guide, "If there be one strain of inferior blood it will never entirely wash out, though twenty, fifty, or one hundred generations after it are crossed from the best known blood, it will show itself one time or another."[54] This was a fantastic claim: After 100 generations, the proportion of one ancestor's contribution to an animal's makeup would be 0.0000000000000000000000000013 percent. But it was good marketing for pedigrees.

The central problem for Thacker was that evidence contradicted the purity meme. If crossbreeding created inferior greyhounds, it would have been easy for Thacker to point to the results of public coursing meets as evidence. He could not. Some of the most successful greyhounds descended from Orford's crosses. Public coursers continued to rely on greyhound crosses in the modern era because those dogs won contests.

Unable to rely on contests for evidence of the purity meme, Thacker introduced a new meme. This meme diverted attention from victory and defeat to an incidental behavior: how greyhounds managed hedges. If a greyhound jumped a hedge rather than forced its way through, Thacker said in 1834, "it betokens a want of pure blood ... and contrary to the acknowledged and admired nature of a true bred greyhound, who runs entirely by sight, and that sight intensely fixed on the hare."[55] A greyhound "of a mixed breed when nearing the meuse will slacken his pace, prick up his ears, curl up his tail, and go through the meuse, but slackly; while the true breed, when once fairly entered, will dash through it without delay."[56] These behaviors were not, in fact, measures of greyhound quality. They mattered only to the extent they affected the outcome of coursing contests, so focusing on them was like saying the purest (meaning best) horse was the one that held its head highest, even if it came in last in races.

Thacker introduced a second meme that diverted attention from contest results. This meme, a classic ad hominem attack, held that cross-breeders had nefarious motives. The purpose of crossing greyhounds with bulldogs, he said, was to aid "the midnight poacher, or for producing flashy speed in coursing; but if you gain in one attribute you lose in another, as regards each separate order of species."[57] Even if true, the fact that poachers adapted greyhounds to their jobs through crossbreeding was irrelevant for evaluating the impact of crossbreeding on coursing performance. Denigrating "flashy speed in coursing" was bewildering. Greyhounds had been bred for speed for centuries. It was their most recognizable trait. Speed enabled greyhounds to win coursing contests, and coursers considered it a virtue.

Given that evidence contradicted the purity meme, we must look outside the greyhound world for its appeal. Thacker's language revealed that his primary concern was the human world, especially class hierarchy. In his 1834 studbook, Thacker declared his goal was "to defend that high spirited and *noble* animal, the greyhound, from the imputation of *ignoble* blood, or of a spurious and cross production from different species, which many modern authors have cast upon him, or of any other than an original creation, intended chiefly to course the hare."[58] Thacker published this argument three years after Parliament democratized greyhound ownership, which suggests he thought greyhounds should have remained a patrician (or, better, noble) monopoly.

Other belief systems encouraged Thacker's purity meme, too. One was Christianity. Thacker called the greyhound "an original creation," which implied God created it for a specific purpose (coursing hares), and it remained unchanged. Thacker said the adaptation of greyhound to hare, and vice versa, showed "the great Creator of all beings" designed them for each other. To buttress this idea, Thacker quoted Genesis 5:2 ("Male and female created he them").[59] Another belief system was Platonic idealism or essentialism. Thacker talked of *the greyhound*, not *greyhounds*. By using the definite articles with a singular noun, he implied that all greyhounds were essentially the same as each other and essentially different from other breeds. He argued that a "true breed" of greyhound needed protection from "the mixed breed" that resulted from crossing the greyhound with "other species of the canine race."[60] It is possible that a fourth influence, human racism, also shaped Thacker's thoughts. Use of *race* alone does not prove this impact. *Race* was a common synonym for *breed* and *species.* Thacker did not explicitly compare breeds to human races. On the other hand, his argument that mixing produced inferior offspring echoed the ideas of human racists.

A version of the purity meme spread to other writers and greyhound owners despite the lack of evidence for its validity. In 1840, Delabere Blaine noted, "The brindled or streaked dog is very generally slighted, as exhibiting the bull-dog cross of Lord Orford, or some other fancy breeder."[61] This bias encouraged many breeders to turn against brindled dogs as inferior for decades. But, because the brindled-inferiority meme grew out of class ideology rather than evidence, it is not surprising that iconoclastic breeders falsified the meme later in the nineteenth century. An 1898 article reported that brindled dogs seldom appeared at public meetings "some years ago," but the success of brindled dogs (such as Fullerton and Young Fullerton) had led brindled dogs to become more popular.[62]

John H. Walsh and others offered a contradictory meme: that crossbred greyhounds were superior in public matches. The crossbred-superiority meme had a crucial advantage over the pure-superiority meme: evidence. As Walsh noted in 1853, "the most successful coursers at Newmarket, in Wiltshire, and in Scotland, for the last twenty-five years have had recourse to the bulldog." Walsh believed "the bull cross develops the animal courage, and that it also somewhat increases the mental faculties, so that the dog is inclined to run cunning but not slack."[63]

Another meme, which promoted inbreeding, gained popularity over the nineteenth century. In previous centuries, breeders looked askance at inbreeding (mating of close relatives) as producing weak, inferior animals. Experts in the nineteenth century moderated this view. They argued that some inbreeding was good but too much was bad. In 1834, Thacker argued that inbreeding "will be beneficial to a certain extent, and become prejudicial beyond it."[64] With time and updates to his guide, however, he became known as "the great advocate" of inbreeding as the only way to ensure greyhound stoutness.[65] Walsh thought inbreeding conferred elegance of shape at the expense of size, stoutness, and bone. But, because some inbred greyhounds had performed well, he thought inbreeding had its place if used carefully.[66]

The Waterloo Cup seemed to offer the strongest evidence for the inbred-superiority meme, but the reasoning was flawed. Breeders long believed "like begets like," so coursers who wanted to win the cup used Waterloo winners as sires. The method worked. Judge won the Waterloo Cup in 1855 and sired three winners by three dams.[67] Breeders took victory of inbred dogs as evidence that the practice was a good one. In 1886, *The Kennel Gazette* concluded, "At this latter stage it is very difficult to see how there can be too much inbreeding ... The winners of the Waterloo Cup for the last ten years have been in nearly all cases the most in-bred occupants of the Coursing Calendar."[68] The problem was that breeders confused superiority in a narrow niche with universal superiority. The narrow niche was the Waterloo Cup, which standardized a job description and habitat. It is not surprising that inbreeding from Waterloo Cup winners, which increased the likelihood that offspring would resemble previous winners, would produce Waterloo winners. But Waterloo winners were not universally superior. They were better in a narrow niche.

A bureaucratic turf battle apparently helped the pure-superiority and inbred-superiority memes drive out the crossbred-superiority meme. In 1873, patricians formed a Kennel Club in London to govern dog shows and breeding. In 1874, the Kennel Club began registering grey-hounds in a studbook. In 1880, the Kennel Club announced that, as of 1883, greyhounds would have to be registered with the Kennel Club to compete in shows. This step was part of a set of complex maneuvers, explained in the next chapter, used by the Kennel Club to gain control over shows. Apparently in response, the National Coursing Club announced it would create a studbook for coursing greyhounds. As of 1883, public coursing greyhounds would have to be registered in the National Coursing Club's studbook.[69] Most likely, the National Coursing Club wanted to prevent the Kennel Club from gaining jurisdiction over coursing and coursing greyhounds.

In sum, human populations evolved in the modern era when memes about breeding changed frequency. Through the mid-nineteenth century, the crossbred-superiority meme was common. Initially rare, the pure-superiority and inbred-superiority memes gained popularity not because evidence supported them but because they appealed to ideas about humanity. Notions of class hierarchy, Christianity, and essentialism boosted the pure-superiority meme. Apparently in a turf battle with the Kennel Club, the National Coursing Club banished the crossbred-superior meme in 1882 when it closed the greyhound population used in public coursing. By that time, inbreeding had gained favor because winners of Waterloo often descended from Waterloo winners. Inbred offspring succeeded because they competed in the same niche as their parents, but it proved easy to mistake adaptation to a narrow niche as evidence of universal superiority.

Greyhound Coevolution

The National Coursing Club's studbook became the weapon for enforcing the pure-superiority meme. The first volume of the studbook appeared in 1882 and listed fewer than a thousand dogs. It helped solidify Waterloo as the measure of greyhound quality by listing the winners and runners up for the Waterloo Cup, Purse, and Plate. No other meeting received this honor.[70] The studbook enabled the National Coursing Club to, in its terminology, "close" the breed in 1882. Henceforth, greyhounds in public coursing contests had to descend from two parents in the studbook. In the twenty-first century, the club claimed that all greyhounds competing in the field and racetracks in the British Isles, the United States, and Australia descended from Waterloo winners.[71]

Greyhounds became "pure" because of an arbitrary, human, social convention: greyhounds in the studbook were pure; greyhounds outside the studbook were not. The declaration of purity had nothing to do with the ancestry of the first greyhounds in the studbook. Most descended from greyhound–bulldog crosses. *Purity* simply meant belonging to an isolated population with members registered in a studbook, no matter what breeds inhabited their ancestral tree. After 1882, greyhounds were pure if descended from two dogs in the studbook. Registration did not erase their pre-1882 bulldog ancestry, except in people's minds. *Purity* did not mean excellence, either. The criterion for inclusion in the studbook was competing in public matches when the first studbook was issued. Some of the dogs in those matches came in last, but they marched into the studbook along with winners.

Closing the breeding pool created a radical transition in greyhound evolution. Prior to 1882, all greyhound populations were open. They had porous breeding boundaries. Breeders usually mated greyhounds with other greyhounds, but they crossed greyhounds with other dogs when they wished to introduce or enhance certain traits. The greyhound population was part of the entire dog population. All traits in all kinds of dogs were available to greyhound breeders. After 1882, the public greyhound population became isolated from all other dogs, including unregistered greyhounds used in private coursing and hare hunting. Now, the only traits available to breeders of public greyhounds were those in the greyhounds in the National Coursing Club's studbook. The range of variation in the population narrowed because the National Coursing Club sampled a subset of all greyhounds, and all dogs, when isolating public greyhounds. Public greyhounds passed through an evolutionary bottleneck.

Sampling effects made the range of variation in public greyhounds smaller than the range of variation in the parent population. Public greyhounds evolved.

Closing the breeding pool was a good way to achieve a human, social goal (protecting turf against the Kennel Club) but a poor way to improve greyhounds. By itself, pure breeding improved nothing. If one bred from the worst performers in the pure population, one reduced the quality of the population. If one bred from the best performers in the pure population, one improved the population – defined, in this case, as winning the Waterloo Cup. But there was no need to close the population to encourage breeding from the best performers. Breeders relied on Waterloo winners as sires before the public greyhound population was closed. The reason was simple: they wanted to win Waterloo. Closing the breeding population had no impact on that goal.

Statistically, closing the breeding pool was counterproductive because it reduced the chance of breeding superior individuals. If coursers wanted to create superior greyhounds, the best way was to (a) widen the variation of desired traits in the population, and (2) select the best performers as parents of the next generation. This was the strategy of Lord Orford and his successors who crossed greyhounds with bulldogs and other dogs. On a graph, this strategy widened the normal (bell-shaped) distribution of traits. On the x-axis was a trait: coursing performance. On the y-axis was the number of individuals who coursed at each level of ability. Widening variation probably (a) pushed the high-performing tail of the curve to the right, and (b) pushed the low-performing tail of the curve to the left. Orford probably produced some greyhounds that were exceptionally bad at coursing (the left-hand tail of the distribution) as well as some that were exceptionally good (the right-hand tail). Coursers kept the best performers and killed the rest. By limiting the range of traits available in the breeding pool, the National Coursing Club made it harder to widen variation, which reduced the chance of pushing the high tail of performance to the right. Pure breeding was good at producing many similar individuals; it was poor at creating rapid change in traits.

The effect of the National Coursing Club's actions was to reverse the monopoly pattern seen in the patrician era. Before 1831, the human population of coursers was closed (monopolized) but the population of greyhound mates was open (not monopolized). Only patricians could own greyhounds, but breeders crossed greyhounds with whatever dogs they wished. Between 1831 and 1882, both populations were open (not monopolized). Anyone could own a greyhound, and breeders could cross greyhounds with any dog. After 1882, the human population of coursers was open (not monopolized) and the greyhound population of public coursers was closed (monopolized). Anyone could own a greyhound, but the National Coursing Club monopolized control over the breeding population. The claim of superiority shifted from the classes of people who could own greyhounds in the patrician era to the classes of greyhounds that could enter contests in the modern era.

In sum, greyhounds coevolved when their traits changed in response to change in human traits. The most radical change came when the National Coursing Club closed the greyhound breeding population. Isolating public greyhounds from other dogs pushed them through an evolutionary bottleneck in which the range of traits narrowed. Closing the breeding pool served human, bureaucratic goals but probably reduced the chance of breeding superior coursers.

Conclusion

Social forces thoroughly modernized the coevolution of greyhounds and people after 1831. The most important forces were democracy, capitalism, bureaucracy, mass communication, and industrial transportation. They modernized coevolution through multiple paths. One route standardized niches – job and habitat dimensions alike – for greyhounds and for people. Standard niches shaped the evolution of greyhound and human populations by rewarding a narrowing of variation in traits. A second route of impact came via breeding. Modern forces helped create a national breeding pool for greyhounds as well as a national meme-sharing pool for people.

Narrowed variation did not mean uniformity for the greyhound population as a whole. Although habitat dimensions narrowed nationally, some variation in habitats remained. Variation also persisted in job descriptions. Contrasts in job descriptions for public greyhounds, private greyhounds, and hare hunters encouraged three populations of greyhounds with distinctive traits.

Human populations coevolved in response to greyhounds and in response to broader social forces. Competing memes spread in the human population in response to the performance of rough and smooth greyhounds. Competing memes emerged regarding the merits of purity and crossbreeding. Coursing contests falsified the claim that "pure" greyhounds were superior, so the popularity of the purity meme probably resulted from broader social forces. A backlash against democracy, along with Christianity and other belief systems, appear to have fostered the purity meme.

The purity meme did shape the evolution of public greyhounds when the National Coursing Club closed the breeding pool in 1882. That year marked a radical transition in the evolution of greyhounds. Dogs that had lived with, and benefited from, porous population boundaries suddenly became an isolated population. Greyhounds passed through an evolutionary bottleneck that narrowed the range of traits available for breeding. It brought seven hundred years of breeding practices to a close and introduced a new era for greyhound evolution.

Notes

1. Hugh Dalziel, *The Greyhound: Its History, Points, Breeding, Rearing, Training, and Running* (London: L. Upcott Gill, 1887), 82–84.
2. Anonymous, "Modern Coursing," *Kennel Gazette*, February 1883, 281–82, see 281.
3. Dalziel, *Greyhound*, 46.
4. John Henry Walsh, *The Dog in Health and Disease. Comprising the Various Modes of Breaking and Using Him for Hunting, Coursing, Shooting, Etc., and Including the Points or Characteristics of All Dogs, Which Are Entirely Rewritten*, 3rd edn. (London: Longmans, Green, 1879), 21, 32.
5. Anonymous, "Revision of the Laws of Coursing and Croquet," *Field*, October 23, 1869.
6. Harding Cox and Gerald Lascelles, *Coursing and Falconry* (London: Longmans, Green, and Company, 1892), 183–86.
7. Cox and Lascelles, *Coursing and Falconry*, 183–86.
8. Anonymous, "Modern Coursing," 281.
9. Dalziel, *Greyhound*, 49.
10. John Henry Walsh, *The Dog, in Health and Disease* (London: Longman, Green, Longman, and Roberts, 1859), 35.
11. Hugh Dalziel, *British Dogs: Their Varieties, History, Characteristics, Breeding, Management, and Exhibition* (London: The Bazaar Office, 1879), 13–14.
12. David Brown, *The Greyhound Stud Book, Established by the Authority of the National Coursing Club 1882*, vol. 1 (Dalry: David Brown, 1882), 36–37.
13. Brown, *Greyhound Stud Book*, 1:36–37.
14. Thomas Goodlake, *Continuation of the Courser's Manual, or Stud Book. Containing the Pedigrees and Performances of Winning Dogs* (London: Simpkin and Marshall, 1833).
15. Robert Abram Welsh, *Thacker's Courser's Annual Remembrancer and Stud Book: Being an Alphabetical Return of the Running at All the Public Coursing Clubs in England, Ireland, and Scotland, for the Season 1852–53; with the Pedigrees (as Far as Received) of the Dogs That Won, and the Dogs That Ran Up Second for Each Prize; Also, a Return of the All Single Matches Run at Those Meetings, and of All Mains of*

Greyhounds, during the Season, That Have Been Made Publicly Known, vol. 13 (London: Longman and Company, 1853). Welsh succeeded Thacker as editor.

16. Robert Welsh, *Thacker's Courser's Annual Remembrancer and Stud Book . . . : With Pedigrees . . . of the Dogs That Ran Up Second for Each Prize . . .* (London: Longman and Company, 1849), 330.

17. Anonymous, "Greyhound Produce," *Field*, February 6, 1869.

18. J. H. Walsh, *Manual of British Rural Sports: Comprising Shooting, Hunting, Coursing, Fishing, Hawking, Racing, Boating, Pedestrianism, and the Various Rural Games and Amusements of Great Britain* (London: G. Routledge, 1856), 163.

19. Walsh, *Manual of British Rural Sports [1856]*, 163.

20. Brown, *Greyhound Stud Book*, 1:36–37.

21. Walsh, *Manual of British Rural Sports [1856]*, 152.

22. Walsh, *Dog in Health and Disease [1859]*, 26.

23. Walsh, *Manual of British Rural Sports [1856]*, 148; Wellesley Pain, "How Greyhounds Are Trained," *Ludgate* 5, February (1898): 435–36; Walsh, *Greyhound [1853]*, 228–40; Delabere Pritchett Blaine, *An Encyclopaedia of Rural Sports: Or a Complete Account, Historical, Practical, and Descriptive, of Hunting, Shooting, Fishing, Racing, and Other Field Sports and Athletic Amusements of the Present Day* (London: Longman, Orme, Brown, Green and Longmans, 1840), 574–75.

24. Walsh, *Dog in Health and Disease [1859]*, 27.

25. Walsh, *Manual of British Rural Sports [1856]*, 148; Blaine, *An Encyclopaedia of Rural Sports [1840]*, 569.

26. Quoted in Charles Hamilton Smith, *The Natural History of Dogs*, vol. 2 (Edinburgh: W.H. Lizars, 1840), 171. See also 173.

27. Smith, *The Natural History of Dogs*, 2:170–73.

28. Quoted in H. D. Richardson, *Dogs; Their Origin and Varieties, Directions as to Their General Management, and Simple Instructions as to Their Treatment under Disease* (Dublin: James McGlashan, 1847), 47.

29. Richardson, *Dogs [1847]*, 47–48.

30. Anonymous, "Coursing.–The Greyhound," *Sportsman's Cabinet, and Town and Country Magazine* 2 (1833): 349–59, see 356.

31. Anonymous, "The Greyhound," *New Sporting Magazine* 4 (1833): 5–8, see 6.

32. Blaine, *An Encyclopaedia of Rural Sports [1840]*, 556–58.

33. Blaine, *An Encyclopaedia of Rural Sports [1840]*, 561–62.

34. Blaine, *An Encyclopaedia of Rural Sports [1840]*, 563–69.

35. Blaine, *An Encyclopaedia of Rural Sports [1840]*, 559–61. Emphasis in original.

36. Blaine, *An Encyclopaedia of Rural Sports [1840]*, 568.

37. Charles Darwin, *The Variation of Animals and Plants under Domestication*, vol. 2 (Baltimore: Johns Hopkins University Press, 1998), 232 (footnote); Charles Darwin, "'Books to Be Read' and 'Books Read' Notebook (1838–1851) CUL-DAR119," accessed October 6, 2015, http://darwin-online.org.uk/.

38. Charles Darwin, *The Origin of Species by Means of Natural Selection or the Preservation of Favoured Races in the Struggle for Life*, 6th edn. (London: Odhams Press, 1872), 31–33, 52–63, 81; Darwin, *The Variation of Animals and Plants under Domestication*, 2:176–236.

39. Smith, *The Natural History of Dogs*; W. C. L. Martin, *The History of the Dog: Its Origin, Physical and Moral Characteristics, and Its Principal Varieties* (London: Charles Knight, 1845); William Youatt, *The Dog* (London: Charles Knight, 1845); William Youatt, *The Dog* (New York: Leavitt and Allen, 1857); Richardson, *Dogs [1847]*; Edward Jesse, *Anecdotes of Dogs* (London: H. G. Bohn, 1858); Walsh, *Dog in Health and Disease [1859]*; John Henry Walsh, *The Dog in Health and Disease: Comprising the Various Modes of Breaking and Using Him for Hunting, Coursing, Shooting, Etc., and Including the Points or Characteristics of Toy Dogs*, 2nd edn. (London: Longmans, Green, Reader & Dyer, 1872); Walsh, *Dog in Health and Disease [1879]*; John H. Walsh, *The Dog in Health and Disease, Comprising the Various Modes of Breaking and Using Him for Hunting, Coursing, Shooting, Etc., and Including the Points or Characteristics of All Dogs, Which Are Entirely Rewritten*, 4th edn. (London: Longmans, Green and Company, 1887); George Richard Jesse, *Researches Into the History of the British Dog: From Ancient Laws, Charters, and Historical Records: With Original Anecdotes, and Illustrations of the Nature and Attributes of the Dog, from the Poets and Prose Writers of Ancient, Medieval and Modern Times* (London: Robert Hardwicke, 1866); J. H. Walsh, *The Dogs of the British Islands, Being a Series of Articles on the Points of Their Various Breeds, and the Treatment of the Diseases to Which They Are Subject*, 3rd edn. (London: "The Field" Office, 1878); John Henry Walsh, *The Dogs of the British Islands: Being a Series of Articles on the Points of Their Various Breeds, and the Treatment of the Diseases to Which They Are Subject*, 4th edn. (London: Horace Cox, 1882); Dalziel, *British Dogs*; E. Gwynne Jones, *A Bibliography of the Dog: Books Published in the English Language, 1570–1965* (London: Library Association, 1971); John Henry Walsh, *The Greyhound: Being a Treatise on the Art of Breeding, Rearing, and Training Greyhounds for Public Running* (London: Longman, Brown, Green & Longmans, 1853); John Henry Walsh, *The Greyhound in 1864* (London: Longman, Green, Longman, Roberts, and Green, 1864); John H. Walsh, *The Greyhound, a Treatise on the Art of Breeding, Rearing, and Training Greyhounds for Public Running, Their Diseases and Treatment, Containing Also the National Rules for the Management of Coursing Meetings and for the Decision of Courses, Also, in an Appendix, an Extended List of Pedigrees* (London: Longmans, Green, 1875); Dalziel, *Greyhound*.

40. Walsh, *Dog in Health and Disease [1859]*, 35–36; Walsh, *Dog in Health and Disease [1879]*, 32.

41. Charles F. Partington, ed., *The British Cyclopedia of Natural History: A Scientific Classification of Animals, Plants, and Minerals; with a Popular View of Their Habits, Economy, and Structure*, vol. 2 (London: Orr and Smith, 1836), 308.

42. William Scrope, *The Art of Deer-Stalking* (London: John Murray, 1838), 334.

43. Smith, *The Natural History of Dogs*, 2:170.

44. Youatt, *The Dog*, 1845, 27–42.

45. W. M., "The Liverpool Waterloo Coursing Meeting," *Sporting Review* 9 (1843): 230–31, see 230.

46. Based on search of Google Books in English from 1500–1900 using Ngram viewer on February 25, 2014. Publication dates are frequently missing or inaccurate in Google Books, so this search may have missed earlier examples.

47. Dalziel, *British Dogs*, 15.

48. Dalziel, *British Dogs*, 14.

49. Dalziel, *British Dogs*, 15.

50. Frederick C. Dietz, *A Political and Social History of England* (New York: Macmillan, 1932), 600–1.

51. Walsh, *Dog in Health and Disease [1859]*, 20–21, emphasis added.

52. Walsh, *Dog in Health and Disease [1859]*, 9.

53. Anonymous, "Coursing," *Sporting Repository* 1, no. 1 (1822): 31–33.

54. Thomas Thacker, *The Courser's Companion, Revised and Enlarged, to Which Is Added the Breeder's Guide, or Breeding in All Its Branches*, 2nd edn., vol. 2 (London: S. T. Probett, 1834):70.

55. Thacker, *Courser's Companion [1834]*, 2:72.

56. Thacker, *Courser's Companion [1834]*, 2:72.

57. Thacker, *Courser's Companion [1834]*, 2:45.

58. Thomas Thacker, *The Courser's Companion*, vol. 1 (London: The author, 1834), 9 (emphasis added).

59. Thacker, *Courser's Companion [1834]*, 1:10–11.

60. Thacker, *Courser's Companion [1834]*, 1:11.

61. Blaine, *An Encyclopaedia of Rural Sports [1840]*, 568.

62. Wellesley Pain, "How Greyhounds Are Trained," *Ludgate* 5, February (1898): 436.

63. Walsh, *Greyhound [1853]*, 229–30.

64. Thacker, *Courser's Companion [1834]*, 2:125.

65. Walsh, *Greyhound [1853]*, 238.

66. Walsh, *Greyhound [1853]*, 237–39, see 239.

67. Dalziel, *Greyhound*, 83.

68. "It Is Not a Little Singular," *Kennel Gazette*, March 1866.

69. Brown, *Greyhound Stud Book*, 1:iii.

70. Brown, *Greyhound Stud Book*, 1:iii.

71. "The Greyhound Stud Book & the National Coursing Club," accessed August 18, 2015, www.greyhoundstudbook.co.uk/.

7

MODERN COEVOLUTION FOR SHOWS (1860–1900)

A radically new niche emerged in the mid-nineteenth century. For more than half a millennium, the job dimension of niches for greyhounds and owners focused on *behavior*. Job descriptions for coursing required (a) greyhounds to run fast and turn hares, and (b) greyhound owners to wager on matches and breed for turning behavior in greyhounds (among other things). Job descriptions for hunting required (a) greyhounds to catch and kill prey, and (b) owners to master the arcane rules of hunting and breed greyhounds that caught and killed prey (among other things). And for more than half a millennium, the habitat dimensions of niches were *outdoor, rural environments*. Coursing and hunting took place in fields and forests. Greyhounds and their owners evolved when they adapted *behavioral* traits to job descriptions and habitats. For greyhounds, selection for behavioral traits shaped physical traits, as when selection for speed led to large chests and wasp waists. Form followed function.

The new niche in the mid-nineteenth century was dog shows. The job and habitat dimensions of show niches contrasted with those in coursing and hunting niches. Instead of prizing behavior, job descriptions in the show niche focused on *appearance*. Instead of demanding outdoor, rural work, the habitat dimension of the show niche required *indoor, urban* work. Greyhounds evolved when they adapted *physical* traits to show niches. The show niche did not demand that greyhounds behave like greyhounds, the essence of earlier job descriptions. Instead, the show job description required that greyhounds *look like* greyhounds. Behavior was all but irrelevant. Greyhounds in coursing and hunting niches had large chests and wasp waists because those traits helped them run fast and far. Greyhounds in the show niche had large chests and wasp waists because those traits helped them *look like* an ideal greyhound, the essence of show job descriptions. The habitat dimension of show niches took standardization to an extreme. Variation in outdoor environments narrowed over the nineteenth century, but variation persisted. Indoor competitions enabled shows to standardize habitats to a degree unavailable outdoors. Holding shows in cities boosted attendance. For people, the show niche focused on behavior more than appearance, but those behaviors focused on making greyhounds look like greyhounds rather than making greyhounds behave like greyhounds.

The show niche, and the evolution it sparked, was thoroughly modern. *Capitalism, industrial transportation, urbanization, mass communication, democracy,* and *bureaucracy* underpinned dog shows. Capitalism played a key role because profit-driven entrepreneurs created and expanded shows. Industrial transportation enabled competitors, greyhounds, and spectators to gather in large numbers at urban shows. Mass communication spread the gospel of shows and show breeding. Democracy enabled people of any class to enter greyhounds in shows. Bureaucracy, in the form of kennel clubs, grew in its power to regulate shows and show breeding. An anti-democratic backlash led patricians to require pedigrees and pure breeding in show dogs.

The trend in evolution for shows was from more to less variation in greyhound and human populations. The main reason was narrowing of variation in the job and habitat dimensions of niches. In the early days of shows, job descriptions and habitats varied widely. Initially, greyhounds had as many job descriptions as there were judges. Shows had no rules for judging, which led each judge to use his own standards to evaluate greyhounds. (All the judges seemed to be men.) Habitats varied, too. Shows took place in outdoor and indoor environments, and entrepreneurs organized indoor space in a variety of ways. Over time, job descriptions for greyhounds and judges narrowed. Shows and clubs issued breed standards for evaluating greyhounds. Variation in habitats narrowed, too. Spatial arrangements converged on indoor benches for showing dogs.

Urbanization, Capitalism, and Industrial Transportation

Urbanization appears to have spawned dog shows. In the early to mid-nineteenth century, London pubs hosted shows for dogs owned by a group of men known as the Fancy (a contraction of *fantasy*, which led to the term *fancier*). The Fancy enjoyed rough sports, such as boxing and dog fighting. Its members showed off their fighting dogs (such as bull terriers) and, oddly enough, dainty pet dogs. An Italian greyhound (a small pet breed) won a silver collar in an 1851 contest. We know nothing about the contest, but it might have been a show organized by the urban

Fancy.[1] Research for this book found no evidence that large greyhounds competed in these early shows of the London Fancy.

Capitalism played a key role in creating show niches for large greyhounds and their owners. In 1859, an entrepreneurial gun maker named Pape took advantage of a poultry show in Newcastle-on-Tyne to advertise his products. He sponsored a companion contest featuring two breeds of gundogs, setters and pointers, which judges evaluated for appearance. Pointing to game birds played no role in the event. So far as we know, Pape did not turn a direct profit from his show. The contest was an investment in marketing that might lead to profit down the road through gun sales. Later the same year, one of Pape's judges, Richard Brailsford, organized a dog show in conjunction with a Birmingham cattle show. Brailsford worked for an aristocrat as a dog breeder and trainer. His Birmingham dog show attracted eighty entries in eleven classes. It turned a profit, so Brailsford organized a second show at Birmingham the next year.[2] It, too, turned a profit.[3] The Birmingham show became an annual event and the leading show in Britain.

Entrepreneurial imitators created show niches, including for greyhounds, in other cities.[4] These entrepreneurs gained income from subscriptions, entry fees, and gate admissions. Show organizers approached wealthy, eminent individuals for subscriptions (donations) while organizing shows. The donations defrayed expenses, and the names of subscribers lent prestige to the events. Organizers charged fees to entrants and spectators. After paying expenses (mainly advertising, space rental, and prizes), entrepreneurs took the net income as profit.

Some participants recoiled from the capitalist ideology of shows, which seemed all about lining the pockets of organizers rather than benefiting entrants or their dogs. One of the subscribers to the Leeds show had the impression his money would be used "for the improvement of the breed of dogs." He realized, though, that subscribers and contestants were "giving our money away and lending our dogs for private speculators to make a profit of."[5] *The Field* was an early proponent of dog shows, and its editor (John H. Walsh) was one of the judges at Pape's 1859 show. After four years of profit-driven shows, Walsh grew disgusted. *The Field* complained in 1863, "We have ceased to place any confidence in that species of speculation."[6]

Some entrepreneurial entrants, on the other hand, approached dog shows with the same spirit of profit as organizers. Greyhound breeders often entered shows to sell their dogs. Organizers encouraged this practice by publishing show catalogs with the purchase price for every greyhound entered. The prices for greyhounds at the 1860 Birmingham show, for example, ranged from 25 to 200 pounds.[7] Entrants who wanted to keep their dogs set astronomical prices, such as 1,000 guineas.[8] Breeders welcomed show prizes as a way to drive up the value of their stock. Some of these breeders were not afraid of conflicts of interest. Dealers serving as judges awarded prizes to dogs they had sold to exhibitors, which helped the dealers gain reputations as breeders of winning dogs, which raised the price they could charge for dogs in the future.[9]

Yoked to capitalism, urbanization helped to create show jobs for greyhounds. More entrants and spectators meant higher profits, so entrepreneurs located shows in large cities to maximize entries and attendance. In locating his show in one of the centers of the Industrial Revolution, Birmingham, Brailsford created a model other entrepreneurs would follow. Large shows appeared in other industrial cities, such as Leeds, Nottingham, and Manchester.

Industrial transportation helped nationalize show niches for greyhounds. Railroads carried dogs, contestants, and spectators from distant regions to shows. Brailsford called his 1860 show The *National* Exhibition of Sporting and Other Dogs, which declared that the show intended to draw entrants from across England.[10] The press and railroads – which expanded rapidly in the 1840s and 1850s – drew in large numbers of competitors, dogs, and spectators. The press announced upcoming shows, and trains enabled people to travel quickly to any show. Entrepreneurs located shows near urban train stations, making it easy to walk to them once arriving in a city, and they advertised details of which trains to take. A Leeds show took place in a building five minutes away from the Great Northern and Midland Railway station.[11] A Nottingham show of 1873 announced that seven railroads were making "liberal concessions" for show participants, and "special trains run from nearly all parts." The catalog included advertisements from railway companies.[12] Participation in shows soared. An 1880 list of one year's exhibitors in dog shows covered 102 pages.[13]

In sum, shows created radically new niches by changing habitats and job descriptions alike. Earlier niches had greyhounds and their owners work in rural habitats. Show niches had greyhounds and owners work in urban habitats. The job dimension of show niches differed, too. Earlier jobs required greyhounds to *behave* in certain ways. Show jobs required greyhounds to *look* certain ways. Greyhounds sat still while judges and spectators peered at them. Job descriptions for some show niches and coursing events conflicted in ways that made it hard for some greyhounds and owners to perform both jobs.[14] The Birmingham show took place during coursing season, so few coursers entered greyhounds in it.[15] This conflict offered an early hint that coursing and show niches would encourage the formation of distinct populations of people and greyhounds.

Standardization of Habitats and Jobs

Early dog show niches varied in habitats. Some took place outdoors and some indoors. For the first Leeds show, organizers erected a temporary roof over a showground. A hard rain drenched entrants and their dogs, creating fears that dogs would sicken and die.[16] Show organizers learned from the experience and moved indoors. The first show in London (other than those organized by the urban Fancy), the Holborn show of 1861, took place under a glass roof that pleased entrants because it provided protection from the weather while letting in light.[17] Once indoors, entrepreneurs began standardizing spaces. An 1863 Islington show set up benches for dogs.[18] Spectators and judges would walk between the benches inspecting the dogs, which were chained or caged in place. Other shows followed this example, leading shows to become known as "bench shows." Although outdoor coursing environments grew more standardized over the nineteenth century, they still offered variation in weather, terrain, and hares. Show benches pushed the standardization of greyhound working environments to a new extreme.

Job descriptions in early show niches varied, too. This held true for people as well as greyhounds. Entrepreneurs chose "knowledgeable men" as judges and trusted them to know quality when they saw it. This plan failed. Judges used idiosyncratic criteria, which left contestants confused and angry. At best, exhibitors thought, judges were incompetent. In an angry letter to the editor of a newspaper (angry letters to editors about judging became a popular genre), "A Sportsman" argued that the cure for bad judging was to appoint as judges sportsmen and gentlemen 'who [know] what a dog is.'"[19] Conflicts of interest multiplied problems. Some shows chose competitors to judge the events in which they entered dogs, leading judges to award prizes to their own dogs (that is, to themselves).[20] Judges also awarded prizes to the entrepreneurs who organized shows, making shows look like self-promotional charades.[21]

These complaints, though valid, overlooked a bigger reality: shows created *new* jobs with *new* job descriptions for greyhounds. The central conceit of shows was that physical traits were sure guides to performance in earlier greyhound jobs. By looking at the size of a greyhound's chest and the girth of its waist, show judges could predict a greyhound's speed and endurance. The problem was that physical traits correlated only loosely with behaviors, and some beliefs about correlations were false. As we saw, many coursers believed that rough and brindled greyhounds were inferior to smooth, evenly colored greyhounds. When given the chance, though, rough and brindled greyhounds falsified these claims. The rough greyhound Gilbertfield defeated all but one smooth greyhound in four years of competition, and the brindled greyhounds Fullerton and Young Fullerton became two of the most successful greyhounds of their era.

It soon became clear that shows lacked (a) the ability to evaluate the most important traits in prior canine jobs, i.e., behaviors, and (b) standards to evaluate the most important traits in show jobs, i.e., physical traits. Commenting on an 1862 Islington show, a journalist complained that judges awarded prizes "more to perfection of canine form than to intellectual merit, there being no opportunities of forming an estimate of a pointer's pointing, a retriever's retrieving, a bull-dog's bullying, or an Italian greyhound's aggravating."[22] Judges paid so little attention to behavior that they rated a blind dog highly commended. A woman bought the dog at a high price before discovering its disability.[23] Even when one accepted that shows rewarded appearance alone, the standards seemed wildly inconsistent. In some cases, show jobs seemed to prize beauty. In greyhounds, judges valued size, depth of chest, and symmetry. In other cases, they rewarded ugliness. In bulldogs, show-winning individuals were "bandy, blear-eyed, pink-nosed, blotchy, underhung, and utterly disreputable."[24]

Contestants and judges turned to dog books for show job descriptions, but this strategy failed. Before 1859, naturalists and dog writers wrote books that helped the public recognize breeds and understand their jobs. Two standard works on sporting dogs, including greyhounds, came out just before the rise of shows: William Youatt's *The Dog* (1857) and John H. Walsh's *The Dog in Health and Disease* (1859).[25] Their texts described traits of each breed, but the descriptions noted variation in traits. This approach made sense, because breeders tailored greyhounds to multiple jobs and environments. But, when applied to show greyhounds, these descriptions proved, in Walsh's words, "too loose in detail to serve as guides to young breeders or incipient judges."[26] The show ring converted variation from a virtue into a problem. If Walsh said greyhounds could vary in size, how was a show judge to know whether a tall greyhound was better or worse than a short greyhound?

Walsh led the way to a solution by writing a job description for show greyhounds and other breeds. His position as editor of *The Field*, the premier sporting newspaper in Britain, gave him the ideal platform. In 1865, he began a series of articles in *The Field* listing the ideal *points* (meaning "desirable external traits," not numerical values) for show breeds.[27] The goal was to describe points, concretely and in enough detail, so that breeders and judges had a shared understanding of the traits rewarded at shows.[28] It took Walsh and collaborators years to issue standards for the growing number of show breeds.

Adoption of standardized job descriptions appears to have begun in 1868, when shows began stating the standards for judging.[29] In 1869, a show gave each judge a list of points for each breed, the judges applied them, and most competitors went away satisfied. Competitors could challenge a decision, but only one did so. It must have been the least controversial set of judging decisions to that date.[30] The show failed to make money, but breeders were grateful for the show's book of points.[31] The success of this effort encouraged other shows to adopt breed standards for judging, too.

Because each show defined its own niches, it took almost two decades for the chaotic show world to standardize job descriptions. Shows worked in an unregulated market. No organization governed the sport, leaving decisions about judging in the hands of each show organizer. As it became clear that standards reduced conflicts among judges and competitors, however, the variation in memes about standards narrowed. In 1878, Walsh announced, "we have now arrived at a definite agreement on all points."[32] This agreement led Walsh to revise his 1859 book on dogs to serve the needs of the show world. The new, 1878 edition incorporated revisions of *The Field*'s breed standards.[33] Hugh Dalziel published a similar book with show standards in 1879.[34] Clubs specializing in breeds later took the lead in writing standards.[35]

Shows shaped human evolution by changing the frequency of memes about classification and quality. Two editions of Walsh's *The Dog in Health and Disease* provide benchmarks. We saw in Chapter 6 that in 1859, just before shows became popular, Walsh described "the rough Scotch greyhound and deerhound" before any other greyhound breed. He identified it as one of the oldest and purest breeds in existence. Memes about breeds varied enough that Walsh described this dog as both one breed and two breeds. He said the rough Scotch greyhound and deerhound looked the same, which enabled him to use one image to illustrate both and use the singular *breed*. But the two dogs behaved differently while pursuing prey, which enabled Walsh to split them into two breeds differentiated only by behavior.[36] (See Figure 6.3.) In other words, Walsh offered two memes for classifying breeds before the rise of shows. Appearance was one way. Behavior was another, equally valid, way.

Walsh narrowed the variation in memes while fighting to standardize show judging. Show standards prized smooth coats over rough coats. In the 1879 edition of the book, Walsh discussed the smooth greyhound first. He reversed course on evolution by claiming, "This beautiful [smooth] animal is by many considered to be the original of all our domestic breeds." Walsh equated short coats with quality: "With regard to *coat*, a very high breed is evidenced by its shortness and silkiness of coat." Most of the section focused on show standards for greyhound appearance.[37] A section titled "the deerhound and rough greyhound" appeared second. It deleted the 1859 claims about the ancient and pure nature of the deerhound and rough greyhound. Other than in the section title, the text omitted rough greyhounds. Walsh used the same image as in 1859, but he said nothing about the rough greyhound looking the same as (but behaving differently from) the Scotch greyhound. Walsh described the deerhound as "more ornamental than useful." He included a long section describing show points for the deerhound.[38] In just two decades, then, rough greyhounds went from being the original, pure greyhounds to being written out of the greyhound family because they had no place in the show world. The Scotch greyhound went from a breed distinguished by behavior to a breed defined by appearance.

The show system had invented a new meme for classifying and evaluating greyhounds – as packages of physical traits rather than as packages of physical and behavioral traits. Authors of show standards claimed, however, to value the same traits as coursers. In 1879, Hugh Dalziel listed the physical traits that he believed created the behavioral traits needed in coursing greyhounds. Courage depended on the width of the head: "A greyhound should measure well round the head, across and at back of ears, which is a sure indication of the courage that gives dash and persistence to their efforts."[39] He continued in a similar vein for the rest of the greyhound's physique. It was a form of phrenology (predicting physiology from physiognomy) applied to the whole body.

Despite the confidence of Walsh and Dalziel, the memes published in the late 1870s failed to define show jobs adequately. Breed standards reduced variation in memes about quality, but they reduced variation too little to prevent conflicts. One reason was that the standards were often qualitative rather than quantitative. Dalziel's standard said greyhounds should "measure well round the head." Breeders and judges could interpret qualitative descriptions of this sort in different ways, so the show world moved to quantification. In 1887, Dalziel published a revision of his greyhound standard that reflected this shift. His discussion of the head provides an example: "The Head. – Long and lean, but wide between ears, measuring in girth, just before or close in behind, about 15 in. in a dog 26 in. high, with a length from occiput to nose of about 10 in. to 10–1/2 in."[40] Now show judges could pull out a tape measure and tell anyone whether a greyhound's head or muzzle was of high or low quality. Breeders had to work within half an inch of variation, pushing the sort of extreme standardization of physical traits never dreamed of in the coursing world.

Although shows claimed to reward the same traits as coursing, they did not. Physical traits of show and coursing greyhounds diverged. In his 1887 book on greyhounds, Dalziel provided measurements from three Waterloo Cup winners (to which I have added a fourth) and three "good show dogs [that] may be taken as a fair average."[41] Show greyhounds were larger and less varied than Waterloo Cup winners. (See Figure 7.1.) In addition to the three populations of greyhounds described in the previous chapter, then, a fourth population – show greyhounds – developed distinctive traits in the late nineteenth century.

In sum, shows shaped the evolution of greyhounds and people in several ways. First, they gave people and greyhounds new jobs in new niches. Human and greyhound populations adapted to those new niches. Second, shows narrowed variation in niches. Early shows took place in varied habitats using varied job descriptions for greyhounds. Later shows took place in standard habitats (indoor benches) using standard job descriptions (breed standards). But, because early standards were qualitative, they proved insufficient to prevent conflicts. New breed standards relied on quantification. Third, shows created human and greyhound populations with different traits from other populations.

Patrician Backlash and Bureaucracy

A patrician backlash against democracy became one of the more important forces shaping the evolution of greyhounds (and other dogs) in

Feature	Show dogs average size (inches)	Waterloo winners average size (inches)	Difference in average size (inches or pounds)
head--snout to neck	10	9.2	0.8
head--girth	14.8	14.1	0.8
head--snout girth	8.2	7.8	0.3
tail	18.8	18.3	0.6
foreleg--before elbow	6.8	6.3	0.4
body--girth chest	30.6	27.6	3
body--girth loins	21.3	20.4	0.9
weight	65.2	52.3	12.8

Feature	Show dogs--standard deviation	Waterloo winners-- standard deviation	Difference in standard deviation
head--snout to neck	0.9	0.6	0.3
head--girth	0.3	1.2	−0.9
head--snout girth	0.5	1	−0.5
tail	0.3	1.5	−1.2
foreleg--before elbow	0.3	0.6	−0.3
body--girth chest	0.9	1.9	−1.1
body--girth loins	0.6	3	−2.4
weight	7.3	6.7	0.6

Figure 7.1 Show greyhounds and coursing greyhounds. Shows claimed that they rewarded the traits that made greyhounds good coursers. The upper table shows that show greyhounds were larger, in every dimension, than coursing greyhounds. The lower table shows that show dogs varied less than coursing greyhounds in six of eight traits. (Standard deviation measures variation in a population. The higher the number, the greater the variation.) Waterloo Cup winners provided a conservative measure of variation because all won in the same place under the same rules. Coursing dogs overall would have varied more than Waterloo winners because environments, hares, and rules varied. Table created by author from data in Hugh Dalziel, *The Greyhound; Its History, Points, Breeding, Rearing, Training, and Running* (London: L. Upcott Gill, 1887), 35–36; and David Brown, *The Greyhound Stud Book, Established by the Authority of the National Coursing Club 1882*, vol. 1 (Dalry: David Brown, 1882), 47. The table includes only features for which sources supplied data for both populations.

shows. The leader of the backlash was Sewallis Evelyn Shirley. Born at Stratford upon Avon in 1844, Shirley was a member of the gentry. He attended Eton and Oxford but left before finishing his degree. Inherited privilege rescued him from academic failure. His family owned a large estate in County Monaghan, Ireland, as well as property in Ettington, Warwickshire. In 1868, Sewallis won election to Parliament for County Monaghan as a Conservative dedicated to preserving the Protestant constitution. He had an undistinguished Parliamentary career. He rarely participated in debates and lost his seat to a Liberal supporter of tenants' rights in 1880. He ran again for Parliament in 1885 but lost to an Irish nationalist.[42] As a landlord, Shirley gained a reputation for ruthless opposition to tenant rights. Shirley inherited his father's Monaghan estate in 1882. In 1887, during an agricultural depression, 150 police armed with rifles and batons evicted tenants from Shirley's estate while a crowd numbering more than 1,000 followed to cheer and jeer.[43] Shirley's harsh treatment of tenants made him a target of the Plan of Campaign of 1887, which aimed to reduce tenant rents when agricultural prices were low.[44]

Capitalism joined democracy in revealing Shirley's weaknesses to the world. In 1870, in the midst of his first undistinguished tour in Parliament, Shirley decided to become a dog show entrepreneur. He rented London's Crystal Palace, a prime location, but lost money on the show. This was a feat. Shows in other cities were thriving, and London offered the biggest market in the land. Usually organizers tried to attract entrants and spectators from London to other cities. Shirley had Londoners in his back pocket but failed anyway. He organized a second London show and lost money again.[45]

Pummeled by democracy and capitalism, Shirley responded with a classic patrician strategy: forming an exclusive club to control people and animals. In 1873, Shirley and twelve other men founded the Kennel Club in London.[46] Two kinds of coursing clubs could have offered models for the Kennel Club: (1) the National Coursing Club, founded in 1858, or (2) the exclusive, local, patrician clubs of the transitional decades. The democratic nature of the National Coursing Club was anathema to Shirley, so it is no surprise he avoided its model. The elite nature of patrician coursing clubs was more to Shirley's taste, but these clubs exercised no control over people beyond members.

Shirley wanted patrician control of dog shows on a national scale, which led him to turn to the Jockey Club as his model. Formed in the eighteenth century by aristocrats and members of the gentry, the Jockey

Club sponsored horse races, regulated racing, and served as an exclusive club for men who relished the prestige of horse racing and royal patronage. The Kennel Club followed the Jockey Club's example almost to the letter. It sponsored dog shows, regulated shows, and created an exclusive club for men who relished the prestige of dog shows and royal patronage.[47] The Prince of Wales became the Kennel Club's patron in 1873 and continued in that role upon ascending to the throne in 1901.[48] The Kennel Club was a London gentlemen's club as well as an organization of men with shared interests. It took over a three-room flat on Victoria Street before moving to roomier quarters on Pall Mall in 1877.[49] In 1902, the club moved to Grafton Street in, as *The Kennel Gazette* (the Kennel Club's mouthpiece, edited by Shirley) put it, "the very centre of Club-land."[50] To ensure exclusivity, the club originally limited membership to 100 men.[51] Shirley served as Kennel Club chairman for 25 years.[52]

Patrician control was anathema to the democratic, individualistic, capitalistic world of dog shows. In 1874, one year after its founding, The Kennel Club issued rules for dog shows and asked organizers to adopt them. The Kennel Club claimed that rampant fraud in dog shows demanded an overlord. It was true that competitors sometimes cheated, e.g., by improving a dog's color with blacking, but this focus appears to have been a pretext. The Kennel Club did not document the extent of fraud and did little to investigate or police it. Most show organizers refused to adopt the Kennel Club rules. They saw the club as a group of self-appointed autocrats meddling in their business. In 1880, only 17 percent of independent shows and field trials (tests of gun dogs in the field) used the Kennel Club's rules.[53]

While trying to assert patrician control over shows, Shirley launched a Kennel Club studbook to promote an inherited-superiority meme. Thacker's studbook for coursing greyhounds offered a model, as did the studbook associated with Shirley's idol, the Jockey Club. In the eighteenth century, James Weatherby published a calendar that reported the results of horse races and served as the voice of the Jockey Club. Horse owners sometimes lied about the identity of their horses, so the Jockey Club welcomed Weatherby's proposal to create a studbook to identify horses. In 1791, he published *An Introduction to a General Stud-Book*, which collected information on horses that had raced over the previous fifty years. The Weatherby family, which owned the studbook, published updates over the years.[54] Beginning in 1874, Shirley and the Kennel Club co-published an annual canine studbook, which included greyhounds.[55]

The studbook stated its purpose – proving inherited superiority – on the first page of the first volume. "The value of blood and pedigree is demonstrated on every page as nine-tenths of the later prize winners trace back to prize blood," the editor wrote.[56] Every page did not, in fact, support this claim. No matter. Soon the Kennel Club claimed that pure breeding, in addition to pedigrees, created excellence. In the third studbook (1876), the editor argued that pedigrees would lead to purity and excellence in dogs in the same way that herd books and studbooks had "marvelously refined and elevated the bovine and equine races." He encouraged dog shows to require pedigrees for all entries, "and then, and not until then, shall we have purity of blood."[57]

The democratic, meritocratic world of dog shows had little interest in memes claiming that inheritance, rather than performance, determined superiority. Shows did not require pedigrees for entry, and judges evaluated the greyhounds in front of them rather than ancestors. Of 139 greyhounds that won shows before 1874, 100 (72 percent) lacked information about parents or grandparents on one or both sides.[58] The patrician Shirley found the democratic lack of interest in pedigrees incomprehensible. "It is astonishing how few exhibitors know, or even care to know, the pedigrees of their dogs," he marveled.[59]

The Kennel Club decided to force pedigrees on the show world, which sparked a democratic backlash. In 1880, the club issued a rule that all dogs, including greyhounds, had to be registered in the Kennel Club's studbook before they could compete in shows run under the Kennel Club's rules. Because a minority of shows used Kennel Club rules, the registration requirement had little immediate impact. The Birmingham show refused to require its exhibitors to register their dogs with the Kennel Club, and it joined several notables of the dog world (including Walsh and Dalziel) to found a rival National Dog Club.[60] The key idea of the National Dog Club was elected governance.

Now two clubs, one aiming to perpetuate patrician privilege and the other to promote democratic self-governance, struggled for primacy. *Stock-Keeper and Fancier's Chronicle* noted that

> these clubs represent two opposite principles which never yet in human history have been reconciled, and must ever be from their nature in contention ... – that is, government by self-election or government by election of those practically interested in dogs – it cannot be ignored that the Kennel Club is the embodiment of the former, whilst the National Dog Club adopts the latter principle.[61]

The self-interested patrician motives of the Kennel Club seemed obvious. As *Stock-Keeper and Fancier's Chronicle* added, the "little good the Kennel Club has done is not merely counterbalanced, but smothered beneath the accumulated acts of wrong and arrogant dictation framed to answer personal or class purposes."[62]

The Kennel Club beat the democratic challenge by co-opting it. The club granted two seats on a Kennel Club committee to the Birmingham show, plus an honorary membership in the Kennel Club for the organizer of the Birmingham show. The Birmingham organizer accepted this humiliation (the honorary membership made him a second-class citizen, not a full member of the Kennel Club). Birmingham adopted Kennel Club rules, the National Dog Club foundered, and opposition to Kennel Club rules and its studbook folded in the show world.[63] Deciding to appeal to capitalistic and meritocratic values, the club decreed that the studbook would list prizes only from shows that adopted Kennel Club rules. This was an effective strategy because independent shows wanted their prizes in the studbook, and breeders wanted prizes in all shows listed with their dogs' names to enhance sales and reputation. The rule went into effect in 1883. The number of shows adopting Kennel Club rules soared from seven in 1880 to thirty-nine in 1883.[64]

The Kennel Club probably prompted the democratic National Coursing Club to adopt a purity-superiority meme at the same time. As discussed previously, the National Coursing Club saw no need to compile a studbook or require registration of greyhounds until 1881, one year after the Kennel Club decided to require registration of show greyhounds (and other show breeds). The registration rules of both clubs went into effect in 1883. These decisions helped to separate coursing and show greyhounds by creating separate studbooks for the two populations.

Publishing a studbook and embracing pure breeding (by closing the breeding pool) was not enough, however, to raise the National Coursing Club in the eyes of the Kennel Club. In 1883, *The Kennel Gazette* argued that democracy would deprive the National Coursing Club of the respect that large landowners gave the Kennel Club. Coursers at the open Waterloo Cup elected the National Coursing Club's members. "And might it not have been different if, instead of the radical representative idea, which invariably puts a lot of nobodies into power," the gazette sneered, "the National Coursing Club had started as a representative body of gentlemen of county standing, men who all had estates to be coursed over, and who could discuss the well-being of a sport on an equality, and with a dignity that would have demanded respect?"[65]

The Kennel Club's enforcement of patrician privilege proceeded in eerie parallel with Shirley's efforts to enforce inherited privilege in his personal life. Shirley lost his seat in Parliament to an advocate of tenants' rights in 1880, and three years later the Kennel Club complained that "the radical representative idea ... puts a lot of nobodies into power" at the National Coursing Club. Shirley inherited his father's Monaghan estate in 1882, and one year later the Kennel Club asserted that the National Coursing Club would have commanded respect if its members were "gentlemen of country standing ... who all had estates." In 1883, the Birmingham show refused to knuckle under to the Kennel Club's demand for control over the show. The Kennel Club triumphed by making small concessions while emphasizing that the Birmingham show organizer was not an equal. In 1887, Shirley's tenants protested high rents at a time of low agricultural prices. Shirley conceded a 20 percent reduction in rent but emphasized he was in control by evicting tenants and seizing the property of tenant leaders.[66]

Although initially an unwelcome imposition of patrician privilege on the show world, the Kennel Club studbook grew in predictive value as show niches narrowed. The standardization of job and habitat dimensions of niches rewarded inbreeding from winners in show greyhounds in the same way it rewarded inbreeding from Waterloo Cup winners in coursing greyhounds. The show world standardized indoor environments in the 1860s, adopted standard job descriptions (breed standards) in the late 1860s and 1870s, and narrowed job descriptions (making greyhound standards more precise and quantitative) in the 1880s. The Kennel Club studbook first appeared in 1874, after greyhound show jobs were standardized. The studbook's impact accelerated in the 1880s, when the registration rule expanded pedigrees at the same time that job descriptions narrowed. As with other claims to "improve" animals, show breeders did not improve greyhounds in any universal sense. They did improve their ability to succeed in narrow job–environment combinations created by shows.

In sum, an anti-democratic backlash by patricians created a radical transition in greyhound evolution. A patrician, manhandled by democracy and capitalism, created the Kennel Club as a bastion of inherited privilege among men. The capitalistic, democratic, meritocratic world of dog shows rejected autocratic patrician control of shows and had little interest in pedigrees and purity. After failing to convince the show world to accept patrician memes about inherited superiority, the Kennel Club succeeded in gaining control of shows by appealing to meritocratic and entrepreneurial values. Commercial breeders and recreational competitors wanted their prizes recorded in the Kennel Club studbook. The price of inclusion was competing in shows run under Kennel Club rules, which put pressure on shows to adopt those rules. Other inducements, such as (second-class) membership in the Kennel Club, helped co-opt opponents. These measures enabled the Kennel Club to close the breeding pool of show greyhounds and most likely prompted the same action for coursing greyhounds by the National Coursing Club. Seven hundred centuries of evolution in porous populations entered a new era of evolution in hermetic populations.

Conclusion

Dog shows created new niches that pushed human–greyhound coevolution in new directions. For centuries, the English valued greyhounds for their behavior. Shows ignored behavior and prized appearance. The job of greyhounds shifted from behaving like greyhounds to looking like greyhounds. At first, the greyhounds holding this new job came from the ranks of dogs holding other jobs, such as coursing and hunting. It became clear, though, that show jobs were unique, and show greyhounds split off to form a new population. Shows changed the habitats of greyhounds, too. Instead of working in outdoor, rural habitats, show greyhounds toiled in indoor, urban habitats. Indoor bench shows standardized habitats to a degree unavailable in the outdoors.

These forces converged to push show greyhounds toward extreme uniformity. Shows created the narrowest, most standardized job combinations greyhounds had ever encountered. Coursing and hunting greyhounds had to display many behaviors to win, including seeing, running, anticipating, turning, and sometimes killing hares. All these behaviors came off the table in early shows, to be replaced by one behavior – staying still. Coursing and hunting greyhounds varied in appearance, especially before homogenization in the mid-nineteenth century. Shows forced breeders to conform to breed standards, or written descriptions of the ideal member of a breed. Coursing and hunting greyhounds encountered varied terrain and weather. Show greyhounds competed indoors, which standardized terrain and weather.

The ability of greyhounds and other breeds to compete in shows circled back to shape human experience. Patricians keen to regain status in a democratic age used shows to form an exclusive club and control dog breeding. Many of the ideas we hold about dog breeds today cohered in shows in the late nineteenth century. Shows promoted the idea that breeds were isolated, uniform populations of animals defined by appearance and ancestry (rather than varied populations defined by jobs and behaviors). They pushed the idea of pure breeding and pedigrees as guarantees of superiority, which required a bureaucracy to register and regulate the breeding world. Shows encouraged inbreeding from winners, giving a few dogs the power to shape the traits of many dogs. Shows introduced the novel idea that all breeds could hold the same job. Many of these ideas remain with us today.

Notes

1. John Henry Walsh, *The Dog in Health and Disease: Comprising the Various Modes of Breaking and Using Him for Hunting, Coursing, Shooting, Etc., and Including the Points or Characteristics of Toy Dogs* (London: Longman, Green, Longman, and Roberts, 1859), 46.
2. Anonymous, "Exhibition of Sporting Dogs at Birmingham," *Field*, December 3, 1859, 458; "Catalogue of the National Exhibition of Sporting and Other Dogs, Held at the Midland Counties Repository, Cheapside, Birmingham, on Monday and Tuesday, December 3rd and 4th," 1860, "Council for 1860" (unpaginated), Birmingham Catalogues 1860–67, Kennel Club Library, London.
3. Anonymous, "North of England Exhibition of Dogs," *Field*, July 20, 1861, 55.
4. "Catalogue of the Second Great Annual Exhibition of Sporting and Other Dogs, Held in Extensive Premises in Tennant Street, Broad Street, near Bingley Hall, Birmingham, Monday, Tuesday, and Wednesday, the 2nd, 3rd, and 4th December," 1861, Birmingham Catalogues 1860–67, Kennel Club Library, London; Anonymous, "The Dog Shows Have Now Become so General," *Field*, August 10, 1861, 134.
5. Summum Bonum, "The Exhibition of Sporting Dogs in London," *Field*, August 10, 1861, 134.
6. Anonymous, "Give a Dog a Bad Name, and–," *Field*, February 21, 1863, 165.
7. "Catalogue of the National Exhibition of Sporting and Other Dogs, Birmingham, 1860," 8–9.
8. Anonymous, "A Thousand Dogs," *Leisure Hour* 11 (August 30, 1862): 557.
9. Anonymous, "Dealing Judges," *Stock-Keeper and Fancier's Chronicle*, April 11, 1884, 400.
10. "Catalogue of the National Exhibition of Sporting and Other Dogs, Birmingham, 1860."
11. Anonymous, "North of England Exhibition of Dogs."
12. "Catalogue of the Fourth Annual Exhibition of the National Canine Society, Held by Special Permission of the Corporation in the Market Place, Nottingham, on Thursday, Friday, Saturday, and Monday, October 2nd, 4rd, 5th, and 6th, 1873" (T. Forman and Sons, 1873), 11, Various Catalogues 1868 to 1874, Kennel Club Library, London.

13. Edward Brown, *The Fancier's Directory: Containing the Names and Addresses of All Judges and Exhibitors of Dogs, Poultry, Pigeons, Cage Birds, Rabbits, and Cats, in the United Kingdom, from April 1879 to March 1880* (London: Cassell, Petter, Galpin, 1880).

14. "Catalogue of the National Exhibition of Sporting and Other Dogs, Birmingham, 1860."

15. A Member of "The Former Committee," "National Dog Show," *Field*, May 12, 1860, 390; Sight-Seer, "Birmingham Dog Show," *Field*, December 15, 1860, 498; A Subscriber to the Field and an Exhibitor at the Dog Show, "The National Exhibition of Dogs," *Field*, December 22, 1860, 516.

16. Anonymous, "North of England Exhibition of Dogs."

17. Anonymous, "The Great London Exhibition of Sporting and Other Dogs," *Field*, October 5, 1851, 306.

18. Anonymous, "International Dog Show at Islington," *Field*, May 30, 1863, 515.

19. A Sportsman, "The Leeds Dog Show," *Field*, August 10, 1861, 134.

20. Daniel, "The Birmingham Dog Show," *Field*, December 10, 1864, 410.

21. Old Calabar, "Dog Shows and Dog Trials. The Late Bala Field Trials, Etc. Etc.," *London Society*, 1873; Anonymous, "Would-Be Reformers," *Kennel Gazette*, December 1882, 233–34.

22. Anonymous, "Two Dog-Shows," *All the Year Round*, August 2, 1862, 493–94.

23. A. Wells, "Dog Purchased as Islington Show," *Field*, June 24, 1865, 442.

24. Anonymous, "Two Dog-Shows," 493–94.

25. William Youatt, *The Dog* (New York: Leavitt and Allen, 1857); Walsh, *Dog in Health and Disease [1859]*.

26. J. H. Walsh, *The Dogs of the British Islands, Being a Series of Articles on the Points of Their Various Breeds, and the Treatment of the Diseases to Which They Are Subject*, 3rd edn. (London: "The Field" Office, 1878), iii.

27. Walsh, *Dog in Health and Disease [1859]*, 24.

28. Walsh, *Dogs of the British Islands [1878]*, iii–iv.

29. A Sporting Dog, "Judging at Dog Shows," *Field*, October 31, 1868, 363.

30. Anonymous, "The National Dog Club's First Exhibition," *Field*, June 5, 1869, 466.

31. G. H. Rushton, "A Breeder's Book of Dogs," *Field*, May 7, 1870, 397.

32. Walsh, *Dogs of the British Islands [1878]*, iv.

33. Walsh, *Dogs of the British Islands [1878]*, 56.

34. Hugh Dalziel, *British Dogs: Their Varieties, History, Characteristics, Breeding, Management, and Exhibition* (London: The Bazaar Office, 1879).

35. Canis Amator, "The National Dog Club," *Field*, March 13, 1869, 228.

36. Walsh, *Dog in Health and Disease [1859]*, 20–21.

37. John Henry Walsh, *The Dog in Health and Disease. Comprising the Various Modes of Breaking and Using Him for Hunting, Coursing, Shooting, Etc., and Including the Points or Characteristics of All Dogs, Which Are Entirely Rewritten*, 3rd edn. (London: Longmans, Green, 1879), 19–32.

38. Walsh, *Dog in Health and Disease [1879]*, 32–37.

39. Dalziel, *British Dogs*, 22.

40. Hugh Dalziel, *The Greyhound: Its History, Points, Breeding, Rearing, Training, and Running* (London: L. Upcott Gill, 1887), 32.

41. Dalziel, *Greyhound*, 35–36; David Brown, *The Greyhound Stud Book, Established by the Authority of the National Coursing Club 1882*, vol. 1 (Dalry: David Brown, 1882), 47.
42. Michael Worboys, ""Shirley, Sewallis Evelyn (1844–1904)," in *Oxford Dictionary of National Biography*, ed. Lawrence Goldman (Oxford: Oxford University Press, 2010), www.oxforddnb.com/view/article/100966, viewed July 20, 2017.
43. "Irish News," *New Zealand Tablet*, June 17, 1887.
44. Worboys, ""Shirley, Sewallis Evelyn (1844–1904)."
45. Edward William Jaquet, *The Kennel Club: A History and Record of Its Work* (London: Kennel Gazette, 1905), 4–5.
46. The Kennel Club, www.thekennelclub.org.uk/our-resources/about-the -kennel-club/history-of-the-kennel-club/, viewed 25 June 2014.
47. Anonymous, "Would-Be Reformers."
48. J. Sidney Turner, "His Majesty King Edward VII. Patron of the Kennel Club," *Kennel Gazette*, June (1902): 190.
49. Jaquet, *The Kennel Club: A History and Record of Its Work*, 4–5.
50. Anonymous, "Club and Kennel Notes," *Kennel Gazette*, January 1902, 1.
51. A. Croxton Smith, "How the Kennel World Is Governed," in *The Book of the Dog*, ed. Brian Vesey-Fitzgerald (Los Angeles: Borden, 1948), 813–29.
52. Jaquet, *The Kennel Club: A History and Record of Its Work*, 230.
53. Anonymous, "Dog Show and Field Trial Fixtures," *Kennel Gazette* 1, no. 1 (April 1880): 2.
54. C. J. and E. Weatherby, *The General Stud Book, Containing Pedigrees of Race Horses*, 2nd edn., vol. 5, 10 vols. (London: C. J. and E. Weatherby, 1866); Margaret E. Derry, *Bred for Perfection: Shorthorn Cattle, Collies, and Arabian Horses since 1800* (Baltimore: Johns Hopkins University Press, 2003), 5; Mike Huggins, "A Tranquil Transformation: Middle-Class Racing 'Revolutionaries' in Nineteenth-Century England," in *Reformers, Sport, Modernizers: Middle-Class Revolutionaries*, ed. J. A. Mangan (New York: Routledge, 2013), 44; J. Weatherby, *An Introduction to a General Stud-Book: Containing (with Few Exceptions) the Pedigree of Every Horse, Mare, &c. of Note, That Has Appeared on the Turf for the Last Fifty Years, with Many of an Earlier Date; Together with a Short Account of the Most Noted Arabians, Barbs, &c. Connected Therewith* (London: H. Reynell, 1791).
55. Jaquet, *The Kennel Club: A History and Record of Its Work*, 8.
56. Frank C. S. Pearce, *The Kennel Club Stud Book: A Record of Dog Shows and Field Trials*, vol. 1 (London: Kennel Club, 1874), Preface (unpaginated).
57. Pearce, *Kennel Club Stud Book [1874]*, 1: Preface (unpaginated).
58. Pearce, *Kennel Club Stud Book [1874]*, 1:223–42.
59. S. E. Shirley, "The Kennel Club Calendar and Stud Book," *Field*, November 1, 1873, 453.
60. Crystal Palace Company, "Crystal Palace. Season 1873. Grand National Exhibition of Sporting & Other Dogs. June 17, 18, 19, & 20, 1873. Catalogue" (Crystal Palace Company, 1873), Members of the Kennel Club (unpaginated), Dog Show Catalogues 1873 Crystal Palace, Kennel Club Library, London; Verite sans Peur, "The New 'National' Dog Club," *Kennel*

Gazette, February 1883, 295–96; Communicated, "The Proposed New Stud Book. Birmingham Show," *Kennel Gazette*, December 1882, 234.

61. Anonymous, "The Rival Clubs," *Stock-Keeper and Fancier's Chronicle*, February 9, 1883, 90–91.

62. Anonymous, "Kennel and Field: Profession and Practice," *Stock-Keeper and Fancier's Chronicle*, February 11, 1881, 7–8.

63. Jaquet, *The Kennel Club: A History and Record of Its Work*, 10, 198, 367.

64. Henry St. James Stephen, *The Kennel Club Calendar and Stud Book*, vol. 11 (London: Kennel Club, 1884), vii–viii.

65. Anonymous, "Modern Coursing," *Kennel Gazette*, February 1883, 281–82, see 282.

66. "The Shirley Estate: Failure of the Plan of Campaign," *Weekly Irish Times*, September 10, 1887.

8

EPILOGUE

Greyhounds and owners in England went on a remarkable journey from 1200 to 1900. As a journalist writing as St. Bernard observed in 1897, "Once the minister only to the pastime of kings or the nobly born, once the recognized companion of 'the gentleman' only, the greyhound is now the instrument of 'sport' for the gambling multitude and the lodestar of the mob."[1] St. Bernard packed a lot of history into a single sentence.

St. Bernard was right that greyhounds, and the people for whom they worked, changed radically. Before 1831, greyhounds served royals, nobles, and the gentry (patricians). After 1831, thanks to Parliamentary politics, greyhounds reached all classes. The middle classes dominated public coursing. The working classes (St. Bernard's "multitude" and "mob") swarmed to coursing contests, where they gambled with delight. The culture surrounding greyhounds changed along with the class of their companions. Once symbols of royals and aristocrats, greyhounds became "lodestars" of the working classes. The symbolism of greyhound sports changed, too. When patricians held a monopoly on greyhounds, coursing and hunting were noble sports. When the middle and working classes behaved the same as patricians, coursing and hunting became ignoble (thus St. Bernard's quotation marks around "sport"). Hunting became "pot-hunting," and coursing became a "mob" scene.

St. Bernard's metaphors expressed the economic and technological transformations that shaped greyhounds and their companions. In the medieval and early modern periods, when the economic base of England was agriculture and the engines that transformed energy into work were muscles, greyhounds were servants. They "ministered" to kings and worked for gentlemen as "companions." In the nineteenth century, after the Industrial Revolution introduced factories and trains powered by steam engines, greyhounds became tools. They were "instruments." Not coincidentally, the "mobs" that loved those instruments worked in the factories of the Industrial Revolution. Industrialization transformed their leisure as well as their employment. They rode trains to coursing contests and followed coursing contests in mass media.

Politics, economics, technology, culture, and ecology joined forces to shape the traits of greyhounds and owners as well as their social roles. Populations evolved. In human and canine populations alike, the trend was from more to less variation. The central reason was that people adapted greyhounds and themselves to niches, each of which combined a job with a habitat. In greyhounds, physical and behavioral traits changed frequency as populations adapted to niches. Philosophies of breeding changed over time, but the ability of breeders to fine-tune the evolution of greyhounds to niches was a constant. Breeders did not aim to produce one uniform, all-purpose breed (*the* greyhound). They tailored individual greyhounds to specialized jobs by selecting for alternate versions of more than forty traits. They could have produced one trillion versions of greyhounds, each one unique. Greyhound owners (and other people who interacted with greyhounds) adapted their behavioral traits through learning. People evolved culturally.

English people and greyhounds continued to evolve after 1900. As always, social forces structured niches and shaped evolution. The forces that modernized greyhounds in the nineteenth century pushed greyhounds further in the same direction in the twentieth and twenty-first centuries. These forces included bureaucratization (the Kennel Club and National Coursing Club registered greyhounds in closed populations), rapid communication (including expansion to the Internet), rapid transportation for breeding and contests (with automobiles and airplanes joining trains), industrial technology (with electric lights and motors becoming important), capitalism (profit-driven breeding and contests continued), and democracy (anyone can own a greyhound). The modern trend toward isolated greyhound populations with narrow traits tailored to narrow job descriptions in standardized environments continued. Scholars have argued that the world has entered a post-modern era, but modernity continues to characterize the forces shaping greyhound and human evolution.

In 1926, industry reopened a niche for greyhounds in England. The country dabbled with racing in 1876, when a windlass pulled a mechanical hare pulled down a straight track.[2] Racing then disappeared from England for half a century. The sport popped up in the United States in the 1920s with a mechanical hare pulled around a circular track by an electric motor. Charles Munn and Major L. Lyne

Dixson imported the American model to England in 1926. A Greyhound Racing Association began sponsoring greyhound races on an oval course of 400–500 yards in Manchester. Within weeks, 17,000 spectators per night flocked to the stadium for races. Electric lighting made evening contests realistic. A perception that the sport lacked cruelty attracted women as entrants and spectators. The Duchess of Sutherland entered her dogs in these commercial contests, suggesting that aristocrats as well as women found the setting congenial.[3] Early racing greyhounds came from the ranks of hare coursers, but breeders soon set about tailoring greyhounds to their new job.[4] Over time, greyhound racing lost its elite luster and became known as a profit-driven enterprise favored by working-class gamblers.[5]

Track racing remains one of the most popular spectator sports in Britain. By 2014, more than two million people attended races each year. Gamblers wagered 2.5 billion pounds per year on greyhound races.[6] Bureaucracies control racing and isolate racing greyhounds. The National Coursing Club registers racing greyhounds, which have to appear in the club's studbook to run in races governed by the Greyhound Board of Great Britain (another bureaucracy).[7]

Shows have offered steady employment to greyhounds. The principle of judging on appearance has remained unchanged, although preferences for specific traits have fluctuated with fashion. The Kennel Club continues to register dogs and make breeding information available to the public, now via the Internet.[8] It still functions as a London social club.

Greyhounds have increasingly found work as pets. Many are retired racers. Founded in 1975, the Retired Greyhound Trust reported in 2014 that it was "Britain's largest single breed animal charity." In repurposing racing greyhounds as pets, the trust breaks with the historical pattern of breeding greyhounds for each of its jobs. The trust spends about 100,000 pounds a year advertising greyhounds as pets, and placed its 60,000th greyhound in 2012. (This number gives a sense of the large number of dogs working in the racing industry.) More than 1,000 volunteers helped the trust.[9] Kennel clubs promote show greyhounds as pets, too.

Coursing provided greyhound jobs until 2005, when Parliament shut it down. Responding to lobbying from humane activists and others, Parliament banned all hunting of animals with dogs. The law made it an offense to attend a coursing meet as well as to enter one.[10] The ban boosted lure coursing, which simulates hare coursing by having an electric motor pull a lure ("a bunch of plastic bags") in erratic directions while dogs chase it. Judges score dogs on speed, enthusiasm, agility, endurance, and ability to follow the lure. Lure coursing developed its own bureaucracy, the British Sighthound Field Association, which sponsors contests. The association reinforces breed separation by limiting entry to purebred dogs registered with the Kennel Club or the National Greyhound Association (an American greyhound racing association). Although lure coursing simulates hare coursing, and although greyhounds are welcome to enter, the sport has favored other breeds. Afghans, salukis and whippets dominated the list of winners from 2003 to 2012.[11] The absence of greyhounds reminds us that small differences in job descriptions can reward big differences in traits of dogs.

Bureaucracies have encouraged inbreeding in coursing, show, and racing greyhounds. The Kennel Club offers a measure of inbreeding on its Website. Called the inbreeding coefficient, this number estimates the chance that a dog inherited both copies of a gene from one ancestor (that is, the odds the same dog was an ancestor to the dog's mother and father). An inbreeding coefficient of 0 percent suggests the two copies came from unrelated parents. A score of 12.5 percent would result from the mating of a grandfather to a granddaughter. Greyhounds' score of 8.8 percent implies that, on average, greyhounds are related to each other less closely than grandfathers to granddaughters but more closely than great grandfathers to great granddaughters.[12]

Inbreeding encourages inheritance of genetic diseases. Greyhounds suffer from inherited diseases of the skin, gastrointestinal tract, blood, skeleton, neurosystem, eyes, heart, reproductive systems, and lungs.[13] Kennel clubs have responded by encouraging genetic screening. Anyone can search the Website of the Kennel Club to find out the results of screening tests for any registered dog.[14] Another approach would have been to reward breeding for variation, which would have increased genetic variation and reduced the rate of genetic diseases. Variation would, however, have revived the judging controversies of early dog shows and threatened brand recognition for commercial breeders.

Modernization is a process in which societies place bigger bets on fewer variables than traditional societies. This approach helps maximize gains but increases the risks of failure.[15] Modernizing the evolution of agricultural plants and animals helps farmers maximize production.[16] It also increases the risk of disaster, such as disease and pests sweeping through genetically identical fields of crops. Modernizing the evolution of greyhounds maximized the odds of winning coursing contests, dog shows, and races. These contests featured narrow job descriptions in standardized environments, which encouraged inbreeding for narrow traits in isolated populations. Inbreeding increased the risk of genetic diseases and loss of variation useful in adaptation. Modern breeders believed they improved greyhounds in a universal sense, but they did not. They adapted greyhounds to specific conditions spawned by historical and natural forces.

These findings forced me to change my understanding of domestic animals and plants in general. Books, Web sites, journal articles, county and state fairs, and dog shows had led me to believe in the statue theory of breeds. I thought breeds, once created, were uniform, static, and isolated. They varied a bit at any given time, of course, as anyone who has seen variation in coat color in cows or dogs can attest. I would have expected that breeds changed a bit over time. But variation in space and time seemed incidental, not important. Breeds stood outside of time. And I thought pure breeding was the rule. If an animal was crossbred, I thought, it no longer belonged to a breed. It was a mongrel. Appearance and ancestry defined breeds.

I did not realize that the statue view of breeds was a recent, modern phenomenon. I did not know that projecting this view onto animals and plants in the past blinded us to some of the most important traits of breeds. I did not know that variation, change, and porosity were not threats to breeds in the past. They were virtues. I did not know that people in the past considered crossbred animals to be superior members of breeds. I did not know that many of the breed histories I read were myths designed to rationalize standards for judging animals by appearance. I did not know that people in the past defined breeds by their occupation and behavior as much as by their appearance. My ignorance was vast.

After doing research, I felt foolish. Historians are supposed to know that everything changes over time. Biologists are supposed to know that organisms vary and evolve. Yet these professional habits of thought had not shielded me from imbibing the implicit idea that people had managed to defy these patterns when breeding animals and plants. I knew breeds came and went, but I did not think each breed varied or changed all that much. I would not have made that mistake about, say, soldiers. If anyone said American soldiers today look and behave the same way as ancient Roman centurions, I would have laughed. I would see some continuity in soldiering over time, but I would not assume ancient and contemporary soldiers were identical.

One route to a more accurate understanding of breeds, I suggest, is to view them as part of labor history. Forget for the moment that we are talking about non-human species. Assume instead that we are talking about employees. Domestic plants and animals work in human economies. That employment is what separates domesticates from their wild relatives. Domestic plants and animals have many jobs. They produce food and fiber. They pull plows and wagons. They carry burdens. They provide companionship, guide people with disabilities, point to game animals, and retrieve dead birds. These are occupations with specific duties in human economies.

As human economies change, occupations for domestic plants and animals change. Some new occupations arise. Dogs are now trained to detect cancer, something they did not do for most of their history. Some occupations disappear. Turnspit dogs, which walked in wheels to turn spits of meat, lost their jobs when mechanization made them obsolete. Other occupations persist but undergo a change in the job description. Dogs guiding blind people at one time did not have to press buttons to change lights at street intersections. Now they do.

As occupations change, breeds change. This is one of the easiest points to miss when looking at domesticates. We do not make the same mistake about people. Today, we do not assume that someone named Carpenter is a carpenter. We know that an ancestor probably was a carpenter, but Carpenters today might be computer programmers. We expect computer programmers to behave differently from carpenters. We would do well to develop the same habit of mind with breed names. We should not assume that all dogs called border collies are the same. A show collie is different from herding collie. They have commonalities, but differences in job descriptions produce differences in traits among holders of each occupation.

Plant and animal employees work in specific environments. Employees need traits that enable them to succeed in that environment. Because so many dogs are bred today for the same environment (indoor show rings), it is easy to forget that in the past they had to have traits suited to varied working environments. We expect carpenters working outdoors in winter in Alaska to dress more warmly than carpenters working in the summer in Lesotho. Traits of domesticates also vary as a product of working in different environments. Variation in coat length of greyhounds is an example. Like jobs, working environments change over time. Changes in occupation almost always lead to changes in working environments.

Border collies that worked as herders toiled in pastures. Border collies that worked in shows labored in indoor rings.

For any breed of domestic animal or plant, then, we should not picture it the way we often encounter it: as an isolated individual surrounded by a white space on a poster or book page. We should picture a population and ask, what is its occupation? In what environment does it work? These questions are valid in all places and times. If the job–environment combinations (aka niches) vary in space and time, we should expect a breed to vary in place and time. And we should expect that the breeding methods and breed boundaries will vary in place and time as well.

Because domestic plants and animals work in human economies, radical economic change affects them just as much as it affects human beings. The transition from agrarian economies to industrial economies spawned wrenching changes in human occupations and experience. It also transformed employment for domestic plants and animals. With industrialization, the job of wheat changed from growing reliably to maximizing yield by absorbing as much fertilizer as possible. The environment of wheat changed from soils with little fertilizer to soils treated with factory-produced fertilizers. This new job–environment combination (niche) led to evolution in wheat. Heavy fertilizer led to heavy heads of grain, which caused tall traditional varieties of wheat to lodge. Breeders adapted wheat to the Industrial Revolution by shortening stalks to prevent lodging.[17] Plants evolved in response to the same economic changes that remade experience for their employers, farmers.

Once we have identified the niches of domestic plants and animals, we need to identify the forces structuring those niches. Those forces are both non-human and human. The non-human factors include climate, geology, disease, and more. In most cases, the human and non-human are intertwined. Climate is no longer an independent variable. It is partly a product of human actions. The human factors include all the historical forces that change human experience. Politics, economics, and culture all play essential roles in molding and modifying niches for domestic plants and animals. When we have identified how these forces construct niches, we have gone a long way toward discerning how historical forces have acted as evolutionary forces.

The juncture where niche construction meets trait modification is, for domesticates, anthropogenic evolution. Often this evolution is the product of breeding, though the ideas and practices of breeding have varied over time and space. Sometimes forces other than breeding, such as unconscious selection, play important roles.

So far, I have emphasized the impact of people on domesticates. The other direction of impact is just as important. Domesticates feed the world, and nothing is more essential for human experience than food. Domesticates do not, so far as I know, breed people. Their impact is subtle. One kind of impact is the creation of opportunities for people to behave in certain ways. Wheat creates the opportunity for people to eat wheat, among other things, and people took advantage of that opportunity. The frequency of a behavioral trait, wheat eating, rose in human populations. The populations evolved. Another kind of impact is price exaction. Wheat does not do everything people want by itself. To produce maximum grain, wheat benefits from fertilizers. So, farmers behave in certain ways, such as fertilizing fields, that are the price of accepting the opportunity to eat wheat.

Once we identify reciprocal impacts in human and non-human populations, we have found coevolution. People and domesticates have always coevolved. They have always modified each other's traits in ways simple and complex, obvious and subtle. This process will continue so long as people inhabit the earth.

Notes

1. St. Bernard, "Notable Dogs of the Chase: The Greyhound," *Good Words* 38 (1897): 848.
2. Anonymous, "Coursing by Proxy," *Times [London]*, September 11, 1876.
3. Anonymous, "New Form of Coursing. Greyhound Racing with an Electric Hare," *Times [London]*, October 9, 1926; Mike Huggins, "Going to the Dogs," *History Today* 56, no. 5 (May 2006): 31–35.
4. A. Croxton Smith, *Greyhound Racing and Breeding* (London: Gay & Hancook Ltd., 1927), 5–35; James Matheson, *The Greyhound: Breeding, Coursing, Racing, Etc.* ([London]: Hurst & Blackett, 1929).
5. Norman Baker, "Going to the Dogs–Hostility to Greyhound Racing in Britain: Puritanism, Socialism, and Pragmaticism," *Journal of Sport History* 23, no. 2 (1996): 97–119.
6. Greyhound Board of Great Britain, www.gbgb.org.uk/, viewed November 4, 2014.
7. National Coursing Club, www.greyhoundstudbook.co.uk/, viewed November 4, 2014.
8. The Kennel Club, www.thekennelclub.org.uk/, viewed November 4, 2014.
9. "Retired Greyhound Trust," accessed October 24, 2014, www.retiredgreyhounds.co.uk/About-the-RGT/.

10. "Hunting Act 2004," Text, *National Archives: Legislation.gov.uk*, accessed October 24, 2014, www.legislation.gov.uk/ukpga/2004/37/contents.

11. British Sighthound Field Association, "UK Lure Coursing with the British Sighthound Field Association," accessed October 24, 2014, http://lurecoursing.org.uk/.

12. "The Kennel Club," accessed April 14, 2014, www.thekennelclub.org.uk/.

13. Alex Gough and Alison Thomas, *Breed Predispositions to Disease in Dogs and Cats*, 2nd edn. (Oxford: John Wiley & Sons, 2010), 108–11; David R. Sargan, "IDID: Inherited Diseases in Dogs: Web-Based Information for Canine Inherited Disease Genetics," *Mammalian Genome: Official Journal of the International Mammalian Genome Society* 15, no. 6 (June 2004): 503–6, doi:10.1007/s00335-004-3047-z.

14. Kennel Club, "Health Test Results Finder," accessed October 24, 2014, www.thekennelclub.org.uk/services/public/mateselect/test/Default.aspx.

15. James C. Scott, *Seeing Like a State: How Certain Schemes to Improve the Human Condition Have Failed* (New Haven: Yale University Press, 1998).

16. Margaret E. Derry, *Bred for Perfection: Shorthorn Cattle, Collies, and Arabian Horses since 1800* (Baltimore: Johns Hopkins University Press, 2003).

17. John H. Perkins, *Geopolitics and the Green Revolution: Wheat, Genes, and the Cold War* (New York: Oxford University Press, 1997).

INDEX

(*continued from page ii…*)

Richard W. Judd *The Untilled Garden: Natural History and the Spirit of Conservation in America, 1740–1840*

James L. A. Webb, Jr. *Humanity's Burden: A Global History of Malaria*

Myrna I. Santiago *The Ecology of Oil: Environment, Labor, and the Mexican Revolution, 1900–1938*

Frank Uekoetter *The Green and the Brown: A History of Conservation in Nazi Germany*

Matthew D. Evenden *Fish versus Power: An Environmental History of the Fraser River*

Alfred W. Crosby *Ecological Imperialism: The Biological Expansion of Europe, 900–1900, second edition*

Nancy J. Jacobs *Environment, Power, and Injustice: A South African History*

Edmund Russell *War and Nature: Fighting Humans and Insects with Chemicals from World War I to Silent Spring*

Adam Rome *The Bulldozer in the Countryside: Suburban Sprawl and the Rise of American Environmentalism*

Judith Shapiro *Mao's War against Nature: Politics and the Environment in Revolutionary China*

Andrew Isenberg *The Destruction of the Bison: An Environmental History*

Thomas Dunlap *Nature and the English Diaspora*

Robert B. Marks *Tigers, Rice, Silk, and Silt: Environment and Economy in Late Imperial South China*

Mark Elvin and Tsui'jung Liu *Sediments of Time: Environment and Society in Chinese History*

Richard H. Grove *Green Imperialism: Colonial Expansion, Tropical Island Edens and the Origins of Environmentalism, 1600–1860*

Thorkild Kjærgaard *The Danish Revolution, 1500–1800: An Ecohistorical Interpretation*

Donald Worster *Nature's Economy: A History of Ecological Ideas, second edition*

Elinor G. K. Melville *A Plague of Sheep: Environmental Consequences of the Conquest of Mexico*

J. R. McNeill *The Mountains of the Mediterranean World: An Environmental History*

Theodore Steinberg *Nature Incorporated: Industrialization and the Waters of New England*

Timothy Silver *A New Face on the Countryside: Indians, Colonists, and Slaves in the South Atlantic Forests, 1500–1800*

Michael Williams *Americans and Their Forests: A Historical Geography*

Donald Worster *The Ends of the Earth: Perspectives on Modern Environmental History*

Robert Harms *Games against Nature: An Eco-Cultural History of the Nunu of Equatorial Africa*

Warren Dean *Brazil and the Struggle for Rubber: A Study in Environmental History*

Samuel P. Hays *Beauty, Health, and Permanence: Environmental Politics in the United States, 1955–1985*

Arthur F. McEvoy *The Fisherman's Problem: Ecology and Law in the California Fisheries, 1850–1980*

Kenneth F. Kiple *The Caribbean Slave: A Biological History*